War
and
Depression

America   1914-1939

War

and

Depression

America 1914-1939

Daniel M. Smith

University of Colorado

FORUM PRESS   **ST. LOUIS**

For Aladeen

Library of Congress Catalog Card Number: 72-83318

ISBN: 0-88273-100-9

First Printing May 1972

Cover Design by Dale-Arden

Contents

Preface

Two major interrelated themes emerge from this account of the history of the United States from 1914 to 1939. Domestically, American society continued the process of industrialization and urbanization that had begun in the late nineteenth century. Industry, and agriculture to a lesser degree, increasingly developed into big businesses absorbing vast amounts of capital and controlled by a corporate elite only theoretically answerable to stock holders. "Organizational" or corporate capitalism largely supplanted the earlier more individualistic type; in a very real sense, corporate capitalism thereby nationalized American industry and finance. Urban growth accompanied industrialism and, as more and more Americans lived in the cities, posed vast new social problems of employment, housing, education, health, and recreation. Rural habits, values, and traditions gradually gave way to social modes and thought more suitable to urban life, but the transition often was disturbing and painful. Government also had to adjust and expand its functions beyond its traditional scope. In 1914 the federal government was still comparatively a small enterprise; the challenge of war and depression in the next two decades transformed it almost beyond belief until today it touches in one way or another almost every facet of American life.

The second theme relates to foreign affairs. Because of its industrial growth and vast wealth, and consequent interest in foreign markets, the United States became one of the foremost great world powers whose very existence necessarily affected the global balance of power. American actions as a nation, whether as positive attempts to mold events abroad or as negative efforts to enjoy material abundance in political isolation, could not help but affect the course of world history. Here too Americans found it difficult to adjust to changing conditions. Despite involvement in World War I, which should have made it obvious that the United States could not insulate itself from world distress and conflict, many Americans clung to traditional foreign policy attitudes and refused to allow the nation to play the kind of constructive political role that its own enlightened interests demanded in the Twenties and the Thirties. Yet economic and educational forces, and the sheer exigency of events, gradually broke down the isolationist psychology and prepared most Americans for belated acceptance of the fact and responsibilities of great world power.

Although this volume concentrates on the years 1914 to 1939, the first chapter discusses briefly the Progressive movement and the major achievements of the Wilson administration prior to the outbreak of the First World War. The selective Bibliography after the last chapter acknowledges my indebtedness to the scholarly labors of others and offers the student a guide for further study. I am indebted to my colleague, Professor Robert A. Skotheim, for a critical reading of the manuscript.

Boulder, Colorado   Daniel M. Smith

1

The New Freedom
at Home and Abroad

ON THE EVE of his first inauguration, Woodrow Wilson remarked that "it would be the irony of fate if my administration had to deal chiefly with foreign affairs." Yet events did not respect his absorbing interest in domestic reform; a world soon to be wracked by revolution and war monopolized more and more of Wilson's time and energy. It was ironic indeed that his role as inspired war leader and world statesman eventually overshadowed his notable achievements as a reformer at home.

The old order seemed to be collapsing everywhere during Wilson's years in the White House. Post-Edwardian Europe, resplendent in monarchical trappings and confident in its industrial riches and world-girdling power, drifted toward the abyss of the First World War. As historian Arnold Toynbee so aptly writes, Western civilization was about to enter a "time of troubles," comparable to the self-destructive rage that afflicted the City States of ancient Greece. These dramatic events did not leave the United States unscathed. Within the Western Hemisphere the harried Wilson administration found it necessary to intervene by armed force in the Caribbean and in revolution-torn Mexico. In the Far East an imperialistic Japan challenged the Open Door in China and moved perceptibly closer to a confrontation with the United States. And in Europe the war that began in 1914 ultimately engulfed America as well. Amidst the destruction of war and the collapse of old empires and thrones, the corrosive revolutionary virus of communism triumphed in Russia and threatened to contaminate the entire world.

From the perspective of today, it is clear that the "Age of Free Security" for the United States was ending. As a result of its comparatively isolated geographical position and a century of general tranquillity in Europe, the United

States, despite occasional alarms, generally had enjoyed peace and security without the necessity of maintaining large armies and navies. Many Americans incorrectly attributed these blessings to their forebears' wise decision to abstain from involvement in Europe's rivalries and conflicts. World War I demonstrated, however, that the nation could not isolate itself either economically or politically from the effects of a global war. After weary months of trying to preserve neutrality, the United States found itself drawn into the holocaust. Because of their idealism, Americans then transformed the struggle into a Great Crusade for democracy and enduring peace. As if making amends for its isolationism, the United States resolved to play a permanent and larger role in world affairs through a new organization, the League of Nations. Unfortunately, the hold of the past could not be so easily broken. Oversold on the idealistic war aims so eloquently proclaimed by President Wilson, the American people after the Armistice rapidly became disillusioned with the Great Crusade and longed to return to the less demanding days before the war. Rather than the beginning of a glorious new era for all mankind, World War I came to be seen by many Americans as an unfortunate and avoidable departure from the policies and traditions of the past.

Progressivism

Wilson's political career coincided with the full flowering of the Progressive Era; his victory in the 1912 presidential election can aptly be viewed as the high tide of that reform movement. What were the causes and essential characteristics of Progressivism, which unlike most great reform eras in American history came not in a time of economic depression but in the midst of prosperity? Historians have not been able to agree. The "liberal-progressive" historians of the 1920's and 1930's, such as Charles A. Beard, Arthur M. Schlesinger, Sr., and John D. Hicks, tended to depict the era in terms of economic and class conflict, a revival and extension of the Populist impulse to preserve democracy and curb the giant corporations created by the newly rich moguls of finance and industry. After the Second World War, scholars began to emphasize the urban middle class and its desire to correct the manifest social ills of industrialization and urbanization. Professor Richard Hofstadter explained Progressivism as sparked by a "status revolution," an uprising not of the down-trodden and economically deprived but of the older middle class of professional people and small or medium businessmen who felt acutely aware of their losses in accustomed social deference and political influence, threatened from above by the *nouveau riche* masters of the giant corporations and from below by corrupt political machines based on the immigrant and worker hordes of the cities. Eric F. Goldman agreed that the reform current flowed largely from the urban middle class that sought to perfect American democracy in an industrial age. By the 1960's, all these interpretations were under attack or being revised and modified. Samuel P. Hays and Robert H. Wiebe challenged the theory of a status revolution and attributed much of the reform impulse to new members of the upper-middle and upper classes who valued regularity, efficiency, and the rationalization of industry and government. Businessmen exerted leadership in the movement for city reform and led in the debate over national economic issues, at least in the first phase of Progressivism down to 1908. Progressivism, therefore, represented the triumph of the organizational mentality of the new middle class over the rural and small-town values and attitudes of 19th-century America. Professor Gabriel Kolko, a New Left historian, advances a more extreme revisionist view. He contends that Progressivism, far from manifesting an era of liberal reform, in fact marked the political triumph of conservative business leaders who sought and at least partially obtained the establishment of governmental machinery and regulation beneficial to big business interests. Substantial segments of big business obtained control over politics and used it to promote market stability and security from cut-throat competition and erratic fluctuations of the economy. Moreover, big business preferred federal regulation, which it could hope to shape, to possibly more radical measures that might be forced upon it at local and state levels. The various regulatory laws and new governmental bureaus between 1903 and 1915 were not forced upon business by liberal reformers but on the whole represented the desires and served the interests of big business.

Progressivism, like most reform movements, can be thought of as Janus-faced. Nostalgically it sought to preserve the mores and values of an earlier and presumably more halcyon period. At the same time it tried to adjust to the demands of an industrialized and urbanized era, to harness new economic forces and utilize the resources of government to promote the good life for all Americans. The impetus for reform came from middle-class, business and professional people, but farmers and the laboring class also provided support. Crusading journalists, the "Muckrakers," played a vital part in arousing the nation's social conscience to the need for reforms. Progressivism began on the local and state levels in efforts to clean up politics and to improve city conditions, and swelled to national consciousness during the administration of Theodore Roosevelt. Proclaiming an abiding faith in individualism, political democracy, and the application of reason and science to human problems, progressive spokesmen advocated legislation to regulate business, protect consumers, clean up politics, and to make government more responsible to the electorate. Progressivism obtained a spate of measures during the Theodore Roosevelt administration: Elkins Act and Hepburn Act to regulate the railroads, Meat Inspection Act, Pure Food and Drug Act, Bureau of Corporations, anti-trust suits, and the policy of conservation of natural resources. At the state and national levels, political measures such as the initiative, referendum, and recall, the direct election of senators, and the enfranchisement of women, were adopted or advocated. Social reforms ranged from laws to regulate the working hours and conditions for women and children, more stringent factory safety and sanitation requirements, workmen's compensation, tenement housing regulations and slum clearance, to the establishment of voluntary social settlement houses to work with the urban underprivileged. In its political aspects, Progressivism did not confine itself to any one party, not even the one labeled "Progressive" in the 1912 campaign. Progressivism cut across party lines and affected every section of the nation before finally exhausting its impetus.

Handing over the reins of power in 1909 to his virtually handpicked successor, William Howard Taft, Theodore Roosevelt soon became disillusioned with Taft's cautious and more conservative course. Despite the fact that his administration recorded a number of progressive achievements, Taft came to be viewed as a tool of the conservatives. Taft handled the tariff issue ineptly, unwisely aroused the fears of the conservationists, and proved unable to keep divergent elements within his party in some kind of seeming harmony. Hence the Republican party splintered into an insurgent progressive and the regular or status-quo wings. After his return from an adventurous trip to Africa and Europe, during which he hunted lions, joined Kaiser Wilhelm II in reviewing the field maneuvers of the Germany army, and represented the United States at the funeral of England's Edward VII, Roosevelt was soon persuaded to reenter politics. Ambition and concern for "my policies" caused him to challenge Taft's leadership of the Republican party. Hurt by Roosevelt's attacks, Taft lashed back at what he termed "political emotionalists or neurotics." He sought and obtained renomination to vindicate himself. Roosevelt's militant followers then bolted the party and prepared to battle for righteousness and reform within a new political movement. The new party, the Progressive Party or "Bull Moosers," offered the Democrats an unusual opportunity to end sixteen years of political drought by recapturing control of the White House.

Wilson Becomes President

Thomas Woodrow Wilson (he early dropped the Thomas) led the Democrats to victory in 1912. A Southerner, born in 1856 in Staunton, Virginia, he was molded by his brilliant and exacting, but devoted, father, Dr. Joseph Ruggles Wilson, a Presbyterian minister. His father imbued young Wilson with the profound conviction that Providence had called all men to special vocations. Woodrow Wilson believed without question that he was a moral agent in the fulfillment of God's will, and he approached first the academic world and then politics and foreign policy as a sort of lay minister charged with spreading moral enlightenment. One Catholic politician later wryly described Wilson as a "Presbyterian priest" in politics. Several recent biographers have suggested that young Wilson was devoted to his father but reacted to his demanding standards with feelings of moral and intellectual inferiority, resulting in a life-long aversion to strong-minded men who might challenge his judgment and leadership. Perhaps as compensation for inferiority feelings, Wilson was intensely ambitious. According to Professor Henry Steele Commager his youthful letters to Ellen Axson, his bride-to-be, reveal "something almost terrifying" about his concentration on his career to the exclusion of almost everything else. Despite his sense of isolation, Wilson craved signs of affection. He wrote Ellen Axson on one occasion that he sometimes was "dismayed to look about and see how few persons in the world stand near me and know me as I am — in such wise that they can give me sympathy and close support of heart."

Entering Princeton in 1875, Woodrow Wilson expended much energy and time not only in his studies but in debating and oratory. He was intensely interested in politics and greatly admired the British parliamentary-ministerial system as superior to the American in providing greater scope for effective leadership. In the post-Civil War years, Congress seemed predominant and the presidency relatively unimportant. Subsequently the more vigorous Presidents, Grover Cleveland and Theodore Roosevelt, demonstrated that the office had greater potential and Wilson concluded that a chief executive could be just as big a man as he willed to be. Graduating from Princeton, Wilson first studied law as a gateway to politics but he soon abandoned it in frustration and turned to the academic world. He received the Ph.D. degree from Johns Hopkins University in 1886, publishing his dissertation on *Congressional Government* which has been viewed as a landmark study in politics. He then embarked on a career that saw him publish a number of historical studies, well written if not particularly profound, and eventually to return to Princeton as a professor.

In 1902 Wilson became Princeton's first layman president. He quickly acquired a national reputation as an educational statesman and reformer, over-hauling the curriculum and instituting the preceptorial system. While these changes seemed exciting and daringly innovative at Princeton, they were rather conservative within the national higher educational climate. Wilson revealed little interest in graduate and specialized studies, and more in inculcating certain standards and morality in undergraduates. A phrase frequently on his lips was "Princeton in the nation's service." Despite his achievements, he encountered two serious defeats, involving abolition of undergraduate eating clubs and their replacement by quadrangle residences that he hoped would raise the quality of Princeton's intellectual life, and the location and hence control of the graduate school. These defeats revealed certain serious personality defects. Wilson could not tolerate dissent and refused to compromise; he broke with old friends and colleagues when they disagreed with him; and he maneuvered almost frantically and not entirely candidly in his efforts for victory and self-vindication.

Because of these checks at Princeton and his old interest in politics, Wilson welcomed a chance to run for the governorship of New Jersey on the Democratic ticket in 1910. At that point, he would have to be classified as something of a political conservative in attitude and beliefs, admiring the great English conservative Whig philosopher Edmund Burke and sharing the prevailing opinion of the governing and influential groups in the United States. Prior to 1910 he had indicated a distrust of organized labor as harmful to the true interests of the worker, viewed Populism as ignorant radicalism, and was highly critical of William Jennings Bryan's leadership of the Democratic party. Yet as a believer in individualism and economic opportunity, Wilson disliked the growth of monopolistic trusts and feared that the ever-increasing concentration of financial power threatened to control the economic life of the nation.

Wilson obtained the New Jersey gubernatorial nomination in 1910 largely through the efforts of George Harvey. A wealthy and conservative magazine publisher eager to break Bryan's hold on the Democratic party, Harvey saw great possibilities in Wilson and persuaded New Jersey's bosses James Smith and James Nugent to run the Princeton educator. Stung by reform-minded criticism during the 1910 gubernatorial race, Wilson quickly identified with the progressive cause and won the election. He was one of twenty-six Democratic governors elected that year, which also saw the Democrats capture control of the lower house of Congress. The new Governor broke with the political machine and displayed effective leadership in the enactment of a number of reforms relating to cleaner politics and closer regulation of the utility companies and corporations. As a nationally acclaimed reform governor of an eastern industrialized state he was able to overcome his chief rival at the convention, Champ Clark of Missouri, Speaker of the House of Representatives, to obtain the Democratic nomination for the presidency in 1912.

The 1912 contest essentially pitted Wilson against Roosevelt; Taft obviously had little hope and the Socialist nominee, Eugene V. Debs, even less of winning the prize. Both Roosevelt and Wilson ran on progressive platforms. The primary difference, apart from personalities, lay in their views of how to cope with the abuses of monopoly and big business. Roosevelt called for a "New Nationalism" that would strengthen the federal government to control and regulate big business. He dismissed "trustbusting" as outdated and reactionary. Instead, America needed a Hamiltonian big government, operating for the general welfare, to hold the balance between big business and big labor. Proclaiming distrust of a bureaucratic regulatory government, Wilson instead recommended to the voters the "New Freedom": a vigorous application of the Sherman anti-trust law and other measures to break up evil trusts, and to restore and preserve competition and individual freedom of enterprise. Bigness itself was not evil, only those big businesses that had got that way wrongfully and that destroyed or diminished economic equality of opportunity for others. Although Wilson received only a plurality rather than a majority of the popular vote, he swept the electoral college. The Democrats also captured control of both houses of Congress. The combined Wilson-Roosevelt-Debs vote, totaling around eleven million to Taft's nearly three and a half million, seemed to be an overwhelming national mandate for progressive reform.

The New Freedom

In his inaugural address the new President in solemn almost religious terms summoned his countrymen to the cause of reform: "No one can mistake the purpose for which the Nation now seeks to use the Democratic Party. It seeks to use it to interpret a change in its own plans and point of view. . . . The Nation has been deeply stirred, stirred by a solemn passion, stirred by the knowledge of wrong, of ideals lost, of government too often debauched and made an instrument of evil." Wilson then called for the support of "all honest men, all forward-looking men" in his task, an appeal to which progressives responded with great enthusiasm. Wilson's cabinet was a moderately able one. William Gibbs McAdoo, a very able lawyer from Georgia and New York and Wilson's future son-in-law, became Secretary of the Treasury. William Jennings Bryan took charge of the State Department. Lindley M. Garrison of New Jersey was appointed Secretary of War, succeeded after his resignation in 1916 by Newton D. Baker, reform mayor of Cleveland; Josephus Daniels, a liberal North Carolina editor, became Secretary of the Navy, with Franklin D. Roosevelt of New York as his Assistant Secretary. Albert S. Burleson of Texas, a conservative but able politician, headed the Post Office Department and used patronage effectively in behalf of the administration's program. Another transplanted Southerner, David F. Houston of North Carolina, was Secretary of Agriculture. The remainder of the cabinet secretaries similarly were reasonably good appointees.

President Wilson quickly proved his leadership in the successful struggle to revise the tariff. The Democratic majorities in Congress wanted to make a responsible record by fulfilling campaign pledges and of course eagerly sought patronage plums. They responded, therefore, to the executive lead. The Underwood bill easily cleared the House, providing for moderate protectionism and lowering of import rates on the average to 29 percent from the existing level of 40 percent *ad valorem*. It also established a large free list of imports and, since the Sixteenth Amendment had taken effect, levied a mild income tax (raised in the Senate to a maximum surtax of 6 percent on higher incomes) to compensate for reduced tariff revenues. The scene was vastly different in the Senate, the traditional "graveyard" of low tariff bills, where lobbyists for protected interests attempted to amend the measure out of all resemblance to the House version. President Wilson brought pressure to bear on the Senate by appealing to the public. Complaining that lobbyists were so numerous in Washington that "a brick couldn't be thrown without hitting one of them," and rallying reform elements that viewed high rates as enriching the monopolists at the expense of the consumer and the small enterpriser, Wilson won the battle. The Underwood Tariff of 1913 did not abandon protectionism but it was a distinct improvement over the Payne-Aldrich Tariff of 1909.

A second major reform involved banking and currency. The existing system, established during the Civil War, had revealed its defects in the financial panic of 1907. Conservative elements, however, wanted to repair its inelasticity by chartering a new privately owned and privately controlled central bank, with branches across the United States, which could issue paper currency backed solely by the reserves of the bank. Progressive and agrarian spokesmen strongly objected. They advocated a government controlled system more responsive to local needs. The Pujo Committee in early 1913 underscored popular fears of alleged Wall Street control of the nation's credit and monetary system, revealing that the J. P. Morgan investment firm and two giant New York banks through a complicated network of directorships apparently controlled 112 financial, industrial, and transportation corporations with an aggregate value of $22 billion. A series of articles by Louis Brandeis, "Other People's Money," pointed out how the Wall Street moguls used the funds of many small depositors and banks across the country to fashion a financial octopus ruling the nation's economic life.

Virginia's Carter Glass introduced a measure in 1913 for a privately owned decentralized banking system. Under pressure from progressives, Wilson accepted the addition of a federally-appointed central governing board and the issuance of currency by the federal government. He also agreed to include provisions for short-term agricultural loans. The Federal Reserve Act of 1913 thus represented a compromise between the views of the banking industry and progressive and agrarian reformers. A central reserve board, appointed by the President and confirmed by the Senate, supervised the privately owned banks that belonged to the system and organized them into twelve reserve districts. The new system ensured stability, all sections of the nation obtained more adequate and reliable banking facilities, and the currency could be more readily expanded or contracted in accordance with the needs of the economy. At first distrustful and resentful, by 1929 one-third of the country's banks had entered the system. The Federal Reserve Act marked one of the most important and constructive legislative achievements of the Wilson administration, even though the Great Depression was to indicate that it had certain defects. Its enactment illustrated the movement toward order in business and the accompanying governmental regulations.

In dealing with the trusts, Wilson soon began to de-emphasize the trust-busting creed of the New Freedom and to turn toward a regulatory approach resembling Roosevelt's New Nationalism. To be sure, the Clayton Act in 1914 strengthened the Sherman anti-trust law. The act prohibited certain trade practices reducing or eliminating competition, although a move to declare monopolistic any business controlling one-third or more of a particular field of enterprise met defeat, and it threw a sop to labor and farm organizations by a provision that they would not be considered as illegal combinations in restraint of trade as long as they utilized legal methods. Samuel Gompers of the American

PLAYING TO THE GALLERIES

Nelson Harding, *Brooklyn Daily Eagle*, 1912.

Federation of Labor hailed the act as labor's Magna Carta, although he had wanted a clear-cut exemption of unions from the scope of the anti-trust laws. But the administration increasingly placed its reliance not on anti-trust suits but on regulating and advising business through the Federal Trade Commission, also authorized in 1914. Anxious to assuage business distrust — the economy experienced a recession in 1913 — Wilson appointed individuals friendly to the business viewpoint to the F.T.C. and to the Federal Reserve Board. One of his appointees to the Federal Reserve Board, Thomas D. Jones of Chicago, had to be withdrawn when an outcry broke out against Jones' connection with a firm then under anti-trust proceedings. An angry Wilson publicly regretted the attitude of suspicion toward big businessmen manifested by many reformers. Reflecting the administration's conciliatory approach, the Justice Department offered friendly advice to businesses doubtful of the legality of their corporate structures and instituted fewer anti-trust suits than it had during the Roosevelt and Taft administrations.

Wilson further revealed his rather conservative or limited variety of progressivism by his resistance to other proposed legislation. He approved the LaFollette Seamen's Act in 1915, freeing merchant seamen from a kind of contract slavery and improving safety measures at sea. But he objected to a proposal to establish a system for long-term agricultural loans as unwise special class legislation. Similarly, on states' rights grounds, he declined to support a federal child labor law or women's enfranchisement. Nor did he approve of a national race commission, proposed by Oswald Garrison Villard, a founder of the National Association for the Advancement of Colored People, and he made only limited efforts to counter the racial segregationist tendencies manifested by several of his cabinet members in their executive departments. He did resist the wishes of some Southern politicians to segregate blacks from whites on the capital's streetcars and to discharge or downgrade all black office holders, but he acquiesced when the Post Office Department and the Treasury segregated their employees. Obviously Wilson shared some of the racial views of many white Southerners.

In view of the President's obvious reluctance to tackle other reforms, more advanced progressive spokesmen felt greatly disappointed, especially when near the end of 1914 Wilson, in a letter released to the public, declared that his administration had accomplished the basic changes necessary to rectify the wrongs of the country, and proclaimed the dawn of a new era of cooperation and harmony between business and the general community. Essentially, Wilson had continued the rather moderate approaches of Roosevelt and Taft toward modernizing the machinery of government and increasing its role in regulating an industrial society.

The Diplomacy of Morality

Wilson brought to the presidency few definite aims in foreign policy except to promote peace and to use America's moral influence to elevate the tone of international relations. As we have seen, he approached both politics and foreign policy almost as a lay minister spreading moral enlightenment. From his boyhood in the Civil War and Reconstruction South, Wilson derived an abiding abhorrence of war and its suffering. Yet he was not a pacifist; some wars, he believed, were justified by the principles and moral issues involved.

Growing to manhood during a period of prolonged peace, when the great reformer and his boyhood hero William E. Gladstone guided British affairs, Wilson saw the great issues of the times as primarily questions of domestic reform. Despite his academic background in history and political science, he revealed little interest in foreign affairs, or much knowledge of them, prior to his presidency. To be sure, like most other educated Americans, the Spanish-American War and the acquisition of an empire in the Caribbean and the Pacific convinced him that the age of isolationism had passed and that the United States would have to play a larger role on the world scene. Yet in contrast to the well-developed view of world politics held by Theodore Roosevelt, Wilson's knowledge in 1913 seems rather superficial.

The new Secretary of State, William Jennings Bryan, a Nebraska lawyer and newspaper editor and thrice the Democratic nominee for the presidency, was ill-equipped for his new responsibilities. Decidedly less of an intellectual than Wilson, Bryan judged domestic and foreign politics from a moral point of view. He easily persuaded himself that the world advanced steadily toward universal peace and democracy. A world tour after the 1904 election provided him with abundant, if misleading, evidence that his fondest dreams were coming true. Seldom has a man of his political stature learned so little by travel. Spiritually Bryan never left home – rural, small town America.

Bryan received a continuous shower of mocking criticism while in office. His spoilsmanship in creating and filling vacancies in the diplomatic service particularly became a target. He replaced able men with amateurs and political hacks. If not restrained by President Wilson, Bryan would have liked to have made a clean sweep of diplomatic and consular posts, though it must be noted that the President himself bore direct responsibility for many political appointments. Critics of the teetotalling Secretary of State expressed savage amusement at his "grape-juice diplomacy" – the substitution of grape juice for alcoholic beverages at state dinners. The hostile New York *Times* gleefully reported the distress of Washington hostesses whose dinner table color schemes were disrupted when Bryan was served dark grape juice while the other diners drank pale golden champagne – one clever hostess solved the problem with a special brew resembling real wine. Sophisticates were dismayed by Bryan's lower middle-class habits – he personally shopped for groceries and took a workman's dinner pail to the State Department – and at his paid lectures on the Chautauqua circuit, supposedly sandwiched in with magicians and other circus-type entertainers. In fairness to Bryan it should be noted that many other distinguished Americans also lectured; he viewed it as a means of maintaining contact with the masses of American citizens.

Wilson and Bryan resolved to use American power and influence in world affairs to serve not only the national interests but also the best interests of other peoples. They envisioned a world-wide system of political democracy and liberal capitalism beneficial to all mankind. Of course, the United States by its enlightened political system and its advanced industry was destined for universal pre-eminence. American diplomacy, therefore, must advance not only the legitimate material interests of the nation but must accord with the highest standards of morality and principle. Laudable in theory if not always in practice, they advocated what has been described as "missionary diplomacy."

The "cooling off" treaties revealed both the noble ideals and the naivete of "uplift" diplomacy. Bryan shared the dream and convictions of the American peace movement and never doubted that a civilized and Christian world had outgrown warfare. Taft had negotiated broad arbitration treaties with Britain and France in 1911, but a Senate jealous of its powers and inclined toward Anglophobia and isolationist sentiment mutilated the pacts to such a degree that they had been abandoned. Bryan sought to solve the problem by negotiating "cooling off" bilateral treaties to submit *all* issues otherwise insoluble to special commissions. During the time used by the commissioners to draw up their report, expected to take about a year, signatories pledged not to resort to arms. Of course, after the report they could make war, but Bryan felt confident that the delay would preserve peace by cooling tempers and restoring sanity. His simple plan overlooked the fact that peace did not have the same high value to all governments and that many nations still viewed war as a legitimate tool to advance their interests.

Bryan successfully negotiated thirty "cooling-off" pacts — Germany declined to sign, to Bryan's disappointment — and the Senate ratified twenty-two of them. Peace advocates praised the treaties as notable advances toward eliminating war; more practical observers sneered. Jules Jusserand, the French Ambassador, reportedly quipped after signing for France: "There! At last there will end for all times the ceaseless wars between France and the United States. What a happy hour!" Bryan proudly viewed his pacts as his greatest achievement and President Wilson shared much of his satisfaction. None of these treaties were ever invoked, though the mere existence of one with Britain and none with Germany may have affected American relations with the belligerents during World War I.

Other policies also revealed the strengths and the weaknesses of moralistic diplomacy. Shortly after the inauguration, Wilson and Bryan decided to withdraw diplomatic support from the Six Power Consortium, formed in 1911 to lend money to the Chinese government, on the grounds that terms of the loan impaired China's sovereignty. Although widely applauded, the decision did nothing to solve China's financial needs and merely deprived her of a relatively disinterested protector in the loan. Ironically, the administration later became apprehensive about Japanese financial predominance in China and revived the consortium in 1918 but with indifferent results. Without waiting for similar action by other powers interested in China, Wilson and Bryan also extended full diplomatic recognition in 1913 to the military regime of Yuan Shih-kai. They hoped to shore up the weak republic established after overthrow of the Manchus in 1911-12 and to demonstrate American friendship for the new China. On the more positive side of the ledger of missionary diplomacy, Wilson's handling of the Panama Tolls question not only fully complied with honor but improved Anglo-American relations. The 1901 Hay-Pauncefote Treaty had specified that all shipping using the isthmian canal should be charged equal rates, but Congress in 1912 exempted American coastal shipping passing through the canal from toll charges. Great Britain protested and many Americans concurred that the act revealed bad faith. Although the Democratic platform in 1912 had endorsed tolls exemption, Wilson decided that it indeed impugned the national honor. He urged Congress in 1914 to repeal the exemption: "we are too big, too powerful, too self-respecting a nation to interpret with too strained or refined a reading the words of our promises. . . ." Congress complied, and not only British but Latin American opinion responded favorably to this evidence of American fair dealing.

Although the Gentlemen's Agreement, negotiated in the Roosevelt era, presumably had halted most Japanese immigration to the United States, many Californians continued to agitate for total legal exclusion. Proponents of exclusion in 1913 introduced a popular measure in the California legislature that would bar aliens ineligible for citizenship, such as the Japanese, from land ownership, even though the 50,000 Japanese in California owned only about one-tenth of one percent of the state's acreage. Wilson and Bryan responded tardily because they sympathized with Californians' view of the Japanese as unassimilable and from sensitivity to the right of a state to regulate its local affairs. Wilson had commented in 1912, "We cannot make a homogeneous population out of a people who do not blend with the caucasian race." Yet even after they became aware of the seriousness with which Japan viewed the situation, the division of powers under the American federal system meant that only persuasion could be used upon California. Almost as an envoy to a foreign country, Secretary Bryan made a special trip to California to plead with its maverick Republican governor, Hiram Johnson, and the legislature for less objectionable legislation. He failed to obtain any significant changes in the alien land law but at least his efforts helped assuage Japan's sensibilities. As the New York *Times* remarked editorially, "Mr. Bryan's policy of treating every apparently acute disagreement with a prescription of endless conversation has worked well."

In Mexico Wilson's policy of benevolent interference nearly led to full-scale armed intervention. Wilson appreciated the need of social and economic reforms in a Mexico cursed with poverty, illiteracy, wealthy landlords, and foreign investors, and he wanted to help. Unfortunately he did not see the difficulties inherent in one nation trying to guide reform in another, especially in a country as proud as Mexico with its memory of past wrongs by the United States. The President refused to recognize General Victoriano Huerta because he had come to power by undemocratic means early in 1913, overthrowing the reform administration of Francisco Madero in a palace coup that cost the latter his life. Since Madero had only recently ended the long dictatorship of Porfirio Díaz, it appeared that Huerta would again inflict a regime on Mexico more sensitive to the welfare of foreign investors than to the masses of exploited Mexican peasants. Despite the willingness of other powers to accept the new regime, and the eagerness of many Americans with oil and other interests in Mexico (valued at over one billion dollars) for a return to strong-man rule, Wilson proclaimed "watchful waiting" and sent emissaries to Mexico City to try to persuade Huerta to step aside for free elections and a return to constitutional procedures. Wilson thereby abandoned the traditional policy of recognizing de facto governments, substituting instead moral and ideological criteria. Huerta, a full-blooded Indian much addicted to alcohol and fully as stubborn as Wilson, refused to retire and took steps to strengthen his power. The American President then in effect encouraged forces in revolt against the dictator. The administration lifted an embargo on arms shipments, to enable military supplies to reach Huerta's enemies. Wilson determinedly resolved that Latin Americans must be taught habits of good government.

On April 9, 1914 during fighting between Huerta and his opponents around Tampico, some American sailors landed in the city for supplies (American vessels were in the area, as were those of other powers, to protect nationals) and were briefly arrested by local Huerta authorities. Although soon released, Admiral Henry Mayo of the American force demanded a formal apology and a salute to the American flag. President Wilson brushed aside Huerta's proposal for arbitration and requested Congress to endorse the use of force in defense of the national honor. Widely misinterpreted here and abroad as an exaggerated affair of honor, the President's underlying purpose was to topple Huerta and open the way for democracy in Mexico. On finding out that a ship was carrying arms to Huerta the President authorized the bombardment and seizure of Veracruz. For a brief period larger hostilities seemed almost unavoidable. Fortunately, Argentina, Brazil, and Chile offered their services, Wilson accepted, and the fighting around Veracruz ended. Wilson nevertheless achieved his larger aim, as a weakened Huerta fell from power in July, 1914.

The successful resolution of the "affair of honor," however, did not solve the Mexican problem. General Venustiano Carranza, the leader of the Constitutionalist party, soon established his sway over Mexico and Washington extended him *de facto* recognition in 1915. Carranza, although interested in reform, harbored strong anti-American feelings and firmly resisted Wilson's tutelage. Carranza not only threatened expropriation of foreign owned lands and oil concessions, but disturbed American Catholics by his anti-clerical policies. Pancho Villa, one of Carranza's rebellious generals, deeply resented Washington's recognition of his former chief, and in retaliation raided across the border into New Mexico. On March 9, 1916, his soldiers or "bandits" sacked the town of

Columbus, killing seventeen Americans. Wilson ordered General John Jacob Pershing to lead a force into Mexico to pursue Villa. The presence of Pershing's force deep in northern Mexico ignited a storm of threats from Carranza until finally Wilson recalled Pershing early in 1917. After the United States entered the World War in 1917, Carranza's rather unfriendly neutrality led to further distrust in Washington and there was talk of seizing the vital Tampico oil fields. Yet despite these frictions, in part the result of Wilson's own moralistic meddling in Mexico's internal affairs, the administration successfully resisted pressures for full-scale armed intervention.

Wilsonian ideals and practice seemed particularly divergent in the Caribbean. On the one hand, Wilson and Bryan disavowed the "dollar diplomacy" of their predecessors and proclaimed a new approach toward Latin America based on mutual respect and sovereign equality. On the other hand, the new administration soon came to appreciate the need for order and stability in the area around the vital Panama Canal. Moreover, Wilson determined to teach the disorderly, revolution-prone Caribbean republics habits of constitutional government and stability.

Wilson declared that cooperation with Latin American states could occur only when supported by "the orderly processes of just government based on law, not upon arbitrary or irregular force." He warned that he would have no sympathy with self-serving persons who seized power. Thus despite Wilson's pledge at Mobile, Alabama, in October of 1913, to seek Latin America's friendship on the basis of honor and equality, his administration obviously valued the promotion of democracy and stability in the Caribbean above respect for the sovereignty of those republics. Consequently there were more financial protectorates and more armed interventions in the Caribbean than ever before, causing the New York *Times* to comment that Wilson and Bryan made Taft's dollar diplomacy look like "ten cent diplomacy."

In Nicaragua which was close to the Panama Canal with an alternate canal route that the United States preferred to reserve for itself, the Taft administration had established a financial protectorate. Taft had stationed a company of marines in Managua, the capital, a so-called "legation guard" that in fact supported in power a pro-American regime. Under Wilson these policies seemed the only alternatives to chaos and revolution. Bryan negotiated the Bryan-Chamorro Treaty for a perpetual option to the alternate canal route in exchange for the payment of $3 million. Prior to the approval of this treaty by the American Senate, not granted until 1916, the State Department with Wilson's approval also felt compelled to resort to dollar diplomacy, persuading American bankers to advance loans to the needy Nicaraguan government. Not to have done so, Wilson and Bryan believed, would be to abandon Nicaragua to disorder or to force it to turn to European financiers with all the attendant dangers of exploitation and armed intervention.

Turbulent Haiti, where a small elite ruled two million illiterate and poverty-stricken Negroes, possessed a strategically important potential naval base at the Môle St. Nicholas which lay athwart main shipping routes in the Caribbean. The Wilson administration, mixing security with benevolent considerations, repeatedly tried to persuade Haiti to lease the Môle to the United States and to accept a financial protectorate similar to the Dominican and Nicaraguan models. A succession of short-lived regimes, each coming to power by revolutionary means, rejected these proposals. Washington feared that such chronic revolutionary turmoil might encourage foreign intervention dangerous to the strategic interests of the United States. In July, 1915, when President Guillaume Sam ordered the killing of a number of his political enemies an enraged mob dragged Sam from the French Legation in Port-au-Prince, where he had sought refuge, and hacked his body into pieces. Thoroughly out of patience, Wilson ordered the landing of American marines who first occupied the capital and subsequently the entire country. As the President remarked to the Secretary of State, "I suppose there is nothing for it but to take the bull by the horns and restore order." Behind a facade of native self-government, American marines and naval personnel remained in control of Haiti until 1934. American authorities launched a series of reforms: sanitation projects, roads and other public works, fiscal controls to pay off Haiti's foreign debt, and reorganization of the military into a more disciplined and smaller constabulary that hopefully would be subordinated to civilian controls. The State Department embodied these long-term reforms in a treaty signed with the native "government" in 1915 and in the new Haitian Constitution adopted by Haitians in a marine-guarded plebiscite in 1918.

The Dominican Republic had experienced a measure of stability and progress under the financial protectorate established by President Roosevelt in 1905-07. Supervising the collection of the customs revenues, American officials disbursed the funds to pay off the republic's foreign debt and to cover legitimate Dominican governmental expenses. Unfortunately, revolutionary agitation broke out again in 1911-13, as eager Dominican politicians found new ways to waste the government's share (45 percent) of the customs. Wilson and Bryan thus inherited a limited protectorate that increasingly seemed to fall short of the benevolent goals of promoting constitutionalism and progress. Moreover, they were ill-advised by the American Minister in Santo Domingo, James M. Sullivan, a political appointee and ex-boxing promoter who personally became entangled in unsavory private financial activities. Prior to his recall in 1915, Sullivan repeatedly urged Washington to adopt more drastic measures to promote order. In the spring of 1916 American marines landed to occupy the capital and then the entire republic. When Dominican "rebels" resisted the occupation, the American forces proclaimed martial law, carried out arbitrary arrests, and censored the native press. Not surprisingly, a number of sensitive Americans became greatly disturbed by their country's benevolent imperialism in the Caribbean, and the obvious contradiction it pointed out between the democratic

MISSIONARY DIPLOMACY
IN THE CARIBBEAN
1901–1921

500 MILES

UNITED STATES

MEXICO

Mexico

Tampico

Veracruz
U.S. INTERVENTION
1914

GULF OF MEXICO

FLORIDA

Havana

CUBA
U.S. OCCUP. 1898 - 1902
PLATT AMEND, 1902–34

BAHAMA
(BR.)

ISLANDS

ATLANTIC OCEAN

DOMINICAN
REP.
T. ROOSEVELT
CUSTOMS
INTERVENTION
1905

San
Domingo

PUERTO RICO
U.S. TERR., 1898
TERR., 1917

VIRGIN IS.
PURCH. FROM
DENMARK, 1916

Port
au Prince

HAITI
WILSON ARMED
INTERVENTIONS
1915–1916

JAMAICA
(BR.)

CARIBBEAN SEA

BR. HONDURAS

GUATEMALA

Guatemala

San Salvador
EL SALVADOR

HONDURAS
Tegucigalpa

NICARAGUA
TAFT CUSTOMS
INTERVENTION, 1911

Managua

CORN IS.
U.S., 1916

PROPOSED
CANAL

San José

COSTA RICA

PANAMA CANAL
PERPETUAL LEASE
1903

Panama

PANAMA
REVOLUTION
1903

COLOMBIA

Bogotá

VENEZUELA

Caracas

PACIFIC OCEAN

TRM

principles advocated by the United States and the armed occupation of these small republics. A congressional investigation, undertaken after the end of World War I, hastened the eventual American departure.

The interventions failed to achieve Wilson's goal of promoting orderly self-government. The principal legacy, after the eventual American withdrawal, seemed to be more efficient and brutal military dictatorships based on the American trained constabularies. Yet given the prevailing moral climate in America and Europe, the belief that creditors must be protected and debtors compelled to meet their obligations, and Washington's sense of its security requirements in the Caribbean, it is difficult to see how the Wilson administration could have escaped the commitments of its predecessors or have avoided further involvement. Probably it would have been wiser, however, to have limited interventions to the financial sphere.

President Wilson made important contributions to Pan-Americanism and served as a precursor of the later "Good Neighbor" policy. Of course, there were adverse reactions to his interventionism and a consequent growth of Yankee-phobia in Latin America. For example, Argentina's literary giant, Manuel Ugarte, a bitter critic of the United States, encouraged a movement for hemispheric cooperation that would exclude the hated Yankee. Yet many thoughtful Latin Americans felt greatly impressed with the liberalism and idealism of President Wilson. In 1915 Wilson proposed a Pan American Treaty between all the states of this hemisphere, to guarantee the territorial integrity and political independence of each and to promote peace and stability. Although the pact failed of adoption, because of continuing Latin American suspicions of the "Colossus of the North," it made a favorable impression and Wilson subsequently embodied its essential provisions in the Covenant of the League of Nations. When the United States entered World War I, thirteen Latin American states indicated their support of Pan American solidarity by either declaring war on Germany or by severing diplomatic relations with her. In the last year of the Wilson administration, the State Department began to close the gap between American ideals and behavior with the announcement that it intended to end Caribbean interventions and Wilson's last Secretary of State, Bainbridge Colby, undertook a brief but highly successful good-will tour of South America in late 1920.

New Freedom diplomacy, often criticized by scholars, was not a complete failure. The Caribbean at least had been stabilized, Latin American good-will had been cultivated, and the "New China" had been befriended. Even in turbulent Mexico, Wilson had managed to avoid full-scale intervention despite repeated vexations and clashes. In any case, all these problems and frustrations paled when contrasted with the challenges posed by the outbreak of the European War in 1914.

2

The Challenge to American Neutrality

IN REMOTE SARAJEVO on June 28, 1914 an assassination ignited a crisis that culminated in a major world war. Gavrilo Princip, an ardent Serbian nationalist and member of a terrorist group, the Black Hand, mortally wounded Archduke Franz Ferdinand, heir to the Austro-Hungarian throne, and his beloved wife Sophia. Blaming Serbian authorities for the political murder, the Austrian government decided to crush or humiliate Serbia and end its constant threat to the stability of the multi-national Hapsburg empire. When Belgrade failed to comply fully with its ultimatum, Austria-Hungary declared war against Serbia on July 28. Because of Europe's rival alliances and age-old ambitions and passions, the war could not be localized. Within a few bewildering days, the principal powers found themselves engulfed in war. Germany joined her ally Austria (the Central Powers) against Russia, France, and Great Britain (the Entente or Allied Powers) in a titanic struggle for the mastery of the continent. Germany violated Belgium's neutrality in an attempt to eliminate France from the war, Japan came in as Britain's ally in the Far East, and Italy joined the Entente in 1915. Eventually Turkey, Bulgaria, Rumania, and Greece also became immersed in the great struggle.

To most Americans it seemed incredible that the most civilized powers of Europe should plunge the world into war. Thoughtful if optimistic people had ignored previous crises threatening a large armed conflict in Europe, confident that the world had outgrown such madness. After recovering from the initial shock, Americans rejoiced that their country stood apart from the folly of the Old World, saved by its geography and by its policy of abstention from foreign alliances and entanglements. They applauded President Wilson when he proclaimed official neutrality and urged his fellow citizens to impartiality of thought as well as speech. One newspaper editor summed up the prevailing sentiment: "Peace-loving citizens . . . will now rise up and tender a hearty vote of thanks to Columbus for having discovered America."

Propaganda Campaigns

Impartiality of sentiment proved to be an impossible goal. The major ethnic groups in America's melting pot understandably sympathized with the countries of their origin. In 1914 approximately one-third of the American population of nearly ninety-two million people were "hyphenated Americans," either foreign born or with one or both parents immigrants. Eight million German-Americans sympathized with the cause of the Central Powers, joined by many of the four million Irish-Americans embittered by centuries of English rule of Ireland, and by many of the Russian-hating American Jewry. Old-stock Americans, on the other hand, tended to align with the Entente Powers, reflecting cultural and economic bonds with England and the traditional Franco-American friendship. Moreover, German-American relations had been slowly deteriorating for several decades as a result of economic competition, rivalry over Samoa, and misunderstandings over the Philippines during the Spanish-American War. By 1914 many Americans regarded imperial Germany and its blustering Kaiser Wilhelm II as the incarnation of militarism and autocracy.

Both the Entente and the Central Powers undertook propaganda campaigns designed to win popular approval for their causes in America. German spokesmen depicted their country as fighting a war imposed on it by Russian imperialism and French desires to revenge their defeat in the 1870 Franco-Prussian conflict. A secret and effectively organized British propaganda machine, known as Wellington House, came under the direction of Charles Masterman. It had a special branch for America directed by Sir Gilbert Parker, aided by the young historian Arnold Toynbee among others. Utilizing such guides as *Who's Who,* Parker's staff compiled a carefully selected mailing list of influential Americans, who ultimately received a stream of propaganda pamphlets, books, and other materials. Weekly surveys of the American press facilitated the shaping of propaganda to appeal to ethnic, religious, and social groups. British propagandists depicted the Entente as fighting a defensive war against a ruthless and inhumane enemy who had cruelly violated Belgian neutrality (a "scrap of paper"), and emphasized the necessity of upholding democracy and decency against German autocracy and militarism. German propagandists found it difficult to portray the Central Powers as waging a defensive war when their troops stood on Belgian and French soil. Moreover, Germany introduced new weapons

"The Kaiser Ravishes Belgium," *New York World,* **1914.**

and tactics that seemed barbarous: poison gas, dirigible aerial bombardments of cities, and submarine attacks against noncombatant enemy passenger and merchant vessels. Because Britain controlled the seas and the trans-Atlantic cables, German propagandists also had much difficulty in getting direct news from Germany into the United States. The majority of major American newspapers and magazines, such as the New York *Times,* tended to adopt a pro-Ally line in editorials and coverage of the war.

Although few historians now attribute our intervention in the wai to the effects of propaganda, the more intensive British campaign undoubtedly had a cumulative impact on the American public. British propagandists effectively utilized blunders such as the German execution in 1915 of Nurse Edith Cavell, a British nurse caught as a spy in occupied Belgium, and the alleged German atrocities and war crimes related in the famed Lord Bryce Report in 1915 to portray Germany's rulers as barbarous and utterly ruthless. The Bryce Report, endorsed by eminent British historians and journalists, contained exaggerated or unproved stories of deliberate German massacres, rapes, and destruction supposedly inflicted upon occupied Belgium and France. The famous affair of Dr. Albert's briefcase followed closely on the heels of the first submarine crisis and the release of the Bryce Report. Dr. Heinrich Albert, one of the German officials in America responsible for propaganda, somehow lost his briefcase on a New York city elevated train; American agents following him quickly picked it up. Its contents, published in the American press, revealed German propaganda activities and touched off a major spy scare that discredited the German effort. Of course, a majority of Americans had been at least mildly pro-Ally when the war began, before British propaganda and German blunders had any real effect. Yet British efforts strengthened that favorable predisposition and probably helps explain why the United States accepted Allied maritime war measures more readily than it did those of Germany. British propaganda probably also made it easier for the United States eventually to enter the struggle against Germany. Nevertheless, the majority of Americans during 1915 and 1916 agreed with President Wilson that the United States should reamin neutral.

The German "Menace"

An influential "realistic" minority in the United States viewed the European war as deeply significant for the security and economic interests of the American nation. For some years a number of Americans had observed Germany with distrust, suspecting the Kaiser's government of seeking coaling stations, naval bases, and perhaps even colonies in the Caribbean and in South America. These fears reflected the fact that both the United States and Germany, industrially progressive and dynamic nations, emerged nearly simultaneously as great powers on the world scene. Army War College and Navy General Board planners saw Germany as the one major power most likely to challenge American hegemony in the Western Hemisphere. Theodore Roosevelt, Admiral A. T. Mahan, Henry Cabot Lodge, journalist Walter Lippmann, and academicians George Louis Beer and Amos S. Hershey, to name a few, at one time or another held that Germany was a potential menace and valued British sea power as protecting the Western Hemisphere.

In an article in *The Independent* in 1909, Amos S. Hershey, Professor of

Political Science at Indiana University, illustrated these fears. He described Germany as a threat to American interests and to world peace, and he urged an Anglo-American alliance to meet the danger. Hershey predicted that "the people of the United States could hardly remain neutral in a war between Germany and Great Britain which might possibly end in German naval supremacy." An English observer, the well-known journalist Sydney Brooks, concluded in 1909 that an influential minority of Americans perceived that Germany was America's problem as well as Britain's. Brooks foresaw that in case of an Anglo-German war the United States would practice a benevolent neutrality toward England. If Germany should threaten American trade in foodstuffs with the British Isles, he concluded, the United States might enter the war on Britain's side.

When the European conflict began in 1914, a number of thoughtful Americans concluded that America's own interests — security, economics, and the preservation of democratic institutions — required an Entente victory. They feared that a German triumph would replace British with German sea power and would dangerously isolate the United States in the Atlantic and Pacific Oceans. These Americans, of course, were not simply "realists"; underlying their concepts of endangered national interests lay a strong conviction that democracy was threatened by German militarism and statism. "Prussian autocracy" soon became the stereotype to symbolize that ideological threat as well as the security danger. Whether primarily realistic or idealistic, this body of opinion made it easier for the United States eventually to enter the war against Germany.

A number of high administration officials and advisers held similar views, particularly the influential Colonel Edward M. House and Robert Lansing. House, an able and wealthy politician from Texas, attached himself during the 1912 elections to Wilson. With an acute understanding of Wilson's psychology, the Colonel astutely mixed flattery with an apparently selfless interest and quickly became the new President's most intimate adviser. In his "gray eminence" role as a power behind the throne House became an important factor in shaping Wilson's policies. Lansing, the son-in-law of a former Secretary of State, John Watson Foster, and uncle of a later Secretary, John Foster Dulles, entered the State Department as Counselor or second-in-command in 1914 with an extensive background in international law and arbitration. Formal, precise, and with a keenly analytical mind, Lansing also exerted much influence in framing neutrality policies. Wilson and Secretary Bryan depended heavily upon Lansing's knowledge and experience in international relations, particularly during the early months of neutrality.

Colonel House made several wartime trips to Europe on special missions for President Wilson. These convinced him that Germany represented unrestrained militarism dangerous to the peace of the world. He commented on one occasion, late in 1915, that the Allies should know that "we considered their cause our cause, and that we had no intention of permitting a military autocracy [to] dominate the world if our strength would prevent it." Yet for a long time

House thought that the preferable outcome of the war would be not total defeat for Germany but a limited Allied victory to curb Germany but still leave her powerful enough to restrain the expansionist tendencies of Czarist Russia.

Lansing essentially agreed with the Colonel but he thought German power should be completely shattered. A German victory or even a stalemate in the war would be harmful to the security and economic interests of America. Moreover, in his view, democratic principles and institutions necessitated the defeat of German autocracy and militarism. In a private memorandum, in July of 1915, Lansing wrote: "I have come to the conclusion that the German Government is utterly hostile to all nations with democratic institutions because . . . [its leaders] see in democracy a menace to absolutism and the defeat of the German ambitions for world domination." Therefore the United States should do no more than mildly protest against Allied acts while holding Germany fully accountable for her violations of neutral rights. He also hoped to reduce or eliminate German influence and intrigue in Latin America, especially in Mexico, and to enhance American security by purchase of the Danish West Indies (which he obtained in 1916 for $25 million).

How should the historian evaluate the fears of House, Lansing, and other "realists" that a German victory would endanger the vital interests of the United States? Did they reflect too uncritically English apprehensions (and hopes) that had been transmitted across the Atlantic before and during the war? Was their realism simply a reflection of long-held American views about the superior virtues of democracy versus monarchy and aristocracy? Any answer must be speculative, of course, but it does seem that these realists greatly exaggerated conflicting German-American interests and the danger from a German triumph in Europe. A victorious Germany probably would have been too exhausted to attack the United States in the near future, even if so inclined. Moreover, its navy would have faced severe handicaps, including lack of bases, in trying to mount a campaign in the Western Hemisphere. Obviously also, German attention would have continued to focus primarily upon the continent of Europe. On the other hand, it probably is true that a decisive victory by imperial Germany would have increased her political and economic influence in Latin America, have weakened the American position in the Far East by reducing British power, and would have made many Americans feel dangerously isolated in a threatening world.

President Wilson shared to some degree the "realistic" views of his advisers. He initially reacted to the outbreak of the European war with sympathy for Great Britain and France as fighting defensively against the aggressive Central Powers. He soon achieved a more balanced and less emotional view that the causes of the conflict were more complex and responsibility more diffuse than he had thought. Yet, because of his deep admiration of the British government and its traditions, he had a greater trust in the Allied than in the German leaders. The British government appeared to Wilson, at least until 1916, to be seeking more reasonable war goals than its opponents. Wilson apparently agreed with House that a German victory was undesirable and its threat might necessitate American intervention. On one occasion, he agreed with the Colonel's remark that "if Germany won it would change the course of our civilization and make the United States a military nation." Nevertheless the President did not think of Germany as an immediate menace to the vital interest of the United States. He earnestly believed in the wisdon of continued neutrality and he made great efforts to keep the nation out of the conflict.

The Perils of Neutrality

Shielding the nation from the material effects of the war proved as impossible as achieving genuine impartiality of thought and speech. The war disrupted the flow of trade to Europe and worsened an economic recession already underway in the United States. Shortages developed in certain materials normally imported from Europe. For example, the United States had imported dyes from Germany before the war but now, cut off from such imports by the Allied blockade, Americans had little choice but to develop their own dye industry. Finer grades of optical glass could no longer be obtained from Germany and some American astronomers had to delay the completion of planned telescopes until after the war. Entente orders for food, raw materials, and munitions soon began to flow in, however, and the American economy quickly recovered from the slump and went on to a booming prosperity destined to last until the end of the war. Yet the war boom had its penalty, for Allied purchases caused shortages of some materials for home consumption and triggered rising prices. In accordance with its traditional policy and with international practice, the United States opened its markets to all the contending powers and freely permitted private citizens to sell munitions and war materials to the belligerents. Although theoretically even-handed, the trade benefitted the Entente countries because of their control of the seas. American exports to Europe vastly increased. Trade with the Allies by 1917 rose to 184 percent above peacetime levels. Vast quantities of food, fiber, and metals, and over $1 billion worth of munitions flowed across the Atlantic to the Allies.

The one-sided war trade in effect made the United States an integral part of the Entente war effort. Disillusioned postwar critics later charged that these economic forces eventually pulled the United States into the war against Germany. Although the trade produced much bitterness in Germany, the evidence does not support that interpretation. The majority of Americans welcomed the war boom, and the administration naturally defended the commerce as neutral and desirable for the economy, but it never considered entering the struggle merely to ensure continued prosperity. Moreover, most Americans, officials and private citizens, assumed that the Allies would win a war of attrition. Germany's unrestricted use of submarine warfare in 1917 aimed at not only disrupting the war trade with America but cutting off all commerce and starving England into submission.

The burgeoning war trade also brought financial bonds with the Entente Powers. At first the administration, upon Secretary Bryan's recommendation in August, 1914 frowned upon private loans to the warring powers as inconsistent with "the true spirit of neutrality." Wilson and his advisers, however, soon perceived that the so-called loan ban conflicted with the country's interest in the expanding war trade. If the Allies could not obtain sufficient credit and loans to finance their purchases, war orders would dry up and prosperity disappear. Consequently the administration in October, 1914 decided to permit credit arrangements, and it abandoned the rest of the ban in the fall of 1915. As Lansing wrote the President, retention of the ban would mean "restriction of outputs, industrial depression, idle capital, financial demoralization, and general unrest and suffering among the laboring classes" of America. By early 1917, American bankers and private investors had loaned the Allies nearly \$2 1/3 billion, largely guaranteed against an Allied defeat by securities and other collateral.

American neutrality, though not planned that way, clearly operated in favor of the Allied cause. It was almost inevitable granted Allied control of access to the American market. Obviously the United States, whether passive or active in world affairs, could not help but exert an enormous influence in the international arena.

At the beginning of the war Americans argued with the British rather than the Germans over neutral rights on the high seas. As in the Napoleonic Wars, Britain used her vast naval power to strangle her opponents by imposing drastic restrictions on neutral commerce with Europe. She greatly expanded contraband lists of goods subject to seizure and effectively prevented direct trade with Germany even in non-military materials. The Royal Navy halted American ships and often seized cargoes consigned to neutral European countries, presumably destined for overland re-exportation to Germany and Austria. In alleged retaliation to the German submarine campaign, the British government in March, 1915 proclaimed a blockade of the Central Powers and nearby neutrals.

The State Department began a long campaign of protests against these Allied interferences as contrary to international law and the rights of neutrals. Although its notes did not lack sharpness, the State Department never pressed controversies to the point of a possible diplomatic rupture. For example, the long American note to Britain of October 21, 1915 one of its strongest to the Allies, denied the legality of the blockade and condemned interferences with neutral cargoes but it ended with a mild expression of hope that future British action would be guided by law rather than expediency. Most American trade went to the Allies anyhow, and it would have been economically self-destructive to permit disputes over neutral rights to disrupt it. Moreover, Wilson and House trusted and admired English leaders such as Sir Edward Grey, the Foreign Secretary. In fact Grey at first managed relations with America with a large degree of understanding and he made some concessions thereby strengthening the moral as well as economic ties between the two countries. For example, when Britain deemed it necessary to treat cotton as contraband, it softened the effects upon the American South by purchasing surplus cotton. In the State Department, Lansing labored to prevent diplomatic controversies with Great Britain from becoming too acrimonious. In his view, American interests dictated the avoidance of a break, and he was aware of the precedents created by the Union Navy during the Civil War in interfering with neutral commerce. Therefore, in his words, "Everything was submerged in verbosity."

Washington reacted less tolerantly to Germany's submarine warfare. German navalists, their surface fleet virtually bottled up in the North Sea by the British, turned eagerly to the underseas weapon as a means of challenging enemy control of the seas and carrying the war home to Great Britain. On February 4, 1915, allegedly retaliating for Allied mining of the North Sea, the German Foreign Office proclaimed that belligerent shipping in a zone around the British Isles would be subject to destruction even though it would not always be possible to save crews and passengers. Germany cautioned neutral vessels to avoid the area, claiming that Allied use of neutral flags and the ramming of U-boats on the surface made it impossible always to observe the customary procedure of "visit and search." Accidental attacks on neutral ships therefore sometimes could not be avoided. Wilson refused to accept these justifications and in a note sent on February 10 expressed "grave concern" at the Berlin proclamation. Rejecting the legality of the German position, he warned that if violations of American rights occurred it would be necessary "to hold the Imperial German Government to a strict accountability for such acts . . . and to take any steps it might be necessary to take to safeguard American lives and property . . . on the high seas."

The strict accountability note clearly opposed what Germany regarded as the most efficient use of the submarine. In the American view, neutral citizens and ships had the right freely to use the high seas subject only to visit and search by belligerent warships to intercept war contraband goods. Apparently President Wilson and Lansing adopted the strict accountability policy primarily to defend the nation's honor and rights and to protect its economic interests against what they deemed an illegal and inhumane method of warfare. They did not consider other possible alternatives, such as requesting American ships and citizens to avoid the submarine zone.

On May 7, 1915, the German *U-20* was off the Irish coast heading for home port when it unexpectedly sighted the pride of the British trans-Atlantic fleet the *Lusitania* in its periscope. The captain of the *Lusitania,* nearing the end of an uneventful voyage from the United States, failed to take the normal defensive measure of zigzagging and had reduced speed preparatory to the final run into port. The *U-20* stalked its prey and at 2:10 p.m. fired one torpedo into the starboard side of the great passenger ship. The Cunard liner came to a stop and began to list to starboard; it sank within eighteen minutes with the loss of 1198 passengers and crew, including 128 American citizens. A feeling of indescribable horror and outrage swept across the United States at news of the sinking.

Fearing the imminence of war, Secretary Bryan throughout the crisis pled with the President for a mild course. He argued that citizens voluntarily entering the war zone aboard Allied passenger or merchant vessels contributed to their own deaths by negligence and must not be permitted to embroil the nation in controversies likely to lead to hostilities. The government should not seem to argue that the mere presence of an American aboard a belligerent ship immunized it from German attack, for that would amount to a condemnation of U-boat warfare in general. Moreover, he pointed out, the German public already felt embittered at the one-sided American war trade with the Allies. The American government, therefore, ought to make every effort to avoid the appearance of official partiality toward the Allies and inflexibility toward Germany. Bryan was also disturbed by the presence of contraband goods, including cartridges and shrapnel, in the cargo of the *Lusitania:* "A ship carrying contraband should not rely upon passengers to protect her from attack — it would be like putting women and children in front of an army."

President Wilson agreed with Lansing rather than Bryan. Strict accountability applied not only to Americans aboard American ships but also to citizens traveling on Allied passenger vessels. He viewed the attack on the *Lusitania* and the destruction of noncombatant and neutral lives as an indefensible and immoral act contrary to international law and neutral rights. Nevertheless, the President refused to be swept by emotion into belligerency; he remarked at Philadelphia on May 10 that "There is such a thing as a man too proud to fight," "a nation being so right that it does not need to convince others by force that it is right." Therefore he adoped a firm course condemning ruthless underseas warfare and demanding that Germany comply with his interpretation of international law. The first *Lusitania* note sent to Berlin on May 13 vigorously upheld American rights and expressed confidence that the German government would disavow its illegal acts and make reparation.

The German government failed to comply with the American demands. It claimed that the *Lusitania* had carried troops and hidden armament, thus becoming in effect a warship subject to destruction. The evidence failed to substantiate those charges, although the *Lusitania* had carried some munitions. Unable to persuade the President to postpone the issue for postwar settlement, Bryan resigned on June 9, to be succeeded as Secretary by Robert Lansing. Apparently Bryan hoped to mobilize peace sentiment against the administration's policies. He had little success, for the majority of the press while sharply criticizing him for abandoning his post at a crucial time also endorsed Wilson's

WAR ZONES AT SEA, 1914-1917

CENTRAL POWERS

ALLIED STATES

300 MILES

GERMAN SUBMARINE ZONES

RUSSIAN EMPIRE

OTTOMAN EMPIRE

BLACK SEA

RUMANIA

BULG.

SERBIA

GREECE

AUSTRIA-HUNGARY

GERMANY

ITALY

SWITZ.

FRANCE

BELG.

NETH.

DENMARK

SWEDEN

NORWAY

FAEROE IS.

ALLIED MINE FIELDS

UNITED KINGDOM

NORTH SEA

BALTIC SEA

ATLANTIC

OCEAN

MEDITERRANEAN SEA

SPAIN

PORTUGAL

AZORES (PORT.)

cautious but firm handling of the crisis. The second American note went to Berlin on the same day as Bryan's resignation, reiterating previous demands. Again Germany failed to give a satisfactory response, although it offered a pledge of safety for American passenger vessels; the mere presence of neutral citizens on a belligerent vessel, Berlin declared, could not be permitted to immunize it from attack. The German government obviously hoped to avoid war but it was unwilling to abandon use of the submarine. Wilson also wanted to prevent a diplomatic rupture if at all possible. The third American note, on July 21, rejected the German defense as unsatisfactory but only warned that any repetition involving American lives would be viewed as "deliberately unfriendly."

Historians long have debated which course, that of Bryan or Wilson, marked the wiser path for the nation in 1915. In the disillusioned 1920's and 1930's, many hailed Bryan as a discerning statesman and the only genuine neutralist in the Wilson administration; defenders of Wilson and more realistically inclined scholars, on the other hand, have tended to dismiss Bryan as hopelessly naive and ill-informed. From today's perspective, Bryan seems to have been on firm ground when he argued that other courses existed than strict accountability: acquiescence under protest to Germany's acts (as to those of the Allies), or avoidance of the war zones. Events also revealed that Bryan correctly foresaw that Wilson's path probably would end in war. Yet it must be kept in mind that the President in 1915 faced a novel form of warfare, with no precedents to guide him, and that he earnestly sought to defend the nation's material and moral interests. Unlike Bryan, Wilson (and most of his fellow citizens) did not value peace at any price. The United States, in contrast to the smaller European neutrals who bent before the U-boat challenge, as a great world power could not weaken its prestige by acquiescence and still hope to play the mediatory role that Wilson envisaged. While from a later perspective one may regret that Wilson's position against Germany led to war and Germany's defeat — the Kaiser later seemed eminently preferable to Hitler — it is difficult to criticize the President's decisions when considered within the context of the times.

A period of quiet negotiation followed Wilson's third note, as both governments sought to avoid direct confrontation. Wilson had retreated from his initial general condemnation of submarine warfare and in effect accepted use of the U-boat as long as American rights were not violated. Yet the President had committed American prestige and honor to holding Germany fully and immediately accountable for the loss of American lives through undersea warfare. Other alternatives had been ruled out and the policy of the United States toward the issue henceforth was comparatively inflexible.

The torpedoing of another British passenger liner, the *Arabic,* on August 19, ended the brief lull. Two American lives were lost in the attack. Although House and Lansing advised stern measures, the President again sought to defend the nation's rights and still preserve peace. He was aware of the deep cleavage between those Americans who demanded more vigorous measures against Germany and the vast majority of citizens who wanted national rights to be upheld but peace also to be preserved. House recorded in his diary, "I am surprised at the attitude he [Wilson] takes. He evidently will go to great lengths to avoid war." The President directed Lansing to enter into negotiations with the German Ambassador, Count Johann von Bernstorff.

The German Chancellor, Theobald von Bethmann-Hollweg, feared that war with the United States would have disastrous results for Germany. He recognized that the United States would bring almost unlimited financial strength, industrial resources, and fresh manpower into the struggle. Although under pressure within Germany for fuller use of the submarine, the Chancellor temporarily obtained the support of the military leaders, who were apprehensive about increasing the country's enemies. Consequently he found it possible to make sufficient concessions to the United States to avoid a break while not entirely renouncing use of the U-boat. The *Arabic* controversy ended with a German pledge not to sink passenger liners without warning and without provisions for the safety of those on board. Significantly, the pledge applied only to passenger liners and not to all merchant vessels. Only a truce had been achieved; the larger issue remained unresolved.

Politics and the War

As German-American relations worsened, more and more Americans, alarmed at their nation's comparative military weakness, urged a program of preparedness upon the President and the Congress. Patriotic groups such as the National Security League and the American Defense Society called for more money for the navy and especially the army. General Leonard Wood initiated what became known as the "Plattsburg Idea," a semi-military training of civilian volunteers in special summer camps. Colleges and universities also began to place greater emphasis upon military science courses and R.O.T.C. programs for their students. Ex-president Theodore Roosevelt quickly became one of the leading spokesmen for preparedness. As editor of *The Outlook*, Roosevelt at first had supported neutrality but soon he advocated a more aggressive course. He raged at Wilson's apparently interminable note writing with the belligerents as dishonorable and unworthy of a great nation. Morality as well as the national interests required that the country should enter the war on the Allied side, he believed: "it is well to remember that there are things worse than war."

Many progressives and peace advocates, however, strongly resisted the call for military preparedness. Their solution to diplomatic problems lay in ending the war, not preparing to enter it. War, in their view, resulted from selfish economic pressures and competition for markets and resources. Moreover, military preparations and war might well kill the domestic reform movement and erode or destroy democratic rights and liberties at home. They demonstrated their earnestness, if not their practicality, when a group of pacifists persuaded industrialist Henry Ford to charter the ship *Oscar II* for a special peace mission to Europe in December, 1915, to attend what its planners called a continuous "peace conference" at The Hague. Unfortunately for the cause of such pacifists as Rosika Schwimmer, who had sold Ford on the plan, the automobile tycoon had only the vaguest concept of the conference and he was vulnerable to cranks who quickly joined his venture. Ford aroused ridicule when he proclaimed his intention to "get the boys out of the trenches by Christmas." Most of the well-known peace advocates thereupon wisely decided to stay home. Needless to say, Ford's naive gesture failed.

The crises with Germany in the first half of 1915 and the growing popular appeal of the preparedness movement finally persuaded the President. In the fall of 1915 the administration presented a plan for heavy outlays for defensive purposes. The naval program called for construction of ten battleships, six battle cruisers, ten cruisers, and numerous other craft within five years, with parity with the British to be achieved by 1925. The plan also proposed that the regular army be substantially enlarged, and the National Guard in effect replaced by a Continental Army reserve of 400,000 men.

Wilson's recommendations ignited a furious political debate and split progressive ranks. While many progressives could agree with Wilson on preparedness, others fearful of doing anything that might encourage war joined the pacifists. A group of eastern peace leaders, including Oswald Garrison Villard and Jane Addams of Hull House, formed the League to Limit Armament, while Miss Addams also joined other feminist advocates in creating the Women's Peace Party. At least thirty Democratic members of Congress, mostly from the South and West, including Claude Kitchin of North Carolina, the majority leader in the House, openly rebelled against the President's leadership. Wilson appealed to the Republicans for support in Congress and early in 1916 undertook a speaking tour in the midwestern states where he defended preparedness as necessary to safeguard the Western Hemisphere. America, he declared, "must play her part in keeping this conflagration from spreading on this side of the sea." Although compelled to accept a number of compromises, Wilson obtained the approval of Congress for doubling the size of the army (to about 220,000 men), greater federal authority over the National Guard, and a vast accelerated construction program for the navy. Congress created a Council of National Defense to advise the President and authorized a federal Shipping Board to own and operate merchant ships and to regulate the merchant marine.

On March 24, 1916 a German U-boat torpedoed the *Sussex*, an unarmed French channel steamer. Although no American lives were lost and the vessel did not sink, the attack clearly violated the *Arabic* pledge. Lansing advised immediate severance of relations with Germany but Wilson again resorted to diplomacy. On April 18, the President solemnly warned the German government that he would sever diplomatic relations unless ruthless U-boat warfare against belligerent merchant and passenger ships immediately ceased.

Despite mounting demands within Germany for increased use of the submarine, Chancellor Bethmann-Hollweg again managed to persuade the Kaiser and his military chiefs to avoid a rupture. In the *Sussex* pledge of May 4 Germany promised that unresisting belligerent merchant and passenger vessels would not be attacked without warning and without provisions for the safety of those aboard. Ominously, however, the pledge reserved freedom of action if the American government should fail to obtain Allied agreement to "freedom of the seas" for neutrals to trade with either side in the war.

A marked deterioration in Anglo-American relations followed the *Sussex* crisis and apparently increased Wilson's conviction that America must preserve its neutrality. Faced with a desperate war with Germany, the British government felt compelled to tighten its blockade and to increase controls over neutral countries. The ministry subjected neutral mails to censorship and publicly blacklisted neutral firms and individuals suspected of trading with Germany. It released a list of 85 American businesses and citizens to be denied use of all British owned insurance, supplies, and other facilities. Such blatant defiance of American sensibilities caused President Wilson to seek and obtain retaliatory legislation from Congress. An act authorized the executive to withhold clearances and port facilities from foreign ships refusing to transport American goods, but Wilson did not use it for the simple reason that it would interfere with exports to the Allies and thereby endanger America's warborn prosperity.

The popularity of the peace issue in the election of 1916 further strengthened Wilson's neutrality. Since Theodore Roosevelt had returned to the fold and the Progressive Party had collapsed, the Republicans seemed to be in a good position to regain the White House. Charles Evans Hughes resigned from the Supreme Court to accept the presidential nomination on the Republican ticket. Hughes spoke of "straight Americanism" and greater executive firmness in foreign policy but played for the pro-German vote, conferring with German-American and Irish-American leaders and indicating a course of strict neutrality toward the European war. Unfortunately he could not escape the more bellicose support of Theodore Roosevelt, which enabled the Democrats to portray Hughes and the Republicans as pro-war. Moreover, party factional strife between conservative and progressive elements hurt his campaign, especially in California, where he unintentionally snubbed Governor Hiram Johnson, and in other western states.

Wilson appealed to progressive sentiment by supporting a series of reform measures of the type he had earlier opposed as class legislation or infringement of states' rights. He appointed to the Supreme Court the liberal Jewish lawyer, Louis Brandeis, despite furious conservative resistance; he obtained approval from Congress for a system of federal farm loan banks to make long-term farm loans, a federal workmen's compensation act, the Keating-Owen child labor act

"A Mother's Plea for Peace," Leo Feist, New York.

that prohibited goods in interstate commerce made by children under fourteen years of age, and the Adamson Act imposing an eight-hour work day on the railroads. In contrast to the more conservative tone of the Republicans, the Democrats successfully identified their party with the interests of labor and social justice. Into Wilson's coalition came the more advanced wing of the progressive movement, many disillusioned former supporters of Roosevelt, and organized labor, especially the leaders of the American Federation of Labor. After the dramatic response at the Democratic Convention to the slogan that

Wilson had "kept us out of the war," the President capitalized on the obvious peace sentiment of most citizens by charging that the election of Hughes would mean war with Mexico and intervention in the European conflict. As a Democratic newspaper advertisement phrased the issue to the people:

You are Working – *Not Fighting*!
Alive and Happy; – *Not Cannon Fodder*!
Wilson and Peace with Honor?
or
Hughes with Roosevelt and War?

The effort of certain Irish-American and Roman Catholic spokesmen to attack the President's recognition of the anti-clerical Carranza in Mexico and Wilson's allegedly pro-British attitude failed to divert many Irish voters from their traditional Democratic loyalties. When Jeremiah O'Leary of the "American Truth Society," an anti-British and pro-German propaganda organization, sent the President a telegram charging pro-British policies, Wilson replied publicly. "I would feel deeply mortified to have you or anybody like you vote for me. Since you have access to many disloyal Americans and I have not, I will ask you to convey this message to them." This was an effective rejoinder, especially when the Democrats charged a German and Irish-American plot to defeat Wilson by backing the Republican nominee and it became known that Hughes had conferred with O'Leary and other known pro-German spokesmen.

The early election returns indicated a Republican triumph. The Democratic "victory" dinner at the Biltmore Hotel in New York City was described as "a morgue-like entertainment" rather than a celebration. Wilson retired early that evening, resigned to his defeat. Banner headlines in some newspapers hailed Hughes as the victor and next chief executive. Later reports from the western states, however, revealed that Wilson had edged his opponent by an extremely close margin, receiving 277 electoral votes to 254 for Hughes. In popular votes Wilson got 9,129,606 to Hughes' 8,538,221. It was a victory for progressivism and peace, but the congressional results foreshadowed great difficulties for Wilson. The election pared the Democratic margin in the Senate to eight and control of the House of Representatives rested in the hands of a small number of progressives and independents.

The End of Neutrality

Wilson always had been interested in serving as a mediator in the war. In late 1915 Colonel House had worked out with the President and Sir Edward Grey a scheme for mediation-intervention. The resultant House-Grey Memorandum of January, 1916, had provided that the United States, at a time deemed propitious by the Allies, would propose a conference of the belligerents to end the war; if Germany declined or subsequently rejected reasonable terms, the

United States would probably enter the war on the Allied side. Apparently House had intervention primarily in mind but Wilson saw the plan only in terms of mediation. It failed because the Allied governments opposed a negotiated peace as long as any hope remained of victory.

After the 1916 election Wilson made two direct peace moves on his own. On December 18, despite the embarrassment of a German bid for a negotiated peace on December 12, he requested a statement of war aims from all the belligerents. Neither side responded as positively as he anticipated. Undeterred, on January 22, 1917, he addressed the Senate and publicly appealed for a compromise "peace without victory" based on justice and reason, a lasting "peace among equals." His efforts failed. Both sides had expended too much blood and money and passions were too deeply aroused for either to accept a mere restoration of peace without extensive gains. Moreover, neither belligerent camp favored an active role for Wilson in the eventual negotiations.

The failure of these peace efforts was ominous for American neutrality. Events within Germany forced the Chancellor to capitulate to the navalists. Field Marshal Paul von Hindenburg and his guiding genius General Erich Ludendorff in effect had become the wartime dictators of Germany. The navalists persuaded Hindenburg and Ludendorff that unrestricted submarine warfare offered the best remaining hope for circumventing the stalemated land war and winning a decisive victory by starving Britain into submission. The navalists argued that the United States was already fully aiding the Allies, therefore its entry into the war would be a mere formality. The Kaiser concurred. Chancellor Bethmann-Hollweg and a few other officials, still dreading war with America, had no realistic option but to acquiesce. The decisive conference came at Pless on January 7. Bethmann-Hollweg, seeing that further resistance would be futile, described the decision as the "last card." "But if the military authorities consider the U-boat war essential, I am not in a position to contradict them." Hindenburg replied confidently, "We are ready to meet all eventualities." On January 31, 1917, Germany notified the United States that after February 1 all ships, belligerent and neutral, would be destroyed — presumably without warning and without safety provisions — in the waters around the British Isles.

In view of his past warnings, President Wilson had no option but to break diplomatic relations with Germany, which he did on February 3. Still reluctant to take the nation into the struggle, however, he clung to a faint hope that Germany might yet curb its submarine campaign; more than ever, it seemed to him, continued American neutrality offered the only hope to the world for a just and stable peace. Wilson apparently contemplated alternative courses short of full belligerency: the arming of American merchant vessels in defense against the U-boat (when a congressional filibuster in the Senate, led by Senator Robert La Follette of Wisconsin and others, blocked passage of a bill for arming, Wilson armed the vessels on his own authority), or a limited naval war in which the navy would convoy American ships. These options seemed unsatisfactory, having all the disadvantages of war without its sense of national purpose and goals. The destruction of three American ships in mid-March (*Illinois, City of Memphis* and *Vigilencia*), plus the earlier sinking of the British liner *Laconia*, indicated that Germany meant to carry out its threats. The British-intercepted Zimmermann telegram also revealed Germany's hostile intentions. Arthur Zimmermann, the German Foreign Secretary, had proposed to Mexico the conclusion of an alliance against the United States in case of an American-German war — Japan also would be invited to join — and tried to tempt Mexico with the prospect of recovering former territory lost during the Mexican War in 1846-48. The British in late February turned a copy of the decoded telegram over to the State Department which released it to the American press. An aroused American public was convinced of German duplicity and hostility.

Wilson addressed Congress on April 2 and recommended that it formally accept the status of a belligerent, forced upon it by Germany's actions. After reviewing his efforts for peace and Germany's repeated violations of American rights, he declared that neutrality was no longer possible. The President then proclaimed the lofty goals for which America should fight:

> The world must be made safe for democracy. Its peace must be planted upon the tested foundations of political liberty. We have no selfish ends to serve. We desire no conquest, no dominion. . . . We are but one of the champions of the rights of mankind. We shall be satisfied when those rights have been made as secure as the faith and the freedom of nations can make them. . . . It is a fearful thing to lead this great peaceful people into war. . . . But the right is more precious than peace, and we shall fight for the things which we have always carried nearest our hearts — for democracy, for the right of those who submit to authority to have a voice in their own governments, for the rights and liberties of small nations, for a universal dominion of right by such a concert of free peoples as shall bring peace and safety to all nations and make the world itself at last free.

Congress and the galleries cheered and waved flags in wild abandon as the President finished speaking. Republican Senator Henry Cabot Lodge congratulated Wilson for expressing American sentiment "in the loftiest manner." Paeans of praise poured into the White House from the press and in private letters. Opposition to war of course remained within the country and in Congress but it could not resist the tide successfully. Senator La Follette led the rear guard resistance in the Senate and Claude Kitchin in the House. They were thwarted. Congress adopted the war resolution by a vote of 82 to 6 in the Senate and 373 to 50 in the House. Most of the opposition came from certain midwestern areas where large numbers of German-Americans or Scandinavian-Americans lived, and where a type of parochial agrarian progressivism was strongest. The mood in Congress and the nation as a whole was one of reluctant acceptance of a struggle imposed by Germany. The President formally proclaimed a state of war on April 6, 1917.

In the disillusioned aftermath of the war, it became fashionable to argue that intervention had been unnecessary and unwise. Some "revisionist" writers and historians charged that the country had been duped into the struggle by British propaganda and powerful economic and financial forces interested in profits through an Allied victory. They dismissed the submarine issue as merely an excuse, or asserted that at most its unrestricted use by Germany had been caused by American unneutrality. Defenders of intervention, on the other hand, replied that the United States had tried to remain neutral but had been forced into the war because of Germany's illegal and aggressive acts. In recent years, a few writers have argued that the United States fought not for any of these reasons but to defend its security against the threat of a German victory.

There can be little doubt that, despite the official position of impartiality, the United States followed a course in 1914-1917 of benevolent neutrality toward the Allies, while adopting by and large an uncompromising attitude toward Germany. This reflected strong bonds of sentiment and trade between the United States and the Allied Powers, especially Great Britain, and the absence of any such ties with Germany. It would be unsound to attribute the eventual entry into the war solely to the submarine issue, therefore, for other options existed beside the policy of strict accountability. Yet the U-boat provided the indispensable point of contact and hence of conflict between the two powers. The United States finally opposed ruthless submarine warfare because it endangered its legitimate economic interests, violated its neutral rights, and affronted its national honor. Moreover, by 1917 President Wilson viewed Germany as a major threat not merely to the rights and interests of the United States but to the peace and progress of the entire world. American involvement therefore seemed necessary not only to safeguard American rights and interests but to eliminate German militarism and provide the basis for an enduring peace of justice and reason. A majority of Wilson's fellow citizens agreed that Germany's actions left no other choice. Time revealed, however, that they were much less committed to the President's vision of an ideal peace and new world order.

3

War and Peace

MOST AMERICANS IN early 1917, confident that the Allies were winning the war, assumed that the United States would need to send only token forces to Europe while providing economic and financial support to Germany's opponents. Even the administration shared that view. That illusion was quickly shattered when the Allies made known their desperate needs for troops as well as war materials. Arthur J. Balfour led a British war mission to the United States, rapidly followed by French, Italian, Belgian, Russian, Serbian and other groups. Received with pomp and ceremony, these visitors not only helped develop the indispensable machinery for a coalition war effort but also stimulated the enthusiasm of the American public for the great struggle. Subsequently Britain sent over Lord Northcliffe, the press tycoon, and France sent André Tardieu to head permanent commissions in America to manage war purchases. Treasury Secretary McAdoo developed procedures to certify needs and establish priorities as well as financing, while Colonel House led a special mission to Europe in late 1917 to advance inter-Allied coordination of economic, financial, shipping, and military activities. The Allies established a joint purchasing agency in the United States and an Interallied Council on War Purchases and Finance in Paris. In these ways a large measure of order and efficiency began to be brought to the incredibly complex problems of waging a coalition war. Wilson agreed to the establishment of a Supreme War Council in Paris to concert strategy, but he balked when the Allied governments tried to broaden its function to include political decisions. The President thereby made clear his determination to retain diplomatic freedom to formulate liberal peace goals and to prevent the Allies from imposing the terms of the eventual peace settlement.

Mobilizing for War

The great crusade against Autocracy required the United States to convert itself into a nation in arms, mobilizing and directing its economy and manpower to the supreme goal of military victory. Reversing gears from its prewar concern with preserving competition, the administration shifted toward a planned and regulated economy. As one government official informed representatives of the steel industry, "This is a crisis and commercialism, gentlemen, must be absolutely sidetracked." The Council of National Defense had been established in 1916 to advise the President on broad questions including war production and procurement. After the entry into the war, Wilson created a General Munitions Board to supervise the placing of war orders, but owing to difficulties with the military he replaced it with a new agency in July, 1917, the War Industries Board. The W.I.B. floundered under its first two directors, until the President overhauled and strengthened the agency in the spring of 1918 and placed it under the direction of Bernard Baruch, a wealthy Wall Street stock speculator and investor. Baruch's agency had authority to create new facilities for production, convert existing plants to war purposes, set priorities in production and transportation, and allocate scarce materials. It curtailed nonessential civilian production, such as automobiles, and obtained a type of price-fixing on certain basic materials through pressure on industry. Relying largely on persuasion and advice, the W.I.B. encouraged increased efficiency and productivity through standardization of styles and sizes of products, lessons that industry remembered in the postwar years. The W.I.B. placed war contracts on a cost plus basis, leading to charges of war profiteering but providing stimulation for the construction or conversion of industrial plants for war purposes.

Armed with authority from Congress, Wilson created a number of war agencies to mobilize the economy. The Food Administration, directed by Herbert Hoover, vastly increased the production of foodstuffs to feed both the American and Allied peoples, setting high minimum prices for government purchases of wheat and pork and curbing civilian consumption by voluntary rationing, "wheatless" and "meatless" days. Wheat acreage increased from 45 million acres in 1917 to 75 million in 1919. Exports of breadstuffs to Europe rose from about 3,320,000 tons before the war to over 10½ million tons by 1918-1919; the export of meats, fats, and sugar also increased proportionately. The Fuel Administration increased coal production, essential for heat and industry. The railroads posed a special problem. For a decade and a half prior to the war, labor and physical costs had risen, yet the Interstate Commerce Commission had been slow to authorize rate increases. The sudden burdens of moving military manpower and supplies to the east coast resulted in a gigantic traffic snarl in late 1917. Railroad unions, demanding sharp wage hikes, and unhappy shippers favored federal operation of the lines, a solution that many rail executives also privately welcomed. The administration's decision to place the railroads under federal control, operated by the Railroad Administration directed by McAdoo, reflected not only wartime needs for an efficiently integrated system but also progressive views that it was a good opportunity to demonstrate the role of government in promoting the public interest. Shipping posed a related difficulty. For years America had depended for cargo facilities largely on British vessels, but in 1917 German U-boats were sending a phenomenal number of these ships to the bottom of the sea. Even before the war entry, Congress had authorized the Shipping Board to build or acquire merchant craft. Although an ambitious construction program at new shipyards, such as Hog Island near Philadelphia, failed to complete much tonnage prior to the Armistice, the Shipping Board acquired the necessary shipping through purchases, commandeering of vessels under construction in private shipyards, and seizure of the interned German ships and of Dutch vessels in American ports. The War Trade Board regulated foreign trade, and the National War Labor Board and the War Labor Policies Board sought to protect labor's interests and to avoid disputes or strikes hampering production.

Mobilization not only increased productivity but resulted in real advances for labor. The eight-hour day spread widely, at least in principle, wages rose and working conditions improved, a U.S. Employment Service helped bring together workers and jobs, and the A.F.L. grew from two million to over three million members by 1920. Large numbers of women found employment and many Negroes began to migrate from the southern states, attracted by jobs in northern cities. A number of business leaders accepted patriotic service in government agencies as "dollar-a-year men," and many intellectuals from the academic and literary worlds for the first time entered the federal service as expert advisers, technicians, and administrators. Among the less desirable side effects of the mobilization of civilians and soldiers, an influenza epidemic struck America in the autumn of 1918 and caused thousands of deaths. Housing shortages, rising rents, and some racial frictions and clashes in northern cities also resulted from the impact of the war.

Politics, behind a facade of patriotic unity, continued as usual during the war years. Both major political parties maneuvered for advantage. Democrats relied upon President Wilson's great prestige as a war leader to help them retain political power in the forthcoming 1918 mid-term elections, while Republicans seized advantage of real or alleged failures in the mobilization program to attack their opponents. The election of 1916 had given no clear mandate to either party in Congress, especially in the lower house where a handful of independents held the balance between the two factions. Divided, confused, and ill-equipped to manage its own affairs efficiently, Congress nevertheless was inclined to challenge the executive's direction of the war effort.

Theodore Roosevelt, remembering his heroic exploits in 1898, eagerly proposed to raise and lead a division of volunteers to France. Although his plan aroused great enthusiasm across the country and in Congress – and even France favored it as a morale booster in quickly bringing some American troops into action – the administration refused to approve it. Secretary of War Newton D. Baker rejected TR's project as an unwise diversion of arms and supplies; politics may also have played a part. Roosevelt called upon his hated enemy in the White House to plead in a rare display of humility for his scheme. He accepted defeat with very poor grace and the continued maneuverings of his supporters in Congress cost him much popular support.

Although Wilson generally tried to balance Democratic and Republican appointees to the various war agencies, he encountered sharp criticism for playing politics with the war. Coal shortages, railroad tangles, lagging armaments production, and alleged administration favoring of southern cotton growers versus western wheat farmers, provided ample grist for the Republican mill. Aircraft production threatened to become a major scandal until defused by Wilson. The administration had promised overoptimistically to manufacture 100,000 warplanes to sweep the Germans from the sky and thereby save countless soldier lives. Despite the expenditure of $840 million, reports revealed that little had been achieved. Wilson effectively countered critics by ordering an investigation headed by the respected Charles Evans Hughes and reorganized the aircraft production board.

Wilson stoutly resisted all demands by Republican critics for a coalition war cabinet or a Civil War type of joint committee of Congress on the conduct of the war. Instead he asked and received full authority under the Overman Act of 1918 to reorganize, abolish, or establish war agencies and to transfer funds as needed. Though the act was criticized as making the chief executive a war dictator, Wilson used his new powers sparingly.

This wartime government which not only regulated the economy but managed it for the purposes of victory signified an advance toward a more regulated economy. Many progressives welcomed the war as an opportunity to modernize the political economy. The results, temporary though they seemed to most citizens, did not all disappear with the coming of peace.

Benefitting from the Allied example and the American Civil War experience, the administration decided to rely upon conscription instead of volunteering to raise manpower for the armed services. There was to be no hiring of substitutes or purchases of exemption as during the Civil War, nor, as in the Roosevelt controversy, did the War Department want to be encumbered with "political generals" raising volunteer outfits. Many citizens, both liberals and conservatives, opposed conscription as un-American, dishonorable, and a violation of personal liberties. Several administration lieutenants, such as House Speaker Champ Clark, deserted Wilson on this issue. Some southerners also feared dire consequences would result from drafting and arming Negroes. The administration finally persuaded Congress that conscription would be more democratic and efficient than any other method. The 1917 act required all males between 21 and 30 years of age, later extended to 18 to 45, to register with their local draft boards. Draft officials assigned each district a quota and drew numbers from a lottery in Washington to determine the order of induction. The law exempted men with dependents or in vital employment; conscientious objectors on religious grounds were usually given non-combatant duties. The government, however, dealt harshly with political objectors, many of whom received heavy prison sentences. An estimated one-third of a million draft dodgers evaded registration or refused to comply with induction notices. Even so, there was far less resistance to the draft than many, recalling Civil War anti-draft riots, had feared. Ultimately the draft conscripted nearly three million men, which combined with the National Guard and volunteers increased the armed forces to close to five million. The military hastily erected training camps to receive this flood of manpower. Life in the jerry-built camps came as a great shock to most of the trainees, as farmers, immigrants, Negroes, and urban middleclass youth, drawn from every section of the country, were thrown together in a new type of melting pot. The War Department found an appallingly high percentage of the men it called for examination and induction deficient in health and education. The army adopted standardized psychological testing to discern various abilities useful to the military, a technique thereafter to be utilized increasingly in civilian life — another example of the thrust of an industrial corporate society toward greater rationalization. Despite the novel and disrupting experience of military life, morale remained high. Various church organizations, the Red Cross, the Salvation Army, and the Young Men's Christian Association, provided entertainment and comforts for the "boys in service." Soldiers and civilians alike sang popular war songs, such as "Over There" and "Oh! How I Hate to Get Up in the Morning."

General John Jacob Pershing commanded the American Expeditionary Force to France. At first only a trickle of men could be trained, equipped, and shipped to Europe, but these few raised the morale of the war-weary Allies. In the early summer of 1917 the American 1st Division paraded through the streets of Paris to a tumultuous welcome. A Colonel Stanton, however, and not General Pershing, stood before Lafayette's tomb on July 4, 1917, and uttered those stirring words that recalled the days of Franco-American alliance during the American War for Independence: "Lafayette, we are here!" American soldiers found life in France confusing and often complained of dirty villages and greedy merchants. The A.E.F.'s newspaper, "Stars and Stripes," and improving mail services and supplies, helped ease the "doughboy's" adjustment.

Pershing's A.E.F. increased rapidly after the early spring of 1918, numbering about two million men by the time of the Armistice. At the War Department's and his insistence, the American forces were kept together as a unit rather than being dispersed among the Allied armies. Pershing was convinced that Allied morale had deteriorated so far that victory would depend primarily upon the fresh and less daunted American troops. The A.E.F. fought courageously and well at Château-Thierry, Belleau Woods, St. Mihiel, and the Meuse-

Argonne. It helped stem the last great German drive in 1918 and took a prominent part in Allied Generalissimo Ferdinand Foch's counter-offensive that smashed the Hindenburg Line and set the stage for the German request for peace. Although no American-built aircraft saw actual combat duty, the Army Air Service fought in Allied-provided craft. Eddie Rickenbacker became the leading American "ace" with twenty-six kills to his credit, followed by Frank Luke, Jr., with twenty-one aerial victories, and Raoul Lufbery who shot down seventeen enemy planes before he jumped to his death from a burning fighter plane. By the fall of 1918, Pershing commanded around one million troops in the battle zones and held nearly a fourth of the entire Western Front. Although the Americans suffered far smaller battle losses than the Allies (50,000 men killed to 1.7 million Russians, 1.385 million Frenchmen, and 900,000 British troops), the addition of fresh American manpower swung the balance against the German armies and played a decisive part in the defeat of Germany. The navy convoyed supply and troop ships to Europe and engaged in anti-submarine warfare, with some battleships stationed with the British Grand Fleet to watch the German High Seas Fleet in its lair across the North Sea.

The war cost the United States approximately $33½ billion by 1920. The Treasury raised about two-thirds of this vast sum through the sale of Liberty and Victory bonds, and the remainder by taxation. A great furor ensued in Congress and the public over the wisest method of raising taxes. Conservatives favored reliance primarily upon consumption or excise taxes, while many progressives advocated shifting the burden to the wealthier citizens by increasing steeply the income tax and levying taxes on so-called excess profits or "blood money" from war production. The 1917 War Revenue Act, a compromise, increased the rate sharply on the upper income brackets and on excess profits, but also dropped the minimum level to annual incomes as low as $1000. Dissatisifed progressives denounced it as a betrayal of the average man and some called for confiscation of all incomes above $100,000 a year. Such criticism, together with mounting war expenditures, caused the rates on upper incomes to be raised even more steeply in the 1918 and 1919 revenue acts, to 77 percent on the highest income levels and to 65 percent on excess profits. Despite charges of "profit-bloated" manufacturers and financiers, those acts shifted much of the taxation burden to those more able to bear it while farmers and laborers made very substantial gains in income.

Public opinion, by no means universally enthusiastic about the war in 1917, also seemed to require mobilization. A Committee on Public Information, directed by the colorful journalist George Creel, undertook to "sell" the war to the American people. Patriotic "four minute men" speakers, often well known entertainment or sports personalities, helped sell the four great Liberty Bond and the one post-armistice Victory Bond drives. Lurid movies, such as "The Beast of Berlin" and "The Prussian Cur," and war posters aroused the emotions of the American people. One poster depicted an American's reaction to German atrocities with the words, "Tell That to the Marines!" Various groups — the super-patriots, conservatives eager to counter radicalism, and ordinary citizens — demanded drastic measures to suppress opponents or critics of the war. Elihu Root, a former Secretary of State, told a cheering New York City audience in mid-1917 that "there are men walking about the streets of this city tonight who ought to be taken out at sunrise tomorrow and shot for treason." Theodore Roosevelt called for vigorous repression to cope with the opponents of war, whom he described as pacifists, socialists, I.W.W.'s (International Workers of the World, a radical syndicalist union), and "a whole raft of sexless creatures." To cope with disloyalty, Congress enacted the Espionage Act in 1917 and the Sabotage and Sedition Acts in 1918. These harsh laws provided heavy fines and imprisonment for anyone obstructing the draft, inciting rebellion, or aiding the enemy; denied use of the mails to disloyal publications; made sabotage a federal offense; and punished utterances deemed abusive to the American government, flag or uniform, and language intended to obstruct the war effort. The Wilson administration requested from Congress formal censorship powers; however, it was rejected by the legislative branch.

President Wilson warned in his Flag Day Address in 1917, "Woe to the man or group of men that seeks to stand in our way in this day of high resolution. . . ." The government used its legal powers to suppress pacifist and radical dissent. The post-office banned a number of pacifist and socialist books, magazines, and newspapers from the mails. The Justice Department arrested a number of critics of the war who were sentenced to long terms in prison. Eugene Debs of the Socialist Party received a sentence of ten years imprisonment for an anti-war speech. Robert Goldstein drew ten years in prison for making a movie, "The Spirit of '76," that was viewed as anti-British and pro-German propaganda. Many patriotic organizations such as the American Defense Society, the National Security League, the American Anti-Anarchy Association, and the American Protective League, staged witch-hunts for individuals (especially German-Americans) suspected of being less than 100 percent loyal supporters of the war. State and municipal councils of defense and safety also flourished, and the Justice Department encouraged these organizations to investigate disloyalty. Ostracism, boycotts, threats, whippings, and worse occurred. The madness even descended to the level of repudiating German music and culture, and the renaming of such foods as sauerkraut and hamburger ("liberty cabbage" and "liberty sausage"). Wilson made little effort to counter the hysteria, apparently because of his desire to promote national unity and his faith that sanity would be restored eventually. Perhaps too he was not displeased at the silencing of the more radical critics of his war policies. Even after the Armistice, Wilson refused to release Debs and others imprisoned for opposition to the war. Debs was freed in 1921, after Wilson was out of office, but it was not until 1923 that the last of the political offenders left prison.

The Great Crusade

While most Americans succumbed to the war hysteria, others gave much thought to the nature of the postwar world. Many earnest peace advocates concluded that alliances and balances of power, the obvious culprits in 1914, must be supplanted by a world court and law or by an international concert of power to achieve peace and promote disarmament. The secret diplomacy of the past must be abolished and the war ended on the basis of an enlightened peace and universal democracy to lay the basis for the new world order. The League to Enforce Peace came into existence in the United States in 1915 to work for these goals — William Howard Taft, among others joined — and a similar society existed in Great Britain.

By May of 1916, Wilson had identified himself with the liberal peace program. Like most Americans, Wilson long had believed that the United States represented a new Zion among nations, freed of the militarism, autocracy, and reaction of the Old World. Its liberal values — political democracy, social mobility, private property, and economic freedoms — clearly represented the wave of the future. America had an historic mission, a sacred duty, to encourage the spread of these liberal political and economic doctrines and institutions to all mankind. He and his advisers saw World War I as the opportunity to achieve an "open-door" world that would be safe both from Prussian autocracy or old-fashioned imperialism and from the social revolutions promulgated by radical socialists such as the Russian Bolsheviks. Such a world view merged both American interests and its ideals.

Wilson concentrated on a collective security organization as the key to an equitable and enduring peace. A universal organization of states by a mutual guarantee of integrity would be able to prevent any war begun contrary to treaty obligations or enlightened world opinion. Hopefully also it could remove barriers to international trade, with the major industrial powers cooperating in developing backward areas. As the foremost economic state in the world, such an order would benefit America greatly but also presumably everyone else. In his peace moves in late 1916 and early 1917, and in his war message, Wilson clearly stated America's interests in a just peace and an international concert of power to ensure its preservation. After America became a belligerent, he began to develop his thoughts into a more definite program.

Wilson realized that the Allied governments did not share his concept of an ideal peace. In a series of secret treaties and agreements, the Allied Powers had planned a postwar division of territorial spoils, the inevitable though not necessarily evil results of a coalition war. The American government knew most of the details of these arrangements by the time of the peace conference in 1919 but did not officially recognize them. Wilson confidently expected that by the end of the war the Allies would be so dependent upon American economic and financial power that he could impose his own views of a just peace. As part of his strategy of preserving his diplomatic freedom, the United States did not enter into any formal alliances or ties with the Allies. Even in referring to the coalition, Wilson adopted the phrase of the "Allied and Associated Powers," with the United States in the latter category. Although some scholars have criticized Wilson's failure to challenge directly the secret treaties, it should be noted that a coalition war presents special difficulties; any other attitude by the President might well have lowered Allied morale and surely would have led to disruptive arguments with the Allied governments. It is noteworthy that Franklin D. Roosevelt followed essentially Wilson's course during the next world war.

In a series of speeches, President Wilson mobilized American and world opinion in support of his concept of a just peace. He and his aides articulated fully the concept of a world-wide authoritarian menace to political democracy and liberal capitalism. Most of the American intellectual community, as the writings of John Dewey and Walter Lippmann, among others, attested, shared the President's views. These officials and private citizens at first defined authoritarianism or statism principally in terms of Prussian or German autocracy. Thus Wilson in his Flag Day Address, June 14, 1917, attacked "the military masters of Germany" whose plots and aggressive actions had driven the United States into the war. Germany's rulers must be crushed or no nation could be safe from their aggressive designs. Secretary of State Lansing more intemperately described Germany as a "wild beast" led by "assassins and butchers" lusting for world domination. If Wilson and Lansing were bad historians in these versions of German imperialism and the causes of the war, they at least reflected widely-held opinions in America and helped work up popular support for the war. At Mount Vernon, on July 4, 1917, the President flailed the Central Powers for imposing statist controls over every aspect of the lives of their own and subjected peoples, "making every choice for them and disposing of their lives and fortunes as they will." Wilson thereby sought to drive a wedge between enemy rulers and their subjects, and to dampen down extreme anti-Germanism in America by focusing animosity upon the Kaiser and his clique. He repeated that distinction when he rejected Pope Benedict XV's appeal for a negotiated peace in August 1917. There could be no peace, he declared, until the world had been freed "from the menace and the actual power of a vast military establishment controlled by an irresponsible government which . . . planned to dominate the world." Eventually the concept of authoritarianism came to include militarist Japan, which American officials privately viewed as the "Prussia of the Far East," and even more that undemocratic regime of Bolshevik Russia which after 1918 called for class war and world revolution. By 1919 Wilson and Lansing publicly described Soviet Russia as in fact as brutal, autocratic, and statist as the Kaiser's Germany, despite its professed noble aim of liberating mankind. Their idea of an evil authoritarianism was to be revived in the 1930's and 40's as the menace of totalitarianism — applied to Nazi Germany, Fascist Italy, and militarist Japan during the Second World War and to Communist Russia in the Cold

War era. World War I thus saw the emergence of an American rehtoric that was to underlie much of our later attitudes and policies in this century.

Wilson began preparations for peace by establishing the Inquiry, a group of scholars under the direction of Colonel House, to study war goals and to draft reports on the problems expected to arise at the eventual peace conference. Indicating progressivism's faith in experts and social planning, the President hoped these scholars would give him a "guaranteed position" for the peace negotiations – that is, a sound preparation for the independent role he intended to play. Enlisting the services of about 150 experts, the Inquiry undertook detailed geographical, economic, political and historical studies of problem areas. Most of the scholars used turned out to be specialists in American or European history, geography, and archaeology; few experts could be found in African, Middle Eastern, and Asian studies. The Inquiry labored diligently, compiling large numbers of maps and nearly 2,000 reports, ranging from the useful to the trivial. When the American peace commission sailed to Europe after the Armistice, it took many of these reports and a number of the experts to guide its work at the Paris Peace Conference.

Wilson delivered the most famous of his wartime utterances, the Fourteen Points address, to Congress on January 8, 1918. He hoped to liberalize Allied war aims, bind the "liberal" and the "Left" in Europe and America to his cause, and to woo the Russian masses away from the Bolsheviks. Listing the essential provisions of a lasting peace, Wilson stated that the enemy must evacuate all Allied territory and return Alsace-Lorraine to France; an independent Poland should be created with access to the sea; and autonomous development should be given to peoples of the Austrian and Turkish empires. He postulated certain general principles to guide the writing of the peace: open diplomacy (no more secret treaties); freedom of the seas in war and in peace; reduction of armaments to a level sufficient for national security; and the adjustment of colonial claims with consideration of the interests of the colonial peoples as well as the claimant powers. Wilson viewed his fourteenth point as the key to the peace: "A general association of nations must be formed under specific covenants for the purpose of affording mutual guarantees of political independence and territorial integrity to great and small states alike."

In subsequent addresses, Wilson added other points to his prescription for a lasting and liberal peace. Peoples and territories must not be treated as mere pawns to be allocated by the great powers, and due consideration should be accorded to the aspirations for self-government of previously oppressed nationalities. More than any other single leader in modern world history (FDR had to share the lime-light with Winston Churchill in World War II), Wilson succeeded in touching the conscience and the imagination of mankind. His inspired language and exalted vision rallied liberal opinion to his cause and eventually had some effect in encouraging popular discontent within the Central Powers. The leaders of the Allied states, despite their lack of enthusiasm for the President's noble prescription for peace, dared not openly object or criticize. Wilson clearly had become the chief, if self-appointed, spokesman, for the Allied and Associated States.

In essence, Wilsonian goals projected a global New Freedom, envisioning the spread of democracy and the encouragement of freer trade throughout the world. German militarism would be destroyed and a democratized Reich absorbed into a universal system characterized by political democracy, liberal capitalism, and great power cooperation within a League of Nations for peace and progress. Evolutionary change would supplant both reaction and revolution. Although most Americans thought their country alone was without selfish goals — it had no need or desire for territory or spoils — obviously Wilson's world order promised the kind of world in which the United States could be secure and flourish.

"Self-determination" of peoples became one of the most popular slogans of the war. It would be incorrect, however, to attribute the emergence of the new states of Poland, Czechoslovakia, Finland, Latvia, Lithuania, Estonia, and Yugoslavia primarily to Wilson's encouragement. Americans and many Europeans, sharing the old liberal belief in the beneficence of nationalism, of course regarded these independence movements with sympathy, and undoubtedly Wilson's words stimulated nationalist aspirations. But the fact remains that nationalist currents ran strongly in these areas long before the war; the debacle of World War I made it possible to translate these hopes into reality.

Russia confronted Wilsonian liberalism with one of its severest tests. Americans had rejoiced when the March Revolution in Russia in 1917 overthrew the czarist regime and began to transform Russia into a democratic republic. At last, it seemed, the war had become a clear struggle between democracy and autocracy. Elihu Root led a special mission to Russia in mid-1917, and the American government extended financial ($325 million) and other aid to the new regime. Unfortunately, both American officials and private citizens failed to appreciate the depths of war-weariness in Russia, the collapse of military morale, the breakdown in transportation and the economy, and the growing influence of radical political doctrines. They too easily assumed that Russia under moderate democratic leadership would remain in the war and would continue to develop in the pattern of western liberal capitalist democracies.

The Bolshevik Revolution in November, 1917 thus came as a stunning surprise. Exploiting widespread discontent and chaos, the Russian Communist or Bolshevik party clamped a ruthless dictatorial rule on Russia and promptly began to withdraw from the war against the Central Powers. Britain and France feared that Germany would now be able to shift vast numbers of troops from the Eastern to the Western Front to score a decisive victory. President Wilson felt deeply disturbed by the undemocratic nature of the new regime, while Secretary of State Lansing expressed apprehension about Communist ideology and the effort to export revolution and class warfare. The State Department,

INTERVENTION IN SIBERIA, 1918–1925

ZONES OF FOREIGN MILITARY OCCUPATION

500 MILES

therefore, denied the new regime diplomatic recognition. That seemed realistic as well as principled, for the Soviets did not control all Russia and their survival appeared highly unlikely.

The Allies began to besiege President Wilson with pleas for armed intervention against the Bolsheviks and the restoration of an Eastern Front. At first he refused, arguing that the Russian people should be allowed to determine freely their own form of government and the impracticality of the military schemes. He finally gave in after receiving exaggerated reports of deep German penetration of Russia, including the releasing and arming of German and Austrian war prisoners. This German advance apparently endangered thousands of tons of war supplies that had been shipped from America and Europe to Russia and stockpiled at the ports of Murmansk and Archangel. Probably even more decisive to Wilson, between 45,000 to 65,000 Czechoslovak troops, previously allowed by the Russian provisional government to form and fight on the Russian front, found themselves trapped by the Bolshevik withdrawal from the war. While evacuating Russia, clashes between the local Soviets and the Czech legion rapidly turned into large scale hostilities.

Capitulating to these alleged military exigencies, the President in mid-1918 agreed to limited armed interventions in Siberia and northern Russia. He insisted that the intervention should not engage in political activity, but should confine itself to rescuing the Czechs and guarding the war supplies. He hoped, of course, that the presence of Allied and American forces would "stabilize" conditions in Russia and encourage by their mere presence the formation of a non-Bolshevik government. The Allies, however, wanted more; they sought to overthrow the Bolsheviks and restore Russia to the war. Japan increased its forces in Siberia to over 70,000 men, far in excess of the American contingent of 9,000 troops. Obviously Tokyo hoped to extend greatly Japanese influence in the area. Yet while Wilson could not completely restrain the Allies, he managed to prevent a much larger intervention. After the Armistice he refused to broaden the intervention, and he withdrew the American troops from northern Russia in 1919 and from Siberia early in 1920. Though these interventions helped create a legacy of hatred with the Bolshevik government, at least Wilson had helped to avoid a costly and probably futile all-out war.

The Coming of Victory

The Central Powers began to collapse militarily by the fall of 1918. Turkey, Bulgaria, and Austria-Hungary sued for peace. The last great German offensive on the Western Front had been checked, partly by fresh American manpower, and the Allied armies under Generalissimo Foch launched a successful counter-drive that broke the Hindenburg Line and threatened to invade Germany itself. Faced with a military disaster and a war-weary people at home,

Hindenburg and Ludendorff forced the German government to request a peace based on Wilson's Fourteen Points. Although usually depicted as suffering from a temporary loss of nerve, Ludendorff merely overestimated Allied readiness for a new offensive against his weakened armies. Apparently he hoped for generous terms or at least a breathing-spell permitting him to regroup the German armies. Despite fears in Europe and America that he would be duped by the wily Germans, Wilson maneuvered with skill and probably hastened the end of the war by several months and thousands of lives. By the time the German high command decided to continue the fighting rather than accept harsh terms, German morale had shattered and the civilian officials were forced to overrule the army. The government accepted Wilson's terms, Kaiser Wilhelm fled into exile in Holland, and a German republic was formed. The Allied leaders reluctantly agreed to the so-called "Pre-Armistice Agreement" to give Germany a peace based on the Fourteen Points, though they inserted two qualifications dealing with freedom of the seas and damages inflicted upon civilians.

On November 8, Matthias Erzberger led the representatives of defeated Germany to a railway carriage in Compiègne forest where Marshal Foch and his triumphant staff presented them with armistice terms. They were harsh, designed to ensure that Germany could not renew the war. Germany must evacuate occupied territory immediately and surrender vast quantities of guns, ammunition, and other supplies. The new German government had no choice but to sign the Armistice. The guns at last fell silent on the Western Front at eleven o'clock on the morning of November 11, 1918. In the Allied countries and America, people poured into the streets to celebrate victory. Joyous crowds repeatedly burned the deposed Kaiser in effigy. President Wilson confidently anticipated the coming peace conference, for the Allied governments apparently had consented to an enlightened peace based on principle and justice.

To the Paris Peace Conference

Politics continued in America during the war despite lip-service to the slogan "politics is adjourned." The Republican leadership, under National Chairman Will Hayes anticipating a return to power, worked energetically to heal the 1912 breach and to capture a favorable position for the 1918 and 1920 elections. Under the guise of "constructive criticism," Republicans hurled charge after charge of mismanagement and waste at Wilson and the war agencies, and tried unsuccessfully to drive Secretary Newton D. Baker from the War Department. Democrats suffered particularly from their failure to adopt a uniform price-fixing policy and to impose controls on scarce raw materials and manufactured goods. The administration had limited price regulations to certain basic commodities, while inflation mounted, the cost of living rose steeply, and profiteering flourished. Wilson failed to see that his war policies had lost support and counted on the electorate sharing his over-riding concern with world affairs.

Anxious to strengthen his position at the forthcoming peace conference, Wilson appealed to the voters in the 1918 midterm elections to vote Democratic, for "The return of a Republican majority ... would ... certainly be interpreted on the other side of the water as a repudiation of my leadership." Although not unprecedented, the President's appeal proved to be a major political blunder. Republicans charged that Wilson had violated his own earlier plea "that politics is adjourned" and that he had impugned the loyalty of Republican members of Congress who had cooperated in the war effort. When the Republicans won control of both houses of Congress, their leaders declared that the President had asked for a popular vote of confidence and had lost. The outcome thus impaired his position at the peace conference and, probably more important, made the new Congress resentful of his leadership.

In a far more serious error, the President failed to appoint a prominent Republican or any members of the Senate to the commission to negotiate the peace at Paris. He chose four persons as commissioners who either were closely connected with his administration or who lacked major political stature: Robert Lansing; Colonel House; General Tasker H. Bliss; and Henry White, a diplomat and a minor Republican. Wilson gave his opponents additional ammunition when in an unprecedented move he decided to include himself in the commission and to play a direct part in the negotiations. Critics raged that he had packed the group with yes-men and charged him with having a messiah complex. Humorist Will Rogers quipped, "There was so much argument about who was to go, that Wilson says, 'I tell you what, we will split 50-50 — I will go and you fellows [Republicans] can stay.'" Wilson thus brushed aside prominent Republicans whom he could have selected as commissioners: Senator Lodge as personally unacceptable, and Elihu Root and ex-President Taft as too conservative. More-over, the President made no effort to consult powerful senators on the peace terms, despite the obvious fact that any treaty would require approval by the Senate. Apparently Wilson felt so certain of his own rectitude and vision, and so resentful of criticism and opposition, that he ignored the probable consequences of his actions. By so doing he virtually ensured that the Senate would challenge his leadership in foreign affairs and that the treaty of peace would become a partisan issue.

The *S. S. George Washington* sailed for Europe on December 4, 1918 bearing the first American President to visit the Old World while in office. Wilson took with him his wife and members of the American delegation, including scholars and experts from the Inquiry. Europeans went wild with joy at the arrival of the American Prophet. Parisians gave him a tumultuous reception, reportedly unequalled since Napoleon's triumphal entries. Wilson passed under one huge banner proclaiming "Honor to Wilson the Just." He also briefly toured England and Italy. Everywhere the multitudes hailed him as the deliverer of mankind, the hope of the future. Unfortunately, too many of the Allied peoples envisioned justice as crushing Germany into the ground. Equally unfortunately, these wildly enthusiastic receptions apparently strengthened Wilson's conviction that he alone spoke for mankind.

Delegates from 32 governments assembled at Paris for the conference that finally began early in January, 1919. Strictly speaking, this was a preliminary conference of the victors, for the formal peace conference began only when the delegates of defeated Germany arrived in May to receive the virtually completed treaty. In theory, plenary sessions of all the attending states, large and small, controlled the conference, but in fact the Big Four directed it: Wilson; David Lloyd George, the British Prime Minister; the French Premier, Georges Clemenceau, the "Tiger" of France; and, to a lesser degree, Premier Vittorio Orlando of Italy. When issues arose involving the Far East, Japan ranked as a fifth great power. The leaders at first operated in the Council of Ten and subsequently in the Council of Four. To the disgust of newspapermen attending the conference, these smaller governing bodies conducted their affairs in secrecy, despite Wilson's earlier slogan of "open diplomacy." Of course, he had intended that slogan to mean only that treaties and agreements *after* negotiation should be fully published, but the masses interpreted it to signify full publicity – a good example of the dangers of sloganeering.

The unquestioned moral spokesman of the Big Four, Wilson often revealed a more practical and realistic approach than might have been expected. He labored diligently to master the details of the peace-making and impressed many observers with his knowledge and comprehension of complex issues. He tended to isolate himself from his fellow American commissioners, however, except for Colonel House, thereby depriving himself of advice and support that could have been of great benefit to him. Apparently Wilson viewed Lansing, Bliss, and White as tedious encumbrances and he realized that Lansing disagreed with his plans for a league of nations. Lansing, like most American internationalists, objected to the use of collective force or its threat to preserve peace, preferring instead to rely upon arbitration and an international court to settle future world difficulties. The three commissioners naturally felt slighted and humiliated by the President. Lansing even contemplated resignation but refrained lest he impede the peace-making. His role at Paris was secondary, although he did have a constructive part in balking French schemes to dismember Germany. Lloyd George, known as a master politician and opportunist, was much less informed than Wilson on the problems that arose at Paris. In general, however, he agreed with the American President in opposing the more selfish schemes of the other powers. He also relied more than Wilson upon his advisers at Paris. Clemenceau, nearly eighty years of age, tirelessly advocated French interests. He resolved to so weaken Germany through heavy reparations and losses of territory that it could never again menace France. The cynical Clemenceau, who once described Wilson as that "Buddha in Washington," frequently was either amused or puzzled by the President's idealism. On one occasion the French Premier reportedly remarked to Colonel House that "talking to Wilson is something like talking to Jesus Christ!" As for the Fourteen Points, "God gave us the Ten Commandments, and we broke them. Wilson gives us the Fourteen Points. We shall see." Orlando, the last of the Big Four, and the only one who did not speak English, generally played a smaller role at the conference.

The Drafting of the Covenant

President Wilson saw the most important task of the peace conference as the framing of the Covenant of the League of Nations. The American and British delegations generally worked together harmoniously, for basically the Anglo-Americans agreed on many issues at Paris. Unfortunately that collaboration stopped short at the highest levels, because of Wilson's preference for independent action and his distrust of Lloyd George. France tried to mould the league into a military alliance of the great powers but failed. The League Covenant, formulated as a part of the treaty of peace, provided for an assembly composed of all members; a council to consist of the five great powers as permanent members with elected representatives of the smaller states; and a secretariat headed by a Secretary-General for administrative duties. The council, bearing the primary responsibility for preserving or restoring peace, could invoke economic and military sanctions or adopt other substantive measures only by unanimous vote. Article X, the heart of the Covenant, pledged members to respect and uphold the territorial integrity and political independence of all members of the League.

Critics later charged that Wilson's obsession with the Covenant delayed the conference in the vital work of quickly restoring peace to a war-weary world. In fact, the League Commission did most of its work in the evenings when other bodies of the conference had recessed. Some historians also have concluded that it would have been wiser to have separated peacemaking from the framing of the League, to avoid delaying the restoration of peace and to allow time for passions and politics to cool. Such a course, however, might well have meant that the new global organization would never have been adopted. Moreover, the delay of a few months or a year or so hardly would have made the League question any less of a political issue in the United States.

After the Covenant had been drafted and read to the conference, the President left Paris in mid-February for a brief trip to the United States. Various legislative items demanded his attention and he particularly wanted to explain the Covenant to the American people. Already critics, mostly Republicans, had attacked the new organization as a world superstate that would impair American sovereignty. Colonel House urged the President to strike a conciliatory note but his fighting blood was up. He landed in Boston, Senator Lodge's stronghold, and in effect denounced critics as narrow and selfish. Subsequently he did invite members of the Senate and House committees on foreign relations to dinner at the White House where he patiently tried to explain the Covenant, to little avail.

Wilson noticeably failed to win over Senator Lodge, a cold, sarcastic, and arrogant but able man who would become chairman of the Committee on Foreign Relations in the next Congress. The Massachusetts senator heartily detested Wilson, a sentiment that the President fully reciprocated. According to Lodge, his feelings derived from study of Wilson's public record which he viewed as irresolute and even dishonest. Yet personal factors probably played an even larger role than principles in Lodge's relations with the President. A Harvard-trained historian, Lodge long had been known as the "scholar in politics" until the even more renowned Wilson entered the White House and eclipsed him. (Ironically, as editor of the *International Review*, Lodge years before had accepted for publication the first Wilson scholarly article to appear in print.) Lodge eagerly searched for indications that the President did not merit his reputation, and cherished for years a mistake made by Wilson in using a classical allusion to illustrate a point in a 1913 speech. By 1919 the Lodge-Wilson relationship while outwardly icily correct had deteriorated beyond repair. Apart from the usual political motives – Lodge as a Republican leader had to guard his party's interests – it is quite clear that the senator hoped to humiliate and defeat the man in the White House. The League issue seemed to offer the opportunity, even though Lodge himself earlier had endorsed the general concept. In fairness, however, it must be noted that Lodge like most other American internationalists favored arbitration and law rather than a coercive international organization. He remarked of the Covenant, Wilson's handiwork, that "As an English production it does not rank high. It might get by at Princeton but certainly not at Harvard."

In a speech two days after the White House conference, Lodge declared that the Covenant should be separated from the main body of the peace treaty, and he warned of the danger of entangling alliances as a departure from America's traditional policy of diplomatic freedom. He expressed alarm that the League might interfere with domestic questions and, via Article X, impair the Monroe Doctrine. Lodge concluded that the Covenant must be substantially changed before the United States safely could join the new organization. The Republican leadership then used delaying tactics to compel Wilson to call a special session of the new Congress elected in 1918, in order to obtain a vantage-point for continuing attacks on Wilson's work at Paris. A Republican "Round Robin," signed by 39 senators or senators-elect, six more than necessary to block approval of a treaty, declared the Covenant in its present form unacceptable.

Swallowing his outrage at what he regarded as unfair or ignorant criticisms, Wilson upon his return to Paris obtained several changes that he hoped would satisfy his critics. These provided that a member could decline a mandate offered by the League (former enemy territories and colonies were to be administered as League mandates or trusteeships); exempted domestic matters from League jurisdiction; and in effect sanctioned the Monroe Doctrine as a regional understanding permissable under the Covenant. Members also could withdraw from the League, after two years' notice and the full performance of their obligations. Wilson refused to ask for additional changes, especially in regard to Article X. He felt that he had answered legitimate criticism; the Senate would either have to accept the revised Covenant or reject the entire peace treaty.

A Peace of Justice?

In other phases of the peace-making, Wilson tried to steer a middle course between too harsh and too soft a peace. He hoped for a settlement sufficiently moderate to reintegrate Germany into world society, yet he too felt that Germany richly deserved some punishment. Moreover, he faced punitive demands from his own countrymen as well as from the Allies. Consequently, he compromised in a harsher peace than he had desired. Even so, he stood firmly against extreme demands for humiliating and disabling the defeated enemy. With Lloyd George, he resisted French schemes to dismember Germany by annexing the Saar Valley, bringing the Rhineland under French control as a puppet state, and dissolving the *Reich* into several independent states. Loss of the Rhineland, together with the rather harsh military terms already agreed upon for Germany — an army of 100,000 men, abolition of the general staff, prohibition of tanks, military aircraft, and poison gas, and a small navy — would have ensured French revenge and power over an impotent Germany. The American and British feared that dismemberment, besides violating the principle of self-determination, would outrage German nationalism and sow the seeds of a future war. The controversy became so heated that Clemenceau accused Wilson of being pro-German and angrily left the conference room. The peace conference seemed on the verge of disruption and Wilson threatened to return home rather than accede to French desires.

The Big Three finally worked out a compromise that seemed to provide adequate protection for France without dismantling Germany. France would occupy the Saar Valley, with its valuable coal mines, for a period of fifteen years, followed by a League-supervised plebiscite to determine its future allegiance; and the Rhineland would be demilitarized to a distance of fifty kilometers east of the river, with France and Belgium occupying strategic bridgeheads along the Rhine for as long as fifteen years. As an additional guarantee, intended to function only until the League could become operational, Britain and the United States signed bilateral treaties with France promising military assistance in case Germany should launch an attack against France. When the American Senate subsequently failed to act on the pact, Britain unfortunately

CENTRAL EUROPE

AFTER THE PARIS PEACE CONFERENCES

300 MILES

AUSTRIA–HUNGARY, 1914
POST-WAR TERRITORIAL CHANGES
POST-WAR BOUNDARIES

UNITED KINGDOM

London

NORTH SEA

DENMARK

NETH.

Amsterdam

BELG.

Brussels

Sedan

Verdun

FRANCE

Paris

Versailles

Compiegne

Seine

Chateau Thierry

Lyon

LUX.

LORRAINE

Strasbourg

ALSACE

SAAR

RHINELAND

RUHR

RHINE

Koblenz

Frankfurt

Weimar

Bremen

Hamburg

ELBE

Berlin

G E R M A N Y

Breslau

ODER

SILESIA

Munich

DANUBE

SWITZ.

Berne

Locarno

Milan

Genoa

Florence

Rome

ITALY

PO

Marseilles

MEDITERRANEAN SEA

CORSICA (FR.)

SARDINIA (IT.)

HELIGOLAND

BALTIC SEA

Danzig

Gdynia

THE CORRIDOR

EAST PRUSSIA

Memel

LITHUANIA

Vilna

ALLENSTEIN

Warsaw

VISTULA

P O L A N D

Brest-Litovsk

CURZON LINE

Minsk

WHITE RUSSIA

Kiev

U K R A I N E

SOVIET UNION

CRIMEA

BLACK SEA

Odessa

DNIESTER

BESSARABIA

PRUTH

MOLDAVIA

BUKOVINA

Lvov

GALICIA

RUTHENIA

Kaschau

CZECHOSLOVAKIA

BOHEMIA

MORAVIA

Prague

Vienna

AUSTRIA

Graz

SLOVENIA

South Tyrol

Trent

Budapest

HUNGARY

BANAT

TRANSYLVANIA

RUMANIA

WALLACHIA

Bucharest

DANUBE

DOBRUJA

BULGARIA

Sofia

GREECE

Istanbul

T U R K E Y

Zara (IT.)

Fiume

KUSTEN-LAND

CROATIA-SLAVONIA

DALMATIA

BOSNIA

YUGOSLAVIA

SERBIA

Belgrade

MONTE-NEGRO

Tirana

ALBANIA

ADRIATIC SEA

decided that her pledge therefore also became inoperative, leaving France without the hoped-for guarantees.

The reparations issue proved less successful for Wilson. The Americans wanted the amount of civilian damages for which Germany was responsible under the Pre-Armistice Agreement based on reasonable estimates of Germany's ability to pay over a limited period of time. The Allies, however, sought to shift as much of the entire costs of the war as possible to Germany. Thus during the 1918 elections British voters had been promised by their leaders that Germany would be made to "pay to the last farthing." The Americans managed to rule out imposition of the total war costs; Article 231 of the final treaty held Germany and its allies responsible for all the damages of the war (the "war guilt" clause), but Article 232 limited actual reparations to civilian damages. Wilson, however, gave in to Allied pleas that veterans pensions be included in the category of civilian damages, thereby more than doubling the final bill. Moreover, he also abandoned the effort to fix a specific sum in the treaty and to set a reasonable time for payment. Unfortunately the failure of the United States to ratify the peace treaty prevented it from participation in the Reparations Commission that subsequently assessed German reparations at the astronomical sum of $33 billion, payable over a period of 42 years. Disillusioned liberals in America and Britain attacked these provisions as unwise and a violation of promises to Germany, while Germans reacted with deep bitterness at the apparent injustice. Whether Germany could have paid such an amount is irrelevant, for it was not to be paid in fact.

Wilson made some compromises in other settlements at the conference, but in general he stood firmly by his principles. France sought the creation of a large Poland, Czechoslovakia, and Rumania in order to restrain Germany in the future. Although aware of strategic and security factors, Wilson and Lloyd George resisted the more extreme proposals. Poland obtained a corridor across German territory to give it access to the Baltic Sea, but the German-inhabited port of Danzig, instead of being annexed to the new state, became a free city under League supervision. The eastern boundaries of Poland could not be then determined, because of the absence of Russia from the conference. Strategic factors also required inclusion of the Sudeten Germans within the new Czechoslovakia, an arrangement that rankled in Germany and later gave Adolf Hitler a popular grievance to exploit. Italy, although gaining Austrian-inhabited areas in the South Tyrol area and Slavic populations around Trieste on the Adriatic Sea, met defeat in its demands for the port city of Fiume. Fiume had a core population of Italians, surrounded by a Slavic area. The Italian delegation briefly walked out on the conference when Wilson publicly opposed it on Fiume which he believed ought to be reserved as a port for the new Yugoslav state. Wilson scored only a temporary "victory," however, for Italy eventually forced Yugoslavia, in 1920 and 1924, to give way.

The Americans, and the British also, felt deeply concerned at Paris about the danger of Bolshevik revolutions sweeping across the defeated countries and penetrating even into the victorious nations. The Russian question at the peace conference thus involved more than the existence of a detested Bolshevik regime in Moscow and a civil war between the Reds and the anti-Communist or "White" forces. The war had ended German imperialism, only to usher in an era of revolution threatening Wilson's new order by leftist radicals and rightist reactionaries. A communist regime under Béla Kun came to power briefly in Hungary in 1919, until it collapsed before invading Rumanian troops and Allied opposition; Austria seethed with communist agitation; and in Germany, the Spartacists led by Karl Liebknecht and Rosa Luxemburg sought a communist regime. The centrist and moderate Social Democratic government in Berlin beat off these challenges, crushing both a communist and a rightist uprising in Berlin and a "soviet republic" in Bavaria. Even Italy, one of the victors, experienced turbulence and uncertainty from communist and rightist movements.

Within the allied countries and the United States, conservative influences – the forces of "order" – sought a punitive peace against Germany and containment or destruction of the Bolshevik virus, in part out of vengeance and fear, but also to curb or defeat liberal and socialist reform movements at home. Thus within the United States the opposition to Wilson's liberal peace plans and the League Covenant reflected in part conservative desires to blunt the impetus of progressive reforms and to recapture control of the national government. In this atmosphere, conservatives and reactionaries grossly exaggerated the Bolshevik menace and used it as a weapon in politics and diplomacy.

Wilson and Lloyd George came under great pressure at Paris to approve open intervention against the Bolsheviks. Clemenceau hoped to strangle Lenin's regime by an economic blockade and he viewed sympathetically the scheme advanced by Winston Churchill, British War Minister, for sending volunteer troops to Russia to aid the Whites. The Anglo-American leaders, aware of liberal opposition within the United States and Britain to an overt anti-Bolshevik crusade, and fearful of deeper involvement and the triumph of reactionary forces in Russia, refused to agree. President Wilson, clearly an anti-communist, still hoped to cope effectively with the problem by diplomacy and economic aid. The Peace Conference tried to end the civil war in Russia and no doubt eventually to undermine the Bolsheviks, by calling for a truce and inviting the Russian factions to meet at Prinkipo Island in the Sea of Marmara – Lenin agreed but his opponents declined to negotiate with the "Reds." The Americans then proposed an extensive food relief and economic aid program in Russia, attended by a truce. Since the latter clearly would have weakened the Bolsheviks, Lenin rejected it. Finally, Wilson reluctantly agreed to give support to the Omsk regime headed by Admiral Alexander Kolchak, who promised to crush the Reds and extend his rule to the entire country. At Wilson's insistence, Kolchak promised democratic reforms after his movement had vanquished the communists and reunited Russia. Kolchak proved unequal to the task, however, in large part because of the reactionaries who supplied much of his forces and he was defeated by the Red Armies directed by Leon Trotsky in early 1920. Yet "containment" had forced communism onto the defensive in Russia and prevented its success in the rest of Europe.

Probably no feasible alternative then existed to containment. Most Americans would have viewed recognition of the Bolsheviks as unwise, and it would have been unrealistic as the Soviets did not then control all Russia. On the other hand, an all-out intervention to destroy the Soviets also would have been unpopular and probably unsuccessful. Wilson was the first American chief executive to confront a dilemma still not fully resolved, the problem of the correct policy toward communist or communist-inspired revolutions.

In the Shantung controversy, Wilson met more of an apparent than a real defeat for his principles. Japan in 1914 had seized the German leasehold in the Chinese province of Shantung (along with the German islands in the North Pacific). Subsequently Japan forced the weak Chinese government to recognize that conquest and to yield other concessions in the "Twenty-one Demands" crisis in early 1915. The American government refused to recognize these gains obtained by force and intimidation. Viscount Kikujiro Ishii had led a special mission to Washington in mid-1917, hoping to arrange some kind of bargain recognizing Japan's recent gains. He failed because Wilson determined to check Japanese pretensions and to eradicate all spheres of influence in China – a return to the Taft-Knox policy. Lansing, conversely, perceived the relative weakness of American interests and power in China and preferred a "bargain" recognizing Japan's dominant role in exchange for promises of moderation. Probably Lansing's views represented the more realistic course that if followed might well have averted future Japanese-American difficulties. Facing irreconcilable differences but anxious to maintain a facade of harmony, Ishii and Secretary of State Lansing turned to a vague formula capable of interpretation as each side might choose. The Lansing-Ishii Agreement, signed in November of 1917, pledged both powers to observe and uphold the Open Door in China, but it failed to define the meaning of the Open Door or the nature of Japan's "special interests" that it referred to in China. Subsequently Japan interpreted the agreement to signify recognition of her preeminent position politically as well as economically in all China, while the State Department maintained that it merely had recognized that Japan had special geographical relations to its huge neighbor.

At the Paris conference Wilson hoped to compel the restoration of the Shantung leasehold to China, only to face Japanese threats to leave the conference and boycott the League. Fearful that Japan's defection would doom the League – Italy had briefly walked out – Wilson finally consented to a clause in the treaty transferring the former German holdings to Japan. Few provisions of the Treaty aroused more widespread condemnation in America than the Shantung clause. Yet here Wilson acted realistically, adjusting to a Japanese *fait accompli*. Moreover, the Japanese delegation did give reassurances that political control of the

THE **FAR EAST** AFTER **VERSAILLES,** 1919

PACIFIC ISLANDS, FORMERLY GERMAN, MANDATED TO JAPAN BY THE LEAGUE OF NATIONS, 1919 province soon would be returned to China, a promise Japan kept in 1922.

The German representatives arrived in Paris to receive the Treaty of Peace on May 7, 1919. They had only a few days to study the document and propose changes, most of which the victors summarily rejected. Facing the threat of an Allied invasion, Germany reluctantly accepted the peace presented to it at the point of a bayonet. On June 28, the fifth anniversary of the assassination at Sarajevo that had ignited the war, the Allies staged the final tableau in the ornate Hall of Mirrors at the Versailles Palace. Before the assembled Allied and American statesmen and crowds of exultant observers, the unhappy German delegates signed the Treaty of Versailles. Treaties with the lesser Central Powers remained to be concluded, but the most dramatic part of the conference had ended.

Even before the formal signing critics denounced the Treaty — many for giving Germany too generous terms and disillusioned liberals for its harshness. The British economist John Maynard Keynes (*The Economic Consequences of the Peace, 1920*) flailed the treaty for its punitive provisions saddling Germany with extensive losses of territory and its colonies and overseas investments, and imposing heavy reparations. Moreover, he argued that Europe unwisely had been Balkanized or fragmented economically. Self-determination had also been violated by the inclusion of large numbers of German-speaking peoples within Italy and the new states of Poland and Czechoslovakia, and Italian annexation of Slavic lands along the Adriatic Sea. Keynes and other critics concluded that hopes for a liberal peace had been betrayed, primarily because of President Wilson's defects. The clever and unscrupulous Old World politicians, Keynes wrote, had "bamboozled" and deceived the New World prophet, who had turned out to be not a philosopher-king, as many had hoped, but a stubborn and narrow Presbyterian.

Such criticisms were unfair. Wilson had worked tirelessly at Paris and his efforts unquestionably improved the final treaty. No doubt the Treaty of Versailles with its several harsh provisions fell short of a complete realization of liberal peace goals. But in the nature of human affairs ideals rarely can be entirely achieved. Wilson had met defeat on the reparations issue, Germany alone was disarmed, and a number of departures had been made from boundaries drawn along lines of strict nationality. On the other hand, he had helped oppose French schemes to dismember Germany, created the mandate system to administer former enemy colonies and dependencies under League supervision, and balked excessive Italian demands for territorial gain. Above all, he had succeeded in establishing the League of Nations. Wilson recognized that the treaty had defects, but he hoped that in the course of time, as passions cooled, the League would be able to repair them. It was not an unreasonable hope. Given proper support by the United States and the major Allied governments, the Versailles settlement might well have preserved peace and have evolved into a more progressive world order.

The Defeat of the Treaty in America

Even as Wilson left Paris for home, many Americans already had begun to lose interest in the League of Nations. Americans traditionally had given little attention to foreign affairs except in times of crisis, and they revealed a marked tendency after the Armistice to concentrate once more on private interests. Oversold on the Great Crusade for democracy and peace, people quickly tired of idealistic exhortations. War-stimulated patriotism also encouraged many citizens to oppose League membership as a threat to American sovereignty and a departure from the solemn advice of Washington's Farewell Address. Some professed to fear that the League would breach the American tariff wall and prevent restriction of immigration. Large numbers of German-Americans, Irish-Americans, Italian-Americans, and others, criticized the Versailles Treaty for betraying the hopes or the interests of their former homelands. Finally, many liberals who formerly had supported President Wilson and the war to end wars felt alienated by the failure to achieve more fully the liberal peace program. Liberal journals, such as the *New Republic* and *The Nation*, denounced the Treaty as vindictive and a guarantee not of enduring peace but of future wars of revenge and rectification.

Despite growing disillusionment and apathy, however, the majority of Americans as indicated by newspaper editorials and polls, speeches, and public meetings, probably still favored membership in the League. Their support lacked intensity, however, and seemed to diminish as the struggle over ratification of the Treaty continued. Most Americans were "mild internationalists" and wanted to move cautiously in assuming world responsibilities. Probably Wilson would have been more successful in arousing public support if he had put the major emphasis upon the practical advantages of League membership for the United States — security, stability, and trade — instead of America's duty to the world.

On July 10, 1919 the President formally presented the bulky 264-page Treaty to the Senate. Observers noted that he was not at his best in the address, rising to a level of eloquence only when he referred to the League of Nations as the best hope of mankind: "The stage is set, the destiny disclosed. . . . We can only go forward, with lifted eyes and freshened spirit, to follow the vision." While the assembled Democrats applauded his remarks, most Republicans listened to the President in ominous silence. The Republicans held a narrow majority (49 to 47) in the Senate that gave them control of the powerful Committee on Foreign Relations. Republican leaders, flushed with their triumph in the 1918 elections and looking toward the White House in 1920, anxiously sought to reap the maximum gain from the Versailles Treaty. They could not allow Wilson and the Democrats to claim sole credit for waging the war and making the peace.

Moreover, not all Republican senators agreed upon the League issue. A small group of "Irreconcilables" adamantly opposed membership in any kind of league. These were about sixteen senators, ranging from genuine archisolationist Republicans such as California's Hiram Johnson, Idaho's William E. Borah, and the maverick Democrat from Missouri, James A. Reed, to some who were merely anti-war or were disgusted by the harshness of the Treaty. One of the group, ex-Secretary of State Philander C. Knox, preferred an outright alliance with England and France to what he viewed as the impractical entanglements of the League. Others viewed the League as an intolerable diminution of American sovereignty and insisted that the wisest course would be for America to adhere to its traditional policy of nonentanglement. Republican "Mild Reservationists," on the other hand, favored membership with only a few changes to clarify the Covenant. The "Strong Reservationists," led by Senator Lodge, Chairman of the Foreign Relations Committee, advocated sweeping changes before the League would be safe for American participation. The Monroe Doctrine must be safeguarded, League interference in domestic questions such as the tariff and immigration precluded, and the obligation to defend other states under Article X reduced or eliminated. The power of Congress to declare war, make peace, or send troops abroad could not be transferred to a world organization. Most of these fears were groundless, as a careful reading of the Covenant would have revealed. In addition to doubts about the Covenant, many senators of both parties deeply resented the President's ignoring of the Senate during the peace-making; apparently they saw the debate on the Treaty as a legislative versus executive battle for control over foreign policy. And as we have seen, the personal animosity of Lodge and Wilson had an incalculable effect on the Treaty fight.

Lodge directed a well-conceived and brilliantly executed strategy. He decided to draft a number of amendments (eventually reservations) to the Treaty that would unify Republican ranks and embarrass the Democrats. If Wilson accepted them, Republicans could claim that they had remedied the defects in the League; if the President rejected them, Republicans could attribute the responsibility for defeat of the Treaty solely to the Democrats who refused to make the League safe for American participation. Lodge clearly expected that Wilson would spurn his reservations and thereby doom the Treaty and the League. When a Republican colleague, Senator James E. Watson of Indiana, expressed fear that Wilson might accept the Treaty with the reservations, Lodge reassured him: "But, my dear James, you do not take into consideration the hatred that Woodrow Wilson has for me personally. Never under any set of circumstances in this world could he be induced to accept a treaty with Lodge reservations appended to it."

Lodge deliberately stalled for time, taking two weeks to read aloud the entire Treaty before a nearly empty committee room, despite the fact that printed copies were available. He used an additional six weeks in hearings. Secretary of State Lansing, increasingly alienated from his chief and deeply resentful of presidential snubs at the Paris conference, badly damaged the cause of the Treaty in his testimony. Lansing admitted that he and others at Paris had objected to Wilson's capitulation on Shantung and he revealed that his advice had not been often sought by the President at the conference. William C. Bullitt, a young and ardently liberal critic of the peace conference who had resigned in protest from the American delegation, also appeared before the committee. Bullitt violated personal confidences to relate to the eager Republicans that Lansing privately had criticized the Treaty and Covenant in most unsparing language.

The committee reported the Treaty to the Senate loaded with 45 amendments and 4 reservations (ultimately reduced to 14 reservations), designed primarily to embarrass the President and curtail his authority. The most important reservation involved Article X of the Covenant: the United States would assume no obligation to defend the integrity of other states or to use its armed forces at the request of the League without the specific approval of Congress. Other reservations specified that the United States would determine the domestic matters to be excluded from the competency of the League, and declared the Monroe Doctrine entirely beyond League jurisdiction. The last reservation, a clear reflection of Anglophobia, refused to bind the United States to any League decision in which any member had cast more than one vote – the British empire and commonwealth had six seats in the League Assembly. Meanwhile, Republican opponents of the League, backed by financial contributions from Henry Clay Frick and Andrew Mellon, among others, established the League for the Preservation of American Independence and sent speakers across the nation to attack Wilson and the Covenant.

While Lodge's strategy unfolded, President Wilson decided to appeal his case directly to the people. His efforts to conciliate and win support from moderate critics of the League had proved unsuccessful. Wilson would accept mild interpretative reservations provided that they were not a formal part of the act of ratification and therefore would not compel renegotiation of the Treaty. In any case he deemed most of the proposed changes as unnecessary, dishonorable, or ruinous to the League. In September the President began a speaking tour through the mid-western and far-western states. Although warned by his personal physician that his health had been weakened by the toils at Paris, Wilson decided that his duty came first. Despite the late summer heat and the discomforts of railroad travel, he delivered over thirty major addresses in defense of the League before he collapsed at Pueblo, Colorado. Exhausted and suffering blinding headaches, the President reluctantly cancelled the remainder of the tour. Probably it had been ill-advised in any case, for even if the Democrats had won all the Senate seats at stake in 1920 as the result of Wilson's campaign, he would still have fallen short of the two-thirds majority required for Senate approval of the Treaty without reservations.

Soon after his return to the White House, Wilson on October 2 suffered a cerebral thrombosis that left him partially paralyzed. For days he lay near death, and even when he began to recover, could not perform many of his presidential duties. Despite an obvious disability under the Constitution, Wilson's wife and close advisers refused to request the Vice President to assume the executive duties. Secretary of State Lansing, who called cabinet meetings on his own authority, thought seriously of declaring a disability but gave up when Wilson's private secretary and his physician resisted. Wilson's wife and aides imposed a virtual conspiracy of silence around the President's sickroom, and carefully restricted the official business brought to his attention. Even cabinet members could not see the President and had to rely upon brief notes by Mrs. Wilson stating the President's wishes. Yet it would be an exaggeration to accuse her of running the government. In fact, for a period no one was in effective charge and the executive branch functioned largely by inertia.

When the President did begin to recover, he adamantly refused to compromise with Senator Lodge. Wilson's intelligence apparently remained unimpaired by his illness, although he seemed much more rigid, irritable, and suspicious. His aides warned him that the only hope for Senate approval of the Treaty in any form lay in compromise with the Republican leaders. Wilson preferred defeat to what he felt would be a cowardly and hesitant entry into the League under the Lodge Reservations. He still had confidence that the great majority of the people were with him, when in fact signs indicated that a growing number, blaming both Wilson and Lodge for the deadlock, desired a compromise. When the Treaty came to a vote in the Senate on November 19, 1919 and again on March 19, 1920 the President urged loyal Democrats to vote against it with the Lodge Reservations. He thereby ensured its defeat for the Democrats could not muster enough strength to approve the Treaty without changes. In the final vote on the Treaty in March 1920 the tally for the Treaty with the reservations fell seven short (49 ayes, 35 nayes) of the necessary two-thirds for approval.

The "Solemn Referendum"

The President refused to acknowledge defeat. For a while, with his fondness for the British parliamentary system, he thought of challenging senatorial opponents to resign and stand for reelection; if a majority won, he would name a Republican Secretary of State and, with the cooperation of the Vice President, resign the presidency to that Republican. Legal problems and the probability that most Republican senators would not cooperate caused him to abandon that novel scheme for resolving an executive-legislative deadlock. Wilson then determined to make the 1920 presidential contest a national referendum on the League. Apparently he wanted a third nomination by the Democratic Party, but his loyal friends, fearful for his life, prevented his name from being presented to the convention meeting in San Francisco. Instead the convention nominated James M. Cox, Governor of Ohio, with Franklin D. Roosevelt as his running mate. The Republicans chose Senator Warren G. Harding of Ohio, an impressive looking man but a mediocrity; Governor Calvin Coolidge of Massachusetts received second place on the ticket. Cox and Roosevelt supported membership in the League, though they agreed to accept moderate reservations to the Covenant. Cox would even accept the essentials of the Lodge reservation relating to Article X. Without repudiating Wilson, Cox clearly indicated that if elected he would not continue the existing deadlock with the Senate.

Harding's position on the Treaty and League seemed less clear. His acceptance address expressed satisfaction that Republicans in the Senate had rescued America from a "merged government of the world" and preserved American sovereignty and diplomatic independence. Yet some of his remarks during the early phases of the campaign suggested that he favored membership in the League after some changes; on other occasions he seemed to advocate negotiation of a new and better association of nations. Harding's personal feelings inclined toward isolationism, however, and when the Irreconcilables brought pressure to bear he finally repudiated Wilson's League. The League, he declared, was a "stupendous fraud" and the provisions of Article X endangered America's independence and peace. Even so, Harding continued to refer vaguely to some kind of association of nations and such pro-League Republicans as Elihu Root, Charles Evans Hughes, and Herbert Hoover argued that Harding would take the country into the League. They hoped not so much to win votes for the Republican ticket – victory seemed assured – but to prevent Harding in office from spurning membership in any kind of a world organization. In view of all these confusing statements by Republican spokesmen, the voter could be pardoned if he remained unclear about the Republican candidate's intentions.

By their very nature, presidential contests are not designed to provide a mandate on any one issue. Too many factors are involved for such an interpretation. In 1920, traditional political loyalties, personalities, and a variety of local and national issues and grievances obscured or eclipsed the question of the League. Administration war-time mobilization policies had alienated many western farmers, northern laborers, and consumers everywhere; German-, Irish-, Italian-Americans, and disillusioned liberals objected strongly to various provisions of the Versailles Treaty; and highly nationalistic and patriotic groups feared loss of sovereignty through League membership. The progressive coalition that had brought Wilson victory in 1916 clearly had disintegrated by 1920. Moreover Harding made an attractive if uninspiring candidate, and many Americans simply desired a change in government and a return to what Harding called "normalcy."

When the election returns came in, Harding had overwhelmed his opponent, polling 16,152,200 votes (61 percent) to 9,147,353 for Cox or a plurality of over seven million votes. Harding carried the electoral votes of all the states outside the "Solid South" and even won Tennessee. Cox went down to a defeat unequalled by any Democratic candidate since Stephen A. Douglas in 1860. The

Republicans also won heavy majorities in both houses of Congress.

Although historians agree that the election was not a mandate on the League or any other single issue, Wilson by his insistence on a "Solemn Referendum" had helped ensure that the Republican victory would interpret it as a decisive popular rejection of membership in the League. The Republicans in office treated the issue as dead, and the United States joined Bolshevik Russia, defeated Germany, and lesser states such as Arabia, Tibet, and Nepal in shunning the League. A variety of factors explain the final defeat of the Treaty: political and personal partisanship, isolationist sentiment, and genuine doubts by many citizens of the wisdom of too rapid an assumption of world obligations. Above all, Wilson by his insistence on all or nothing contributed mightily to the final outcome. The United States in a very real sense thereby betrayed its own ideals and national interests. It had entered the war to defend imperiled interests and rights and yet, after turning the conflict into a struggle for a just peace and a stable post-war world, abandoned the field when victory was in sight. American withdrawal left a badly weakened France and an impaired Britain to uphold the new settlement.

While Wilson and his internationalist supporters had lost, it proved impossible in the 1920's to ignore the legacy of American intervention and victory in World War I, or to return fully to the nineteenth century pattern of isolationism. The First World War marked the beginning of a great departure for the United States from the neutrality and isolationism of the past to the global responsibilities of the future. The war also marked a movement toward a larger role for government in regulating and directing the American economy. Wilson's Republican successors could no more ignore that fact than they could the implications of the war for foreign policy. The task of the 1920's lay in defining and improving the new relationship of government and the economy, while developing a new foreign policy to protect American interests.

4

A Business Civilization

UNTIL RECENTLY, most historians portrayed the Twenties as an interlude between two great reform eras, Progressivism and the New Deal. The national mood was depicted as weary with crusades at home and abroad, longing to return to the peace and prosperity Harding termed "normalcy." Big business, no longer suspect as in the muckraking era, had gained immense prestige from wartime miracles of production and the service in government of a number of business tycoons as patriotic "dollar-a-year" men. The Republican party seemed the preferred political instrument for a return to the politics of business and the "good old days" of prosperity and contentment. The reactionary and conservative, as well as the bizarre elements in American politics and society during the decade were unduly emphasized.

Yet many of the people who lived in the 1920's, from businessmen to economists and sociologists, viewed the decade as a hopeful new era characterized by material plenty, the gradual elimination of poverty, and technological and scientific advances. It was disillusioned and alienated intellectuals who fastened a misleading label of crassness and reaction on the era. From the present viewpoint it can be seen that the Twenties witnessed profound economic and social changes almost revolutionary in nature. The movement toward greater order and stability in business and finance, the scientific and managerial rationalization of industry, and the growing urbanization and transformation of American values and institutions, long underway, continued apace and gave the decade its major significance. Part of the process of transformation and adaptation, which seemed conservative and even reactionary to some older style liberal critics, came from the growing involvement of government in the economy, the closer relationship between business and the federal government. The reform legislation and regulatory bodies of the Progressive Era, supposedly intended to curb big business, in fact often had been sought by the large corporations and operated to stabilize and encourage business activity. World War I especially brought about an intimate relationship between business and government and a continuous involvement of federal authorities in stimulating, directing, and controlling the economy. The postwar years saw business and government gradually work out the details of their new relationship. The New Deal and World War II contributed further adjustments, until today we live in a society that takes a large degree of government regulation and management of the economy for granted. These economic and political changes and tendencies, and not the colorful but superficial image of flappers, gangsters, booze, and reaction, represent the deeper meaning of the Twenties.

The Rationalization of Industry

Scientific management in industry and business appeared to be triumphant in the 1920's. The prosperity of the decade resulted primarily from enormous increases in productivity, rising 46 percent for all branches in 1929 over the 1920 level, attributable in large part to more efficient management. As early as 1900, Frederick W. Taylor pioneered in scientific study and planning in production, "time and motion" studies, to eliminate waste and inefficiency in the use of time and materials. Industry adopted "Taylorization" and utilized technical research, cost studies, production planning, salesmanship, and market surveys. The Commerce Department also preached the new gospel of efficiency of operation and standardization and simplification of products to businessmen. Greater use of electrical energy also contributed to increased production. Technical advances reduced the cost of electricity, so that while only one-third of industry was electrified in 1914, by 1929 three-fourths used electrical power. Output per worker increased by 40 percent in industry from 1919 to 1925. A growing technological unemployment, however, became a socially undesirable by-product of the increased use of machinery; for example, the continuous strip-sheet rolling mill for sheet steel and tin-plating eliminated 40 to 50 workers per mill; cigar machines by 1930 had taken over 47 percent of what used to be hand labor; and heavy construction was mechanized by use of power shovels, belt conveyors, and concrete mixers doing away with large numbers of unskilled laborers.

Consolidation in business, a trend underway since the late nineteenth century, reflected the desire to promote efficiency and stability, reduce costs, and above all to eliminate cutthroat competition and price wars. During the Twenties, over 6,000 factories and mining companies disappeared, 4,000 utility companies were consolidated into larger units, and there were 1,800 bank mergers. Samuel Insull built a giant utility holding company that operated gas and electric firms in 23 states, while A. P. Giannini of California controlled a chain of 500 banks across that state and became the fourth largest banker in the nation. By 1930 the 200 largest non-financial corporations in America owned nearly half the total national corporate wealth. Four meat packing firms dominated 70 percent of that industry, four tobacco companies manufactured over 90 percent of the cigarettes consumed, and so on. The larger firms, regarded as "price leaders," in effect set price levels for the lesser members of an industry. Such competition that existed was more in brand advertising than in prices. Expansion and consolidation proceeded swiftly in the automotive, radio, and chemical industries, to name only a few. The DuPont firm, benefitting from wartime production of explosives and confiscation of German dye patents, dominated the chemical industry with its new synthetic fibers such as rayon and cellophane. Newspaper chains began in the late nineteenth century but reached a peak in the Twenties. By the end of the decade about 60 chains owned over 300 daily newspapers. Chain stores thrived in the wholesale and retail grocery and merchandising fields; the Great Atlantic and Pacific Tea Company (A & P) had 17,500 stores across the country by 1928. Other chains, such as Woolworth and Rexall, spread across regions or the entire country. Although these chains drove many small independents out of business and dominated one-fifth or more of the retail field by 1929, they were often highly competitive with one another.

During the Twenties, business and government worked closely together. Herbert Hoover, Secretary of Commerce during the Harding and Coolidge administrations, converted the Commerce Department from a minor to a major executive agency to encourage greater business productivity and efficiency. The Commerce Department investigated economic problems, distributed technical information and reports on foreign markets, and facilitated greater standardization of sizes and designs in production. For example, it reduced the varieties of paving brick from 66 to 4 and basic types of hospital beds from 44 to 2. An economic nationalist, Hoover saw the world's welfare as dependent upon American prosperity. He sought American control of vital foreign raw material resources and an expansion of American exports, while at the same time encouraging American economic self-sufficiency. A new era had dawned which was not simply a return to the old order favoring business but one of close government-business cooperation. Hoover envisioned a benevolent government helping business to achieve greater efficiency and productivity, and thereby benefitting the nation as a whole. As President Calvin Coolidge was to remark, the business of America was business. Under Hoover's inspiration, the federal government sought not merely to create a favorable climate for business but to aid business to a more positive approach through persuasion and suggestion.

The prosperity of the Twenties tended to be irregular. Total national income rose from $74.3 billion in 1923 to $89 billion by 1928, and corporate profits increased by 62 percent during the same period. Real wages also rose but more slowly — 11 percent from 1923 to 1929 — and the average work week declined from 47.3 to 45.7 hours. Yet there was much unemployment, especially in such ailing industries as coal mining and textiles. Coal prices remained depressed, in part because of an over-abundant supply and in part due to the more efficient use of coal by industry. In textiles, except for booming sales in rayon and silk, prices were relatively low although production was high. That situation reflected both sharp competition and style changes as clothing and shoes for women and men became lighter. Layoffs of workers and low wages also resulted from the large-scale movement of textile industry from the northeastern states to the southern, exploiting cheaper labor and lower land costs. Farmers received a disproportionately small share of the general prosperity.

Labor in a Business Era

Organized labor also retreated during the Twenties. Labor had made considerable progress during the Progressive era, and especially during the war when worker shortages and a government anxious to avoid strikes had created a favorable climate. After the Armistice, labor leaders determined to preserve and extend these gains and to obtain wage hikes to compensate for inflation. However in addition to employer resistance, the conservative craft-union philosophy of the A.F.L. unions, presided over by Samuel Gompers' colorless successor William Green (1924), made it difficult to organize mass production industries with their hordes of unskilled and semi-skilled workers. Overseas immigration had been curtailed but rural migration, nearly 17½ million between 1920 and 1929, flooded the cities with cheap labor and potential strike breakers. White-collar employees, growing in number, also found unionism unappealing.

Many industrialists had consented with reluctance to the government's wartime labor policies and resolved to end them after the war. Opponents of unionization discouraged national union membership by practicing "welfare capitalism" to remove worker grievances through higher wages and improved employer-employee relations. John D. Rockefeller, Jr., deeply shocked by the violence of the 1914 Ludlow Massacre in Colorado, led the way. Even at its best, welfare capitalism was paternalistic and clearly anti-union. Henry Ford, the automotive tycoon, pioneered the "Doctrine of High Wages" in 1914, inaugurating in his non-union plants the "Five Dollar" workday wage scale. In practice, however, Ford granted no general wage increase between 1919 and 1929, and he laid off 60,000 workers without wages for over a year in 1927 as he retooled for a new automobile model. The National Association of Manufacturers and the U.S. Chamber of Commerce endorsed the "American Plan" or open-shop approach against compulsory unionism. As a condition of employment some employers forced workers to sign "yellow-dog" contracts renouncing national union membership. Mine workers in West Virginia had to sign a contract reading: "I am not now a member of the United Mine Workers. . . . and I enter this employment with the understanding that the policy of the company is to operate a non-union mine . . . and [that it] would not give me employment under any other condition." Employers supported company controlled plant unions and used black-lists drawn up of known national union organizers.

In the reactionary postwar climate, Congress and the Executive, even under Wilson, tended to favor business in disputes with labor. Wilson called a National Industrial Conference but it failed to harmonize the interests of employers and workers. A wave of disruptive strikes swept the nation in 1919, involving about four million workers and threatening to plunge the country into economic paralysis. A coal miners' strike pulled 425,000 miners out of the bituminous coal fields, until broken by federal court injunctions. The miners subsequently received a substantial wage increase.

One of the bitterest conflicts occurred in the steel industry. Over half the laborers worked a twelve-hour day for very low wages. Previous attempts, the 1892 Homestead strike and clashes in 1901 and 1910, failed to unionize these semi- or unskilled workers. Judge Elbert H. Gary served as Chairman of the Board of the giant United States Steel Corporation, which was controlled by Morgan interests. A dignified lawyer and pious Methodist, the iron-willed Gary determined to defeat unionization and uphold the non-union or "open shop." In 1918 the A.F.L. established a committee to assault this bastion of anti-unionism with William Z. Foster, a labor radical but not at that time a communist, providing much of the committee's zeal and leadership. Unfortunately, the A.F.L. rejected a single industry-wide union and tried to organize workers under appropriate craft unions. After initial success, the labor committee encountered resistance from the company – Judge Gary refused even to confer with union spokesmen – and a major strike broke out in September, 1919. Although only about half the workers walked out, the strike disrupted a vital national industry. The press in general reacted sharply against the union organizers, depicting the strike as an industrial war led by radicals and revolutionaries. The *New York Times* called it an attempt to Bolshevize America and others agreed that it was a radical conspiracy. Exploiting this theme, U.S. Steel and the other companies charged that the strike was foreign in origin and without appeal to native born workers. Foster especially became a target of calumny, and he was hailed before a congressional investigating committee. Facing industry intimidation, employment of strikebreakers, and arbitrary arrests by local and state police, the union organizers failed. The strike collapsed by early 1920; not until the 1930's did the steel industry at last capitulate to unionization.

The most shocking postwar labor disturbances took place in Seattle and Boston. James A. Duncan, a radical labor agitator who had outspokenly opposed American intervention in the war and sympathized with the Bolshevik cause in Russia, took advantage of a shipyard dispute to call a general strike of all workers in Seattle early in 1919. This new type of strike which virtually paralyzed Seattle for five days was denounced by Mayor Ole Hanson as a communist plot. Public revulsion caused several of the participating unions to withdraw their support and the general strike collapsed. In Boston, lowly-paid policemen had formed a union and received A.F.L. endorsement. E. U. Curtis, the stubborn police commissioner, refused to permit police to belong to the union and when he dismissed nineteen of their union leaders, over 1100 of the city's 1544 policemen walked out. Criminals looted stores and robbed citizens on the streets, yet Calvin Coolidge, then Governor of Massachusetts, delayed calling out the state guard for two nights of crime and public panic. By the time he finally acted, Boston's mayor already had largely restored order by use of volunteers and state guardsmen living in the city. The newspapers exaggerated the effects of the strike and assured a horrified public that it was the work of communists and other radicals. President Wilson denounced it as a "crime against civilization." Coolidge received national plaudits for his famed telegram to Samuel Gompers: "There is no right to strike against the public safety by anybody, anywhere, anytime."

There was another coal miners' strike in 1922 when operators declined to renew contracts with the United Mine Workers union and announced sharp wage reductions. After the strike dragged on for months and a bloody clash occurred in southern Illinois between strikers and strike-breakers, President Harding ordered the mines opened and endorsed the use of state troops. The miners returned to work on the basis of the old arrangement and a federal investigation into working conditions, but despite the inquiry's findings of deplorable mine conditions, Congress failed to act. In 1925, when the U.M.W. refused to accept wage cuts as the price of coal fell, the Pittsburgh Coal Company, after thirty years of relations with the union, cut wages and reopened with nonunion labor. Wage cuts, strike-breakers, and violence took their toll, and by 1930 John L. Lewis' once powerful United Mine Workers had declined to a fraction of its former size. A railroad shopmen's strike also took place in 1922, again because of a wage slash. Attorney General Harry M. Daugherty obtained a sweeping federal court injunction against the strikers and the strike collapsed.

Communist organizers and agitators during the 1920's challenged organized labor with "dual unionism" (separate communist-controlled unions) and exploited labor grievances to promote communism. In 1928 and 1929, in the cotton mills of Tennessee and North and South Carolina, low wages, unsanitary factories, long hours for women and children, and company town abuses spawned unrest and strikes. Communist agitators helped to arouse workers and there were bloody clashes at Gastonia, North Carolina. Local police, state troopers, and court injunctions smashed the strikes. Union membership in the A.F.L. and unaffiliated unions declined from 5 million members in 1920 to about 3½ million by 1929.

The Plight of the Blacks

After wartime gains, the Negro experienced a considerable deterioration in the Twenties. During the war, Negroes had often been discouraged from enlisting in the armed forces, but 2,290,525 registered under the Selective Service Law and 367,000 were inducted. Although Negroes found the Marine Corps closed to them and obtained only menial positions in the Navy, they served in almost every branch of the Army in segregated units, and some held commissioned rank. Negro soldiers served and fought well, only to return after a "war for democracy" to face intensified discrimination and violence, especially in the South. About 400,000 Negroes migrated from the southern states during the war (reaching a total of over 1,200,000 by 1928), attracted by the prospects of jobs in northern industry. They often encountered intense white resentment over competition for jobs and above all for housing and recreational opportunities. Lynchings increased from 38 in 1917 to 58 in 1918. In July, 1917, a serious race riot in East St. Louis took an estimated forty black lives.

Racial tensions heightened after the Armistice in a national atmosphere of reaction, the Ku Klux Klan, and competition for jobs caused by the brief postwar recession. A reported seventy blacks were lynched in 1919, including ten black servicemen still in their uniforms. A rash of race riots ensued, about 25 in all, the worst one taking place in Chicago. Large numbers of blacks had migrated to Chicago, particularly during the war, bringing the black population to nearly 110,000 by 1920. Mounting tensions set the stage for a riot, touched-off in July, 1919 when whites threw stones at a young black swimmer who had drifted into an area of Lake Michigan "reserved" for whites. The youth drowned and the rumor spread throughout the black sections that he had been murdered (his body showed no signs of stoning). Mobs gathered and fighting occurred between Negroes and whites in several parts of the city. For almost two weeks racial tensions plunged that city into strife and wreckage, finally ended by the state militia after thirty-eight people had been killed and over 500 injured. Negroes suffered the most and over 1,000 families, largely black, were left homeless.

Led by the National Association for the Advancement of Colored People, Negro organizations sought a federal anti-lynching law but, while it passed the House of Representatives in 1921, Southerners filibustered it to death in the Senate. The N.A.A.C.P. published *Thirty Years of Lynching* in 1919 followed by Walter White's *Rope and Faggot, A Biography of Judge Lynch* (1929), based on careful investigation into the circumstances of such outrages. The N.A.A.C.P. also conducted numerous protest meetings against lynchings during the 1920's. Advocates of Negro rights made limited progress in legal attacks on the Southern white primary system and at promoting improved racial relations in the South through education. The majority of Negroes, however, tended to look with some suspicion upon the N.A.A.C.P. and similar liberal organizations as upper class black and white movements remote from their interests.

In this climate of unemployment, low wages, and discrimination in all sections of the country, quite a few poor and under-educated blacks were attracted to Marcus Garvey's black nationalist movement. Garvey came to New York from Jamaica in 1916 with his Universal Negro Improvement Association, preaching racial pride in the Negro's origins in Africa and the beauty and excellence of blackness. In his view, black contributions to American history had been ignored and its culture shattered by whites; therefore racial pride must be restored and a Negro culture rebuilt. Garvey extolled everything black, described whites as of a lower breed or race, and called for a truly black religion free of an alien white deity and theology. Since he deemed it hopeless to try to overcome the racism embedded in white civilization, he accepted segregation or separatism as desirable and launched a mass "back-to-Africa" movement. Organizing an "Empire of Africa," he made himself its president, dispensed noble titles, and enrolled some 75,000 members. His movement faltered and eventually collapsed when Garvey was sentenced for fraud in 1923 and was deported from the United States four years later. While most American Negroes hoped to improve their situation in America, rather than migrate to a new country, "Garveyism" represented the first large-scale expression of Negro discontent and black awareness, themes that surfaced with renewed intensity in the 1950's.

The Culture of a Business Age

In the Twenties boosters bragged that a democratic revolution had occurred in the ownership of stocks in American corporations. The great bull market saw stock-ownership increase from 2 million people in 1920 to some 17 million by the end of the decade. Office workers, clerks, and laborers joined businessmen in purchasing stocks for investment or speculative purposes. John Raskob of General Motors suggested that anyone could get rich within twenty years by investing $15 weekly in stocks and letting them grow in value. Hoover voiced the prevailing optimism and "get-rich-quick" urge in 1928: "We seem only to have touched the fringe of our potentialities."

These optimists usually overlooked a darker side to the dispersion of stock ownership. Diffusion of ownership did not mean that large corporations became more responsible to their small stockholders, but only that insiders, owning a minority of the stocks, found it easier to control and even wreck the corporations. Many stocks in fact were non-voting issues; one textile firm issued 2,000 voting stocks out of a total of 600,000 stocks outstanding. The holding company device, with one holding company pyramided over a number of lesser holding and operating companies, facilitated a ruinous manipulation by the few speculators in control at the top. Small stockholders and the assets of the actual operating companies could be fleeced through overcapitalization, excessive service charges, and other techniques. Samuel Insull erected a holding company on top of holding companies until his system defied analysis; it collapsed in 1932 with an estimated loss to investors of a billion dollars.

Businessmen became the popular heroes of the day. No longer under the "robber-baron" onus of the muckraking era, big businessmen often spoke in the Progressive rhetoric of public service and the common good and identified their cause with democracy and progress. Booster clubs, trade associations, and chambers of commerce extolled the new hero and the American "way of life." President Calvin Coolidge commented that "Brains are wealth and wealth is the chief end of man." "The man who builds a factory builds a temple," he proclaimed, and "the man who works there worships there." The parlance of business crept into every facet of American life. An article in *The Independent* praised the business community for providing the "sanest religion" in America, for "any relationship that forces a man to follow the Golden Rule rightfully belongs amid the ceremonials of the church." Bruce Barton, in the best seller *The Man Nobody Knows* (1925), described Jesus Christ as the world's most successful businessman who had recruited twelve disciples "from the bottom ranks of business and forged them into an organization that conquered the world."

Industry transformed American society and life. Probably the automobile had the greatest single impact on the economy and society. At first highly experimental and expensive, by 1910 standard production type automobiles had been developed. Henry Ford, the high-priest of assembly-line production, flooded America with the cheap but durable Model T; his assembly technique reduced the time required to produce a car from over 12 hours to less than 2 hours. Satisfied with a small unit profit on a large volume of sales, Ford reduced the price of a Model T from $950 to $290 by 1924. Ford owned the majority of stock in the Ford Motor Company and zealously guarded his family firm from raids by the great bankers and financiers. Ownership of an automobile changed from a symbol of social status that it had been prior to 1914 to a commonplace convenience. Ford became a national hero, rated by a group of college students as the third greatest figure in history, behind only Jesus Christ and Napoleon. His many admirers overlooked his anti-union policies, his peculiar politics, and his anti-semitism. General Motors ranked next in the automotive field, organized by William C. Durant but falling under the control of J. P. Morgan and the DuPonts after the First World War. Ford and General Motors between them shared 60 percent of the automobile market. The rising sale of General Motors' Chevrolet forced Ford to introduce a new car, the Model A, in 1928. Third among the giants, Chrysler Corporation competed with its Plymouth in the low price field.

The automobile created a whole new industry, involving not only the makers of the product and the suppliers of metals and fabrics for the vehicles but petroleum refineries and innumerable service stations, garages, and highway inns to care for the car and its occupants. The industry consumed annually 90 percent of the country's refined petroleum products, 80 percent of its rubber, 75 percent of the plate glass, and 25 percent of the machine tools. By 1929

Americans drove 26 million vehicles and annual passenger car production reached 3 million units. Highways vastly increased in mileage, spurred by matching grants to the states inaugurated under the 1916 Federal Highway Act and subsequent legislation. Authorities expended an estimated $1 billion per year during the decade on highways and $400 million on city streets. Trucking and bus transportation also grew steadily, to the corresponding loss of the railroads.

The automobile helped break down rural isolation and made possible the rapid growth of city suburbs and vacation retreats. A fantastic real estate boom in Florida, touted as America's Riviera, reached incredible proportions by the mid-Twenties. Miami grew from 30,000 in 1920 to 75,000 by 1925. Around the city, and indeed over much of the entire state, land values rose exorbitantly and developers launched scores of construction projects for housing, hotels, and resorts. Lots, some bought unseen and subsequently discovered by unwary purchasers to lie under water in swamps or the sea, sold for prices as high as $25,000 to $75,000 each, until that bubble burst in 1926. Among other less desirable effects of the automotive age were highway congestion and a mounting toll of accidents. Moreover, the automobile made crime more mobile and, in the view of many, encouraged juvenile delinquency and sexual immorality.

Aviation, born around the turn of the century with the pioneers Wilbur and Orville Wright, was stimulated greatly by military needs in World War I. The industry made slow progress thereafter, however, until the stimulus of the 1925 Air Mail Act. Thereafter a number of major manufacturing and transportation companies began to emerge, and by 1929 forty-eight commercial airlines provided connections between 355 cities.

Advertising, the quintessence of "boosterism," became a major industry of nearly $2 billion by 1929. It brought with it an emphasis on brands and on psychological obsolescence. To clear the way each year for a new flood of consumer goods and gadgets advertisers persuaded the public that this year's model was incomparably superior to last year's. Industry also indulged heavily in public relations, hiring publicists to extol its merits and discredit critics. Much of the increased purchasing resulted from a vast expansion of credit or installment buying, that mixed blessing that permits one (briefly) to live beyond his immediate means. By the end of the decade, 15 percent of all goods sold were on credit, accounting for $5 billion of sales annually by 1929.

Development of the radio and the motion picture industry brought a growing sophistication in tastes and manners. From an infant industry in 1920, by 1929 one out of every three households (four out of five by 1940) owned a radio and broadcasting networks such as the National Broadcasting Company and the Columbia Broadcasting System supplied local stations with entertainment and information. Motion picture cameras and projectors, developed by George Eastman, Thomas A. Edison, and others in the late nineteenth century, spawned a new industry by the early 1900's. Prior to World War I, David W.

Griffith produced lengthy film stories and Mary Pickford, Charlie Chaplin, and others achieved fame and fortune. After the Armistice, motion picture theaters across America — 22,731 by 1931 — regaled viewers first with silent and then with sound movies (the first "talkie," in 1927, starred Al Jolson in "The Jazz Singer"). Average weekly attendance at the movies numbered 95 million by 1929, consuming a diet of gangster, western, and boudoir films. The movie idols of the day were personalities such as Clara Bow, the "It" girl, Theda Bara the "Vamp," and Rudolph Valentino the "Sheik."

Increased leisure, as well as affluence, led to a growth in recreational activities. Municipal and private golf courses, tennis courts, and swimming pools multiplied. Professional sports — baseball, football, and boxing — provided both entertainment and popular heroes for spectators: Babe Ruth in baseball, boxers Jack Dempsey and Gene Tunney, and the immortal Red Grange, an Illinois fullback, to name only a few. When Dempsey fought George S. Carpentier in 1921 for the heavyweight boxing championship, 91,000 people paid over $1 million to see the American flatten the French challenger. Similar receipts flowed in to promoters later when Tunney finally dethroned Dempsey in two highly advertised encounters. College football became semiprofessional and some schools apparently cut back on academics in order to build huge stadia and hire expensive coaches. Fads for Mah Jong, crossword puzzles, and flagpole sitting ("Shipwreck" Kelly) swept the nation. The idol of the decade, the "Lone Eagle" Charles A. Lindbergh crossed the Atlantic in 33 hours in a single-engine airplane in 1927. He landed at Paris to a hero's welcome and, on orders from President Coolidge, returned home in triumph aboard an American warship. No single event of the decade so captured the world's admiration and aroused such hero worship as his flight in the "Spirit of St. Louis."

The Revolt against "Victorianism"

The revolution against "Victorian" morals and standards, actually underway during the Progressive Era prior to the First World War, became fully apparent in the 1920's. The urbanization and secularization of American life had eroded the appeal and authority of past traditions and morals. The "new woman," enfranchised by the Nineteenth Amendment and by economic opportunities, and above all by the growth of the city, sought greater freedom. Large numbers of women left the shelter of home for employment in the professions, industry, and as typists and secretaries in the business world. Over 10 million women were employed by 1930. As more women enjoyed release from past restraints, the number of divorces mounted and the size of families declined as the birth rate fell. New moral standards prevailed, at first among upper-class women but eventually affecting to some degree women of the middle and lower classes. Shorter dresses and rolled-down hose, bobbed hair, increased use of

Life, 1926, New York Historical Society.

cosmetics, dances such as the *Charleston*, drinking from hip flasks and smoking, and more illegitimate births seemed to characterize the new woman. The psychological theories of Dr. Sigmund Freud, widely misinterpreted as having sanctioned sexual promiscuity to avoid neurotic inhibitions and complexes, became fashionable. Testifying to the new and open emphasis on sex, an estimated one-fourth of the radio broadcasting time in 1928 conveyed erotic messages with such songs as "Baby Face," "Hot Mamma," "Hot Lips," and "Burning Kisses." One movie producer advertised a film as offering "brilliant men, beautiful jazz babies, champagne baths, midnight revels, petting parties in the purple dawn, all ending in one terrific smashing climax that makes you gasp." Sex themes also abounded in certain types of mass circulation magazines, such as *Snappy Stories* and *True Confessions*, and "petting" and "necking" entered the nation's vocabulary.

Americans seemed more hedonistic than ever before, observing the Sabbath more with golf, movies, or afternoon drives than by church attendance. Alarmed moralists spoke out: the head of the Christian Endeavor Society condemned the *Charleston* as "an offense against womanly purity"; the Young Women's Christian Association launched a national drive for more modest female attire; and several legislatures debated laws on the proper length of dresses. Judge Ben Lindsey of Denver ignited a controversy by suggesting "trial marriages" to reduce divorce and illegitimacy. Yet the moral rebellion should not be exaggerated; millions of Americans continued to live as before. The cult of youth died out in the early 1930's, because it is the nature of such rebellions to burn out or pall and because of the sobering effects of the Great Depression.

Education scored notable advances during this period, although here too materialistic values seemed to predominate. John Dewey's philosophy of progressive education to adjust the learning process to a changing society was often misinterpreted as a permissiveness in teaching and the abandonment of traditional subjects of study such as classics, literature, and languages for more practical courses. Enrollments and expenditures in the public schools, especially on the secondary level, vastly increased. Advances took place in student health through physical examinations and use of school nurses. Since many new students were not academically oriented high schools instituted vocational training embracing subjects such as the manual arts and secretarial skills. By 1926 one out of every eight American youth attended a college or university. The increases in high school and college enrollments reflected not only prosperity and the traditional belief in the value of education, but the needs of the business world for trained professional people and skilled technicians. Higher education expanded beyond the liberal arts to provide courses in commerce and business, home economics, and applied arts and sciences.

Reaction and the Great Red Scare

Changes as sweeping as those of the Twenties inevitably aroused bewilderment and resistance. Much of the reaction — the upsurge of Fundamentalism, prohibition, and the revulsion of the intellectuals — can be understood as responses to the upheaval of war and rapid economic and social transformations threatening the older ways of life.

Political and social reaction did not begin with the Republican era. As historian David A. Shannon points out, some of Wilson's domestic policies in 1919-1920 were far from liberal and made their own contribution to the postwar climate. The government after the Armistice quickly terminated millions of dollars of war contracts and drastically reduced federal construction projects. The armed forces demobilized servicemen with little effort to ease the shock of return to civilian life and to cope with the increase in unemployment. The government had efficiently operated the railroads as an integrated system during the war. McAdoo, who had supervised their direction, wanted to continue federal operation for five more years to allow time for further study of the problem, while the Railroad Brotherhoods advocated the Plumb Plan for governmental purchase and management. Conservative opposition blocked these solutions but not without some concessions to progressive sentiment. The Esch-Cummins Transportation Act of 1920 returned the roads to their owners but enlarged the supervisory powers of the Interstate Commerce Commission. The I.C.C. could fix rates based on a "fair return" on the value of the property. A "recapture" clause provided that the government would take one-half of any profits above a rate of 6 percent, but it proved unworkable in practice due to lack of agreement over how to determine the value of railroad property. A Railway Labor Board was created to hear worker grievances but it lacked the power to enforce solutions. The Water Power Act of 1920, another progressive achievement, established the Federal Power Commission to control construction of private power-generating facilities on federal lands and navigable streams, but it proved ineffective in practice. With the Jones Merchant Marine Act, Wilson and Congress decided to get government out of the shipping business and to subsidize private shipping by selling government owned vessels at bargain rates, roughly one-eighth of the cost of construction. In 1928, to aid a declining merchant marine, Congress authorized loans and mail subsidies. The 1919 Revenue Act continued to tax large incomes heavily, but in general the government changed rapidly from wartime inflationary policies to deflationary ones of steep taxes and sharply reduced expenditures and thereby contributed to a brief postwar economic recession.

The Great Red Scare of 1919-1920 marked a particularly reprehensible blot on the Wilson administration and the nation. Conservatives had long trembled at the growth of radicalism in America, and the war had provided an opportunity to vent hatreds and suspicions not only on hapless German-Americans but also on radical leaders and movements. Fear of radicalism increased after the Bolshevik Revolution in Russia and the founding in 1919 of the Comintern or Communist International to foment world revolution. Eugene Debs' Socialist Party had been weakened and divided during the war, first by the defection of those members who supported Wilson's war program and then by wartime arrests and repression. The communist wing bolted the Socialist Party in

1919 and two revolutionary Marxist parties were formed, a Communist Party based on some of the foreign language members of the old Socialist Party and other alien radicals, and a Communist Labor Party led by native-born Americans such as the young radical poet and writer John Reed, who was to die of typhus in Russia in 1921 and be buried in the Kremlin Wall. These rival communist groups slavishly emulated the Russian model and bolstered their own morale by confidently predicting imminent revolution in the United States. Ordered by Moscow to amalgamate in 1921, the united party failed to make much headway even among laborers and by the end of the decade was thoroughly Stalinized under the nominal leadership of William Z. Foster. Even so, the puny communist movement aroused widespread fear and reaction in America during the last months of the Wilson era. Labor unrest gave middle-class Americans further cause for alarm.

Despite mounting fear of radicalism, the Justice Department under Attorney General A. Mitchell Palmer at first followed a moderate course. Radicals mailed a number of packaged bombs to high government officials and to such prominent citizens as John D. Rockefeller and J. P. Morgan, timed to arrive on May Day, 1919. Postal authorities intercepted most of them though one blew up, shattering the hands of a maid in a U.S. Senator's home. Investigation failed to reveal the perpetrators but the press and public harbored few doubts in attributing the outrage to the Bolsheviks. On June 2, another bomb shattered both the home and the nerves of the Attorney General. The bomber, who carried anarchist pamphlets, blew up with his own device. Similar attacks also occurred in eight other cities.

Palmer, harboring presidential ambitions, tried to exploit the prevailing hysteria against radicalism. He established a General Intelligence Division under J. Edgar Hoover within the Justice Department to keep radical organizations under close surveillance. Although little if any evidence existed of a serious organized attempt at actual revolution, Justice Department officials succumbed to the panics and fears of the times and further aroused them by exaggerated reports and dire predictions. Palmer considered deporting dangerous radicals as early as June, and he encountered much criticism when he delayed repressive action. Finally, while President Wilson was still seriously ill, he launched the so-called Palmer Raids. Under the 1917-1918 immigration law, aliens advocating violence or the use of violence against the government could be deported. An estimated 90 percent of the members of the two communist parties and the anarchist groups consisted of foreign born individuals, hence the agitation for large-scale deportations. The Union of Russian Workers, an apparently peaceful anarchist organization, became the first target of the Palmer Raids. The raiders arrested about 300 men and women, including citizens not members of any radical group, who were caught in the building housing the Union in New York City on November 7, 1919, the second anniversary of the Bolshevik coup in Russia. Authorities subsequently released most of them, quite a few with bloody heads or bruises, but held 39 for deportation. A total of 650 were seized in New York City and there were arrests without warrants in other cities. Palmer justified these violations of legal rights on the basis that the country faced imminent revolution. On December 21, 1919 the *S. S. Buford*, popularly rechristened the "Red Ark," sailed with 249 alien deportees for Russia. In January of the next year, larger raids swept in between 3,000 to 4,000 suspected alien radicals, again without search warrants. After days or weeks in overcrowded jails and detention centers, most of those arrested subsequently obtained release for lack of evidence.

A Red hysteria seized many otherwise sane Americans. Several state legislatures, continuing the wartime search for subversives, launched investigations and passed laws to curb radical activity. The Industrial Workers of the World (the "Wobblies") had been organized in 1905 as a radical union of skilled and unskilled workers, dedicated to the overthrow of capitalism and the creation of a socialist society. Too revolutionary for most Americans and prone to violence and internecine brawling, the I.W.W. appealed mostly to the logging camps and mines in the western states. The I.W.W. opposed American intervention in 1917 in what it called a capitalistic war and the government singled it out for legal attack and repression. A number of states enacted anti-syndicalist laws, while the Justice Department convicted and imprisoned 180 Wobbly leaders under the Sedition and Espionage Acts, blows from which the union never recovered. Still other members fell into the hands of local patriotic groups and suffered "tar and featherings," beatings, and even lynchings. On Armistice Day, 1919 three parading American Legionnaires were killed as they marched past the I.W.W. headquarters in Centralia, Washington. Although it seems clear that the legionnaires had provoked the incident, an irate mob demolished the union hall and the authorities arrested twelve members of the I.W.W.; one was lynched and the others imprisoned for long terms. In the aftermath of Centralia, more state legislatures hastened to pass anti-syndicalist laws.

Illustrating the hysteria of the brief Red Scare, South Carolina's James F. Byrnes called for use of federal forces to suppress an alleged communist-directed Negro rebellion in the southern states. Kenneth McKellar of Tennessee proposed converting the remote island of Guam into an American Devil's Island for dangerous native radicals who could not be deported to Russia. And evangelist Billy Sunday suggested saving space on our ships by executing some of the radical leaders by firing squads. The hysteria subsided in the spring of 1920 as a number of Americans became alarmed at the excesses. The Labor Department, charged with responsibility for aliens and immigration, recoiled from Palmer's indiscriminate zeal and insisted on legal counsel and due process for the accused. Consequently, over one-half of those arrested in 1920 were released; when called before Congress to explain, Labor's Assistant Secretary made an effective case. Finally, Palmer's reputation suffered a severe eclipse when a mass radical uprising predicted for May Day, 1920 failed to materialize. Appalled by the wild charges and the violations of civil liberties, thoughtful citizens denounced the scare and Palmer's presidential aspirations faded as sanity began to return to the nation.

To many liberals then and since, the Sacco-Vanzetti case symbolized the reactionary nature of the postwar era. Police arrested Nicola Sacco and Bartolomeo Vanzetti, Italian aliens and admitted philosophical anarchists, and accused them of murdering a shoe factory paymaster and a guard in South Braintree, Massachusetts, in 1920. Although the evidence seemed unsubstantial to many observers, and the trial judge, Webster Thayer, was obviously highly prejudiced against alien radicals ("those anarchist bastards," he once commented), the two men were convicted in 1921 and sentenced to death in the electric chair. They spent the next six years in prison while their defenders made repeated attempts to save them. Intellectuals and liberals rallied to their cause, along with the radicals and the communists at home and abroad. On the other hand, many conservatives resented all the agitation in behalf of the two aliens and no doubt agreed with the sentiments of evangelist Billy Sunday, "Give 'em the juice." Despite world-wide sympathy and numerous appeals for mercy and justice, Sacco and Vanzetti finally were executed in August, 1927. Debate about their guilt or innocence persists to the present and the case did more than any other single event to fasten the label of reaction on the America of the 1920's.

The Nativist Upsurge

Influenced by such racist books as Madison Grant's *The Passing of the Great Race* (1916) and the writings of Lothrop Stoddard and William McDougall, a eugenics cult flourished during the decade. It had long been widely believed that the superior "Anglo-Saxon" or Nordic racial strain in America was being swamped by the influx of inferior immigrants from Southern and Eastern Europe. Responding to the supposed peril, 29 states enacted racial integrity laws prohibiting interracial marriages. The Ku Klux Klan, revived in 1915 by William J. Simmons of Georgia, fell into the hands of skilled organizers and salesmen. Under the leadership of its new Imperial Wizard, Texas dentist H. W. Evans, the Klan spread across the South and most of the nation. It carried with its pretentious ritual and elaborate secret hierarchy sinister hatreds of minority groups and foreigners, Catholics, Jews, and Negroes especially. Although the Klan professed to be a fraternal patriotic order, it inspired not only white-sheeted parades and nighttime cross burnings but whippings, mutilations, and lynchings. After reaching a peak membership of between four and five million and achieving political influence in a number of states, northern and southern, the movement eventually subsided under the weight of its own excesses. The Klan, long thought to have been confined largely to Protestant rural and smalltown America, also drew great strength from lower middle-class Protestants in the cities (many only recently from the farm) who resented the influx of blacks from the southern states and Catholic and Jewish aliens from Southern and Eastern Europe. Like fascism in Europe, the Klan represented a troubled Protestant and "native" America frantically seeking a return to an older and simpler past, a "native, white, Protestant America."

In such a fevered nativist climate, Congress passed the Immigration Acts of 1921 and 1924. Immigration had declined during the war but rose in 1920-1921 to over a million and a quarter, of which about two-thirds came from Southern and Eastern Europe. The 1921 emergency immigration act set limits for annual entry of 3 percent of those nationalities present in the United States based on the census of 1910. Congress designed the 1924 National Origins Act even more clearly to curtail or halt immigration of undesirable or "inferior" aliens, imposing an annual quota to admit no more than 2 percent of those nationalities present in the United States according to the census of 1890, when heavy immigration from Southern and Eastern Europe first had become noticeable, and prohibiting entirely Oriental immigration. Northern Europe, which did not need it, received larger quotas in contrast to Southern and Eastern European areas. In 1929 even smaller quotas were set, based upon the 1920 census. During the Great Depression, President Hoover made still more drastic reductions. An historic era of free immigration to people America, starting in 1607 and 1620, for all practical purposes had ended. By the early 1930's, the combined effect of the law and the depression reduced annual arrivals to less than those leaving the country. Now at last the melting pot presumably could function to "Americanize," though not entirely eliminate, the foreign language enclaves in the great cities. It should be kept in mind, however, that while immigration restriction reflected racist and nativist sentiments, it also in a sense had progressive overtones. Many progressives had long advocated such curtailment on a planned, scientific basis, which the law seemed to embody.

The Noble Experiment

The Eighteenth Amendment to the Constitution in 1919 imposed prohibition upon the United States. Implemented by the Volstead Act, the law forbade the manufacture, transportation, or sale of alcoholic beverages containing over ½ of 1 percent of alcohol. Long sought by reformers who attributed most human ills to alcohol and who viewed prohibition as a panacea for slums, poverty, and crime, the amendment had been hastily pushed through Congress and the states as a patriotic war measure to protect servicemen and conserve grains. Many progressives also had favored it as a means to disrupt malodorous ties between political machines and the liquor interests. Rural Protestants were particularly dedicated drys, expressing their distrust of the "corrupt" cities and alcohol-imbibing aliens. When the ban went into effect on July 16, 1920 (many gathered to mourn as well as to cheer) Billy Sunday summed up the hopes of the prohibitionists: "The slums soon will be only a memory. We will turn our prisons into factories and our jails into storehouses and corncribs. Men will walk upright now, women will smile, and the children will laugh. Hell will be forever for rent." Yet many other citizens viewed prohibition as an intolerable violation of individual rights and an unworkable attempt to legislate morality. Resentment ran strongly among many minority groups, such as the German- and Italian-Americans, accustomed to the consumption of beer and light wines with meals.

Prohibition ran counter to the hedonistic characteristics of the 1920's. It was widely flouted, especially in the cities and among the upper classes. Illegal bars called speakeasies sold alcoholic beverages, often with bribed police protection. Organized crime quickly took over much of the lucrative whisky traffic, manufacturing liquors (usually redistilling industrial denatured alcohol) or smuggling them in from abroad (rumrunning). "Scarface Al" Capone and his gang grew rich and powerful in Chicago, and criminal elements often combined other forms of crime, such as prostitution and narcotics, with bootlegging. Many stores openly sold equipment and supplies for the illegal home brewing of wines, beer, or even whisky. Enforcement on the whole was a farce, with neither Congress nor the executive particularly vigorous in its duty. Violations in any case were so extensive as to defy rigid enforcement, yet even so the courts were clogged with a vast backlog of cases. Although surveys indicated that by 1926 large numbers of citizens favored repeal or modification of the Volstead Act, politicians feared the largely rural dry vote and continued to pay lip service to the noble experiment in legislating morals. Not until the Twenty-first Amendment repealing prohibition was adopted in 1933 did government and the people at last admit failure and even then only over the strenuous opposition of the dry forces.

Religious Currents in the Twenties

The flowering of new religious cults and a popular "mind-cure" seemed symptomatic of the growing dismay at the loss of traditional values and beliefs. Jehovah's Witnesses, established in 1884, preached the imminent end of this world and the beginning of the reign of Christ. The Witnesses aroused much hostility when they refused to permit their school children to salute the flag. The Four Square Gospel of Aimee Semple McPherson was less orthodox and more bizarre. A former schoolteacher and carnival barker, and a divorcee, Sister Aimee invaded Los Angeles and within a few years built an enormous Angelus Temple and won 30,000 members. Her theology was crude and simple, but its stress on love and hope, and her highly unorthodox services marked by filmy gowns, bright lights and color, musical bands, and dramatized sermons, proved enormously appealing. The temple owned its own radio station, KFSG, and sent missionaries into the Pacific slope and midwestern states. A mystic cult, the

"Great I Am," flowered in California, while a number of New York blacks and whites ascended to Father Divine's earthly Heavens. Frank Buchanan launched the Oxford Movement, or Moral Rearmament its later name. He gave theology little attention and advocated individual "spiritual silence" and group confessions to obtain "God guidance" in life. Many other Americans in this secular decade seemed to find Coué-ism more appealing than any religious approach. Combining ideas drawn from mental healing and psychoanalysis, Emile Coué of France advocated auto-suggestion to assert the primacy of the will over the emotions and the body. Spreading to America, Coué-ism soon had large numbers of Americans chanting to themselves at all hours:

> Day by day, in every way,
> I am getting better and better.

The principal reaction to the growth of religious liberalism and skepticism in urban America, however, came from an upsurge of Protestant fundamentalism and religious conservatism, particularly strong in rural areas and small towns but also affecting the cities. The "warfare between science and theology" that had characterized the late nineteenth century had seemed to be over, as an increasing number of Christian ministers and laymen — "Christian modernists" — had come to terms with the implications of science and evolutionary theories and had adopted the social gospel to improve the social and civic aspects of American life. Yet after World War I an upsurge of religious conservatism, determined to cleanse the church, seminaries, and public schools of modernism, seemed to threaten the preservation of intellectual freedoms. Fundamentalism apparently owed its name to the efforts of two oil millionaires in Los Angeles, California, who in 1910 had subsidized the publication of ten small pamphlets entitled "The Fundamentals: A Testimony to the Truth." These rejected the findings of modern science and the Biblical Higher Criticism, and presented as essential Christian doctrines belief in the inerrancy of the Bible and its account of creation, the virgin birth of Christ, the incarnation and historical resurrection of Jesus, and other dogmas. Fundamentalists distributed over three million copies of these pamphlets through churches, schools, and other organizations.

Apparently stimulated by the postwar reaction, many of the religious traditionalists attributed all of America's strains and stresses, from radicalism to crime, to a departure from strict Scriptural faith and standards. Appealing largely to the rural and less educated, fundamentalism reflected a fear of change and a quest for certainty, and was intensely emotional and even violent in denunciation of such leading exponents of liberal or modernist Christianity as the Rev. Harry Emerson Fosdick. Some fundamentalists described Fosdick as a seducer of the minds and souls of youth. Evangelists such as Billy Sunday continued to exhort audiences with the simplistic old time religion at revival meetings across America. Such organizations as the World's Christian Fundamentals Association, the Bible League of North America, and the Bible Crusaders of America assumed the offensive against the tides of liberalism, skepticism, and atheism. The Bible Crusaders even sought a constitutional amendment to proclaim America a Christian nation.

In 1922 the World's Christian Fundamentals Association launched a drive for state laws prohibiting the teaching in public schools and colleges of Darwinism and other scientific theories contradicting the Biblical account of the creation of the world. William Jennings Bryan with magnetic oratory threw himself into the leadership of this crusade to refute scientific heresies. As he put it, "It is better to trust in the Rock of Ages than to know the age of rocks." Local school boards, especially in the southern and midwestern states, banned books on evolution and pressured teachers into compliance. An obscure Georgia legislator expressed the anti-intellectualism of the fundamentalist current: "Read the Bible. It teaches you how to act. Read the hymn book. It contains the finest poetry ever written. Read the almanac. It teaches you to figure out what the weather will be. There isn't another book that is necessary for anyone to read, and therefore I am opposed to all libraries."

The anti-evolutionists made some progress in the South in their drive for prohibitory legislation. Although checked in North Carolina, where educational leaders courageously spoke up, crusading fundamentalists scored partial victories in Oklahoma and Florida. The Tennessee legislature passed a bill that prohibited all state supported schools from teaching "any theory that denies the story of the divine creation of man as taught in the Bible and to teach instead that man has descended from a lower order of animals." Educators remained silent and the governor felt little choice but to sign the measure in 1925. Bryan wired him his congratulations: "The Christian parents of the State owe you a debt of gratitude for saving their children from the poisonous influence of an unproven hypothesis. . . . The South is now leading the nation in the defense of Bible Christianity." Fear of other states following Tennessee's example caused the American Civil Liberties Union to resolve to challenge the law in the courts and to offer aid to anyone involved in such a case.

The opportunity came in the small community of Dayton, Tennessee. John T. Scopes, a twenty-four year old teacher of science in the local high school, allowed himself to be arrested and tried on a charge of violating the new law. The trial commanded national and world wide attention as a supposed battle to the death between Christianity and evolution. Scores of reporters, observers, and the curious flocked to Dayton and the little town took on all the color and excitement of a circus. The World's Christian Fundamentals Association persuaded Bryan to aid the prosecution, while the noted criminal defense lawyer and agnostic, Clarence Darrow, joined the defense. Darrow came to Dayton fresh from his triumph in a celebrated trial where he had helped Nathan Leopold, Jr., and Richard Loeb, two brilliant youths from wealthy families in Chicago, escape the gallows by receiving life sentences for their senseless murder of thirteen year old Bobby Franks.

At Dayton the key issue of academic freedom versus the right of local authority to control education seemed almost lost sight of in the feverish atmosphere. Although Bryan declared that the real question was the right of the taxpayers to regulate their schools, he too acted as if the trial were one between Christianity and evolution. Many felt disappointed when the judge ruled against the plan of the defense to call noted scientists and liberal clergymen to testify that no real conflict existed between science and the Bible. Unfortunately for his cause, Bryan then unwisely allowed himself to be called to the stand as an expert on the Scriptures. Darrow's merciless examination revealed that Bryan was abysmally ignorant of science, history, and comparative religion and philosophy. Moreover, Bryan's replies seemed to indicate that even he did not interpret literally everything in the Bible. Although the court found Scopes guilty and fined him, it seemed to many that fundamentalism had been convicted by the enlightened public opinion. Bryan, humiliated and perhaps partially discredited even before his own followers, died a few days after the conclusion of the trial. Deprived of his leadership, fundamentalism went into eclipse, although it did not disappear. The spread of education, the battle over the repeal of prohibition, and the coming of the Great Depression soon shunted aside the anti-evolution crusade.

Alienation of the Intellectuals

Whereas the prewar literary generation had rebelled against the genteel tradition in art, literature, and morals, and had exuded optimism about the promise of American democratic life, the postwar generation tended to be pessimistic about social issues. The attitude of this so-called "Lost Generation," whose youth presumably had been sacrificed in the recent war, often was corrosive and fatalistic. As Professor Henry F. May comments, World War I had ended the ago of American innocence — moral idealism now seemed to many ridiculous, and faith in human progress through reason and science had been shaken or destroyed. Yet the alienation of the intellectuals had begun before the war. The influence of William James's pragmatism and psychology, Dewey's instrumentalist thought, and Freudianism, among other currents, inspired avant-gardists prior to 1917 to challenge the optimism and faith in progress of the Progressives. The disillusioning experiences of the Great Crusade merely deepened the currrents of pessimism and the rejection of traditional ideals and beliefs.

While businessmen and many others, including historians and economists, contentedly regarded the decade as a "new era," marked by the use of scientific technology and efficiency to produce prosperity for all, much of the intelligentsia could only see decline and retrogression. Professor Frederick J. Hoffman writes of these "disinherited sons and daughters" of the middle class: "The vigor of anti-bourgeois criticism in the 1920's came, not from the proletarian critics, but from middle-class men and women who were disgusted with their cultural heritage." Rebelling against middle-class culture, standards, and morals, these rebels often loosely used the term "Puritanism" to describe society as repressive of the natural desires and potentialities of human beings. Americans seemed to them hopelessly materialistic, with "moral and cultural philistinism." In 1922, Harold E. Stearns published a symposium of thirty essays on *Civilization in the United States*, a savage criticism of virtually every aspect of American life. America, in the view of the critics, was a cultural wasteland. A number of disillusioned intellectuals denounced democracy and praised European fascism; many demonstrated their disgust with American life either by flocking to the bohemian retreat in Greenwich Village, in New York, or left for self-exile in Europe.

H. L. Mencken, editor of *The American Mercury*, reigned as the chief iconoclast of the Twenties. A mordant critic of middle-class democratic society, he mercilessly attacked almost everything admired by the average citizen whom he described as the "booboisie." He described democracy as an unworkable but amusing form of government and jabbed at crass politicians, smug businessmen, and "Bible Belt" rural Protestants. But though a generation of rebellious youth saw only revolt in Mencken's writing, in fact he surgically exposed the ills of the times. His most enduring contribution was far removed from satire: *The American Language* (1919), a scholarly study of American speech.

Theodore Dreiser was the major representative of literary naturalism in America. Born in Indiana in 1871, the son of a poverty-stricken German immigrant, his career as a novelist spans much of modern American history – he died in 1945. From his own bitter experiences and influenced by Darwinist currents of thought, Dreiser derived the major themes of his writings, the conflict between human instincts, desires, and ambitions versus social convention and restraints. Dreiser therefore has been classified as a naturalist or realist novelist, guided by a philosophy of scientific determinism. His first important novel, *Sister Carrie* (1900) focused upon a sensitive young girl trying to escape her lowly environment through use of her sex. *An American Tragedy* (1925) presented the central figure of Clyde Griffiths caught in the trap of biological forces and society, culminating in the drowning of his sweetheart and his own subsequent execution in the electric chair. This work was not a tragedy in the Greek sense but rather was a tragedy of biology and society.

Sinclair Lewis, a native of Sauk City, Minnesota, wrote in a type of regional vein, concentrating on the area of rural countryside and small towns and cities that he knew intimately. He became the best known novelist of the decade by 1930, when he won the Nobel Prize for literature. Literary critics view Lewis as less of a rebel against the older ideals, though he was often so interpreted, than as against their corruption and distortion in the Twenties. *Babbitt* (1922) portrayed the crassness and materialism of life in the city of Zenith, while *Main Street* (1925) does the same for the small town of Gopher Prairie where nearly everything is measured in terms of money. *Arrowsmith* (1925), one of the first novels of medicine, depicted the conflict between ideals and a commercial society, while *Elmer Gantry* (1927) described evangelical Protestantism as corrupted also by crass materialism. Yet, as *Dodsworth* (1929) revealed, Lewis did not lack sympathy for businessmen; he sought reform, not the supplanting of old values.

F. Scott Fitzgerald, another Minnesotan, attended Princeton and after the Armistice plunged into the gay, frenetic, party life of the postwar period. He expressed the generation's shaken faith in noble ideals and crusades for reform and democracy, and a restless cynical hedonism in *This Side of Paradise* (1920), *Tales of the Jazz Age* (1922), and *The Beautiful and Damned* (1922). In *The Great Gatsby* (1925), his most tightly written novel, the idealist is a bootlegger. Rich and famous after his first book, Fitzgerald married Zelda Sayre of Alabama and plunged into dizzy revelry here and in Paris. He returned to the United States in 1931, with funds exhausted and Zelda insane; drinking heavily, Fitzgerald went to Hollywood to write, where he died of a heart attack in 1940.

Encouraged by Gertrude Stein, the high priestess of the American postwar exiles living in Paris, Ernest Hemingway developed a clear and simple writing style glorifying the more basic physical and emotional experiences of men. Born in Illinois in 1898, the son of a physician, Hemingway had been a reporter — he remained one off and on throughout most of his life — and he served in the First World War as an ambulance driver in Italy where he was seriously wounded. He reflected the disillusionment and pleasure-loving mood of the '20's in *The Sun Also Rises* (1926), in which postwar expatriates in France and Spain aimlessly spent their days in love-making, drinking, and watching bull fights. *A Farewell to Arms* (1929) is generally considered his best novel and one of the best of all the novels arising from World War I. Obviously based on Hemingway's wartime experiences, the novel at one point has the hero remark:

> I was always embarrassed by the words sacred, glorious, and sacrifice and the expression in vain. . . . I had seen nothing sacred, and the things that were glorious had no glory and the sacrifices were like the stockyards at Chicago if nothing was done with the meat except to bury it.

In many of his subsequent novels and stories prior to his apparent suicide in 1961, Hemingway concentrated on a nihilistic world of action and adventure for its own sake.

William Faulkner, a contemporary of Fitzgerald and Hemingway, came from a distinguished Southern aristocratic family and spent most of his life in Oxford, Mississippi. Using a stream of consciousness technique in *The Sound and the Fury* (1929), followed by *As I Lay Dying* (1930), *Sanctuary* (1931), and later novels, Faulkner wrote of the decay of the older Southern way of life. Critics at first viewed him as a naturalistic novelist of a world of decay, terror and cruelty, but now they see him as utilizing romantic and naturalistic techniques to arrive at ethical ends. When he accepted the Nobel Prize in 1950, he briefly stated his creed: "Man will not merely endure: he will previal . . . because he has a soul, a spirit capable of compassion and sacrifice and endurance." Therefore, "the writer's duty is to write about these things."

John Dos Passos, a realistic novelist who had not given up hope for social reform, joined a number of radical causes during these years. *Three Soldiers* (1921) expressed disillusionment with the Great Crusade, and in his trilogy *U.S.A.*, published in the 1930's, he penned a trenchant indictment of the materialistic and corrupt aspects of American life.

A literary-artistic "Black Renaissance" centered in New York City. Developing growing confidence as well as race consciousness, black writers bitterly attacked racial oppression in America and demanded equality and opportunity for their race. Among the more significant black writers must be listed W. E. B. DuBois, *The Gift of Black Folk* (1924); James Weldon Johnson, *The Book of American Negro Poetry* (1922); and Langston Hughes, *Not Without Laughter* (1930) and *The Ways of White Folks* (1934). Black artists and performers, such as Paul Robeson and Marian Anderson, received increasing recognition from white Americans. Growing out of black life while borrowing from many other sources, jazz in its various moods, joyful funeral marches, "hot" music, and sad "blues," has been described as one of America's few original contributions to western culture. It swept across the United States in the 1920's and was taken up by white musicians. George Gershwin utilized it in his "Rhapsody in Blue" and other compositions.

The great Armory Show in New York City in 1913 displayed not only the realistic paintings of the "Ash Can School" but also called attention to new trends in European art. One of the most talked of pictures at the display was Marcel Duchamp's *Nude Descending the Staircase*. Cubism, derived from Henri Matisse and Pablo Picasso in France, sought to probe beneath the outward appearances of objects to their underlying geometric forms. This movement in America received great encouragement with the founding of New York's Museum of Modern Art in 1929 and the Whitney Museum in 1931, the latter devoted to American art. Throughout the 1920's and 1930's, the artistic world divided into realistic painters and the abstractionists. Although the pendulum swung back toward such realistic painters as Grant Wood, Thomas Hart Benton, and Edward Hopper in the Thirties, new modes of abstractionism such as expressionism and surrealism invaded America from Europe. Whatever its artistic merits, abstractionism in its several expressions has been interpreted as a graphic mirror to the ambiguity, confusions, and chaos of modern life and thought.

Irving Babbitt, a literary critic, wrote in 1924 that while American achievements might be impressive quantitatively, they were not qualitatively. What else could one expect, he asked, of a country that lavished admiration and even hero worship on such individuals as Bryan, Billy Sunday, and Henry Ford. Yet behind all the glitter and crassness of the materialism of the Twenties there lay a genuine idealism that a life free from poverty and drudgery was possible for all in America. To be sure, the rich got richer but the middle and lower classes also made advances. Unquestionably life for the majority of Americans became far more pleasant during this decade than it had ever been before. Living and health standards improved, leisure time increased, and both recreational and educational opportunities were available on a hitherto unimaginable scale. Material advance cannot be equated with cultural development but it does make it possible; and despite the attacks of the self-disinherited critics of the 1920's, the decade also witnessed much of lasting value in the arts and literature. Finally, the progressive impulse had not vanished during the decade. Conservation of natural resources broadened to include the preservation of natural beauty. Social service groups remained active and, though their goals often had to be deferred, they contributed much to the coming New Deal in the fields of women and children labor legislation, unemployment and old age insurance, public works and housing, and collective bargaining. The New Deal drew upon these ideas and called many former social workers to high positions in government.

5

The Politics and Diplomacy
of a Business Era

THE ELECTION of Warren G. Harding in 1920 inaugurated a decade of Republican predominance in the national government. These were lean years for the Democrats, the lowest dip in their political fortunes since the Civil War. Progressivism seemed dead and political conservatism supreme. Yet the progressive impulse in fact was still alive and the period cannot be dismissed merely as one of conservatism and reaction in politics. The trend toward governmental involvement in the economy continued as Republican administrations sought to cooperate with business rather than attempting to regulate it.

Warren G. Harding

In so far as the Harding administration had a policy it was the politics of business leadership. The business community asked and received from the new administration more economy and efficiency in government, tax reductions, the elimination of government competition with private enterprise, and freedom for business self-regulation.

Warren Gamaliel Harding provided an apt symbol of the new age of business politics. He often compared himself with William McKinley, whose administration had represented the quintessence of the middle-class ideal in the late nineteenth century. Born in Ohio in 1865 and raised in a rural community, young Harding moved to the town of Marion, Ohio and tried first salesmanship and then journalism. He married a divorcee, the daughter of the wealthiest man in the town, and became the owner-editor of the Marion *Star*. Attracted to politics, Harding was aided by his handsome looks, florid oratory, and genial manner. A "joiner," he belonged to the Elks, Odd Fellows, and the Moose, among other organizations. In the course of politicking, he met a lawyer, Harry M. Daugherty, who became his lifetime friend. Yet while many writers have assumed that the allegedly lethargic Harding was managed by his wife, whom he called the Duchess, and by Daugherty, in fact he was an ambitious and skillful politician who made his own key decisions. Daugherty merely exploited his relationship with Harding to rise from obscurity to power and eventual eclipse.

After holding several state offices in Ohio, Harding won a seat in the U.S. Senate in 1914, one of the first to be chosen by popular vote under the Seventeenth Amendment to the Constitution. There he compiled a conservative record in a progressive era and cooperated with Lodge in the Treaty fight. His nomination in 1920 was not an accident nor was it the result of a boss-ruled convention. A dark horse candidate from Ohio, Harding moved cautiously at the convention while the front-runners monopolized public attention. Hiram Johnson, a contender for the nomination, charged his competitors, Leonard Wood and Frank Lowden, with spending millions of dollars in attempts to control the convention and buy the nomination. The three candidates cancelled themselves out and threatened a deadlocked convention. Not one but many smoke-filled rooms occurred at the convention as delegates sought a compromise between the bitterly divided contending forces. Harding emerged with the great prize because he was highly available, a man with few enemies, from a key state, and with a politically attractive personality. Senator Lodge in formally notifying the candidate of his selection lectured him on the new balance to be sought between the executive and legislative departments of the federal government and Harding humbly promised to accept Senate tutelage. Lodge was to be disappointed in his hopes for a subservient president.

Harding offered a sharp contrast to his predecessor in office. He could not be accused of advocating social reform at home or idealistic crusades abroad. Something of an isolationist in foreign policy, he disliked the League of Nations and advocated an independent nationalistic course for the United States. He shared the political outlook of rural small-town America, which no doubt helped account for his victory in 1920 and his unquestioned popularity. Harding viewed America as a classless society, with economic equality of opportunity for all, functioning in a free market climate of private property and initiative. He greatly admired the very rich and shared the speculative and booster spirit of the age. Harding's private morals were not beyond reproach — according to recent biographers, it seems that he had at least two mistresses, one of whom, Nan Britton, unfortunately for his reputation was later to write *The President's Daughter*. Easy-going Harding often could be found in the White House playing cards and drinking whisky with his cronies. As Alice Roosevelt Longworth, Theodore Roosevelt's daughter and a caustic observer of the Washington scene, later remarked, "Harding was not a bad man. He was just a slob."

The cabinet appointed by Harding contained a mixture of competent and incompetent men. Virtually ignoring the Senate, whose leaders had expected to dominate him, Harding named the very able Charles Evans Hughes as Secretary of State, Herbert Hoover became Secretary of Commerce, and Henry C. Wallace Secretary of Agriculture. Andrew Mellon, reputedly the second richest man in the country, headed the Treasury Department. Other appointees tended to be mediocre. Harding's good friend, Daugherty, became Attorney General, and Senator Albert B. Fall, a known foe of conservation who was later sent to prison for bribe-taking, served as Secretary of the Interior. Lesser appointments, to Harding's subsequent regret, went to a group of old supporters and hangers-on known as the "Ohio Gang." This group maintained a sort of headquarters at "the little green house" at 1625 K Street. There Harding cronies received bootleg whisky and engaged in the selling of government influence and favors.

The Return to Normalcy

In his inaugural remarks, Harding called for "an end of government's experiment in business and . . . more efficient business in government administration." One of the first acts signed by Harding was the Budget and Accounting Act. Heretofore each executive department had approached Congress separately for its appropriation, thus precluding overall budget study and planning. The act provided for a Director of the Budget to help the President plan an annual executive budget and a Comptroller General to audit accounts and to oversee expenditures in a more efficient way. Faced with a postwar economic slump, Harding frankly stated that business cycles were inevitable and that all government could do was to curtail its own expenditures and to maintain the national credit. World War I veterans had formed the American Legion in 1919. Arguing that "stay-at-home" civilians had prospered while doughboys risked health and life in the army camps and trenches, the Legion asked for veterans a bonus of one dollar a day for each day of service at home and a dollar and a quarter for overseas service. Harding appeared before the Senate to block passage of such a bill in 1921, but as the congressional elections approached Congress capitulated to pressure and passed a bonus in 1922 in the form of paid up insurance. Harding vetoed it as unwise special interest legislation and costly to the Treasury (it was finally passed over Coolidge's veto in 1924). Secretary Mellon urged Congress to repeal the wartime excess profits tax and to reduce income tax rates on higher incomes, claiming that they penalized initiative and investments. He obtained a large part of his request in the 1921 revenue act, eliminating the excess profits tax and cutting the maximum income rate to 50 percent. Subsequently he obtained further reductions and he also gradually cut back the war swollen national debt.

Agricultural distress and the postwar economic slump caused a return to protectionism, long a cardinal plank of the Republican Party. Conservatives as well as many progressives supported protectionism. Farm prices had declined sharply as European agriculture recovered and American production increased. Although a higher tariff was of doubtful benefit to most farmers, since the United States was primarily an exporting nation, the Emergency Tariff of 1921 threw the "Farm Bloc" in Congress a sop by imposing nearly prohibitive duties on twenty-eight agricultural items. The 1922 Fordney-McCumber Tariff, with an average rate of 33 percent, continued farm protection but also raised sharply the rates on industrial goods. Protectionists obtained extremely high duties, intended to virtually embargo imports of dyes, chemicals, silk and rayon, textiles, cutlery, and other products of Japan and Germany. Yet the act retained the low Underwood Tariff rates on most other items. The Tariff Commission, first established in 1916, was authorized to study the costs of production at home and abroad and to recommend to the Executive further rate increases, or decreases, based upon its findings. Originally conceived as one of the progressive reforms using impartial experts in government, the Commission in the '20's became highly protectionist. In fact, of 37 changes it recommended that were adopted by Harding and Coolidge, 32 involved increases in rates. The high tariff by its restrictions on imports probably increased industrial profits and the tendency toward monopoly by large businesses. It also had an adverse effect on trade with Europe, eased only by the fact that vast amounts of private American capital then flowed to investments in Europe. Consequently the European debtor countries found it difficult to repay the war debts, while their total private indebtedness to the United States also increased.

The federal government withdrew from competition with business as rapidly as possible. Harding's appointees to the Shipping Board sold government-owned vessels for a fraction of their value. He named men to federal regulatory agencies such as the Federal Trade Commission who were interested less in regulation and more in cooperation with business interests. The Justice Department also revealed a marked disinterest in enforcement of the anti-trust laws. In this favorable climate, trade associations and cartel arrangements with foreign firms were able to monopolize markets and fix prices. For example, two American sulphur firms formed an agreement with an Italian company, a large supplier, and through the Sulphur Export Corporation controlled the supply of sulphur; and in 1928 General Electric and Krupp of Germany regulated the price of tungsten carbide in Germany and America. Trade associations had been organized earlier to limit competition and stabilize markets, and the movement increased during the war mobilization period. Each trade association had its own code of fair practices and changed competitive industries into semi-non-competitive ones. Standardization of products and greater efficiency resulted but at the cost of free competition. The federal government in the 1920's looked kindly on these developments and the courts upheld them as long as there was no overt price fixing.

The progressive current lingered on in the 1920's, though more divided and weakened than before. Theodore Roosevelt's party bolt in 1912 had damaged progressive influence within the Republican party and his return to the fold in 1916 further disorganized progressive ranks. What can be viewed as the Wilsonian mainstream of progressivism had largely accomplished its reform ends by 1917; in any case war and disillusionments with the peace had wrecked Wilson's coalition by 1920. The postwar decade, therefore, found progressivism lacking both unity and dynamic leaders of the prewar type and unable to capture control of either major party. It still manifested some influence in the Congress but not much in the White House.

Progressivism's political role in the postwar Republican era was to be largely negative, as the fight over the disposal of Muscle Shoals revealed. During the war the government had built two plants at Muscle Shoals, Tennessee, using power from federal dams to manufacture nitrogen for the munitions industry and as fertilizer for agriculture. The Harding administration wanted to turn the entire complex over to private enterprise. Henry Ford bid for its lease at a small part of the original cost and, in addition, wanted exemption from federal regulation and a one hundred year renewable lease. Progressive-minded senators, led by George W. Norris of Nebraska, Chairman of the Committee on Agriculture, successfully prevented congressional approval of this lease. Norris advocated cheap public power and wanted the government to use Muscle Shoals as the key to the development of the Tennessee Valley. Congress twice passed such a measure only to encounter vetoes by Coolidge and Hoover. Progressive sentiment was strong enough to frustrate the executive but too weak to compel action.

On the positive side of the ledger, enactment of the Sheppard-Towner Act in 1921 illustrates the link provided by the Twenties between the Progressive Era and the New Deal. Supported by women's groups and endorsed by President Harding, the bill provided for modest federal support of state-established maternity and infancy health programs designed to reduce high mortality rates. Congress passed the measure despite opposition from conservatives and from the American Medical Association, whose House of Delegates denounced the proposal as an "imported socialistic scheme." The government finally permitted federal funding to lapse in 1929, not to be revived until 1935 by the New Deal's Social Security Act. Other progressive contributions involved an enlarged concept of conservation to include preservation of areas of natural beauty and recreation as well as of natural resources. Social service groups continued to advocate reforms, and although their goals usually had to be postponed during the Twenties, they formulated programs in the fields of women and child labor legislation, unemployment compensation and old age insurance, public works and housing, and bargaining rights for labor that contributed greatly to the coming New Deal.

The Harding Scandals

The Harding administration shares with the earlier Grant regime the dubious distinction of being the most scandal-ridden in American history. Both chief executives governed in postwar eras characterized by disillusionment, moral slump and material prosperity. Private and public chicanery flourished. Even as individuals Harding and Grant had certain similarities, for both men were personally uninvolved in the scandals, victimized by their poor choice of friends and subordinates.

Harding had appointed Charles R. Forbes as director of the Veterans Bureau. On hearing that Forbes was misusing federal funds and accepting payments from contractors, Harding forced his resignation. Forbes's second-in-command, Charles F. Cramer, committed suicide during a congressional investigation and Forbes subsequently received a prison sentence for his conduct. Jess Smith, a crony of Attorney General Daugherty, also committed suicide when he feared his activities in influence peddling in government were about to be exposed. A later investigation revealed that Smith had worked closely with the Alien Property Custodian, Thomas Miller, in fraudulent settlements. Miller, after dismissal from office, was tried and convicted in 1927 of accepting bribes. Many suspected Daugherty also of being involved, but after Harding's death and Daugherty's resignation at the request of President Coolidge, he managed to escape conviction when brought to trial. Daugherty refused to testify personally and intimated, probably falsely, that he was shielding the dead President's reputation.

The top scandal, breaking after Harding's death, involved his Secretary of the Interior and the lease of naval oil reserves. A rancher in New Mexico, and a former prospector, the picturesque and arrogant Albert Fall had formed a friendship with Harding while both men served in the Senate. Fall's appointment to the Interior Department — he was regarded as a friend of those interested in despoiling the public domain — had greatly disturbed conservationists such as Gifford Pinchot and Harry A. Slattery who kept close watch on him. As Pinchot had remarked of Fall's appointment, "On the record, it would have been possible to pick a worse man for Secretary of the Interior, but not altogether easy." Conservationists also regarded Edwin Denby, Harding's choice for the Navy Department, as questionable. Earlier in the Taft presidency, the government set aside two great oil reserves, at Teapot Dome, Wyoming, and Elk Hills, California, for the Navy's future needs. Shortly after he took office, Fall with Denby's concurrence had these reserves transferred from the Navy to the Interior Department by an executive order approved by President Harding. Slattery and the conservationists were disturbed by the transfer and also at Fall's attempt to have the Forest Service moved from the Agriculture to the Interior Department. Fall resigned in early 1923 on the grounds of private financial sacrifices; apparently his departure also reflected his resentment of Harding's refusal to approve all his plans. Reports leaked out that Fall was prospering on his ranch at Three Rivers, New Mexico. A Senate inquiry, after Harding's death, eventually uncovered evidence that Fall had secretly leased, without competitive bidding, offset drilling rights at Teapot Dome and Elk Hills to two oil men, Harry F. Sinclair and Edward L. Doheny. In return for these favors, Fall had received so-called loans and gifts of $100,000 from Doheny, delivered in cash in a little black bag, and $25,000 from Sinclair. Although Doheny and Sinclair escaped punishment, Fall was convicted of accepting bribes in 1929, fined $100,000, and sentenced to a year in prison.

Most of these scandals became public only after Harding's death, but he knew enough of them to be deeply disturbed as he embarked on a political fence-mending western tour in mid-1923. According to the Kansas Republican newspaper editor, William Allen White, Harding complained, "My God, this is a hell of a job. I have no trouble with my enemies. . . . But my damned friends, my God-damn friends, White, they're the ones that keep me walking the floor nights!" Harding had long suffered from heart trouble – his wife had not wanted him to run for the presidency in 1920 for that reason – yet he could not relax on the tour, making 85 speeches in five weeks, playing bridge almost constantly in the intervals and sleeping little. He collapsed in Seattle, where physicians at first diagnosed his condition as a digestive illness; rushed to San Francisco, he died of a cerebral attack.

Although several recent studies have attempted to rehabilitate Harding, revealing that he had more intelligence and decisiveness than is usually credited, it seems unlikely that his administration will ever be regarded as more than mediocre. Perhaps the fairest evaluation is that he had tried to cope with a job too large for his modest talents. At the time of his death, however, that seemed less clear. A great outpouring of popular grief and mourning attested to his genuine popularity. Only later, when the scandals became fully known, did his reputation plunge. Liberal journalists and muckrakers, alienated by the passing of the Progressive Era and the crasser aspects of the 1920's, also aided greatly in fastening the image of failure to Harding.

Coolidge Prosperity

Vice President Calvin Coolidge fell heir to Harding's office and policies. The new President's personality, his politically skillful but undemanding and unchallenging leadership, coinciding with a period of booming prosperity, seemed to fit the mood of the times. Sometimes called a latter-day Puritan presiding in a most non-Puritan age, Coolidge continued the pro-business policies of his predecessor.

Born in Vermont on the Fourth of July, 1872 Calvin Coolidge grew up in a small town in a small state that clung to the rural Yankee folkways of the past.

Young Coolidge absorbed the values of hard work, thrift, and frugality from his unimaginative and conservative family and community. His mother died when he was twelve; his father, prosperous by local standards, seems to have been an extraordinarily withdrawn, laconic man. Young Coolidge, frail of health and with a thin, quacking voice resulting from nasal congestion, also grew up extremely shy and withdrawn, uncommunicative and outwardly unemotional. His dour visage once caused Alice Roosevelt Longworth to quip that he looked as if he had been weaned on a pickle. Graduating from Amherst and entering law practice, Calvin Coolidge settled in Northampton, Massachusetts. In 1905 he married Grace Goodhue, a gracious and outgoing lady who compensated for many of her husband's social deficiencies.

An astute student of politics, if prosaic and of limited horizons, Coolidge served in both houses of the state legislature, then as Lieutenant Governor, and was elected Governor in 1918. As Governor, he lived in two rented rooms in the capital and saved much of his salary, as he did also when he dwelt in the White House. Coolidge's political principles perhaps are best summarized as economy, honesty, and efficiency in government and order and stability in society. Coolidge respected wealth and confidently believed that the wealth and prosperity created by businessmen would trickle down to benefit the masses of the people. Riding the crest of his unearned fame for ending the Boston police strike, Coolidge won an overwhelming gubernatorial re-election in 1919 and was mentioned as a dark horse candidate for the Republican presidential nomination in 1920. After Harding had won the first prize, the convention ignored the leaders' wishes and nominated Coolidge for the vice presidency in a burst of rebellious enthusiasm.

After the inauguration, Harding invited Coolidge to attend cabinet meetings, but the President only rarely consulted him — Mrs. Harding apparently disliked both of the Coolidges. Coolidge became known as "Silent Cal," a somewhat exaggerated taciturnity that nevertheless had a certain political usefulness. With few close friends and overshadowed in politics and at social functions, Coolidge within his family and staff occasionally sought emotional release in fits of rage and tantrums, sulking and shouting his frustration at those around him. Apart from politics and the reading of history, he had few interests or pastimes except walking and riding a mechanical hobby-horse. Like many of his predecessors and successors, Coolidge regarded the vice presidency as a mockery, an empty and powerless pretension.

Suddenly Harding's death catapulted this discontented man into the White House. At the news, Senator Lodge exclaimed to a reporter, "My God! That means Coolidge is President!" Taking the presidential oath administered by his father, a notary, by the light of an oil lamp in his Vermont home, Coolidge assumed his new responsibilities determined to continue the cabinet and the basic course of the Harding administration.

Coolidge envisioned his presidential duties as essentially to execute the laws while Congress, an independent branch of government, legislated. He wanted to promote stability, unity, and harmony; he thought that big business would promote general prosperity, good for the nation and good for the individual. Accumulated wealth provided the fountain of prosperity and of art and learning as well. Coolidge rejected anything resembling federal paternalism; in his view, the government should keep its own affairs and finances in order and not try to run the economy but help it to run itself. Legislation should never be hurried and government should act or spend only when absolutely necessary. As columnist Walter Lippmann wrote, "Mr. Coolidge's genius for inactivity is developed to a very high point. It is far from being an indolent inactivity. It is a grim, determined, alert inactivity which keeps Mr. Coolidge occupied constantly." Coolidge himself once said that Theodore Roosevelt had kept himself constantly in trouble by prematurely taking a public stand on issues: "It seems to me public administrators would get along better if they would restrain the impulse to butt in or be dragged into trouble. They should remain silent until an issue is reduced to its lowest terms, until it boils down into something like a moral issue." These concepts of economical and highly limited government accorded with the mood of a majority of Americans during the 1920's. Coolidge's administration, therefore, was to be a popular and even a successful one within the context of the times.

If the policies remained the same, the atmosphere of the new administration changed sharply. Alice Roosevelt Longworth commented that the White House under Coolidge, in contrast to Harding, was "as different as a New England front parlor is from a back room in a speakeasy." Coolidge enjoyed his role as master of the White House and minutely supervised its operations. He rose early and went to bed early and social affairs were few and stilted. He met reporters, usually twice a week, and often lowered his guard as he selected written questions for comment, although he would not permit direct quotation. The record of his press conferences reveal dry wit and political astuteness but also lack of interest in ideas or abstract speculation. Coolidge's speeches, boringly delivered, were platitudinous and pedestrian. He depended heavily on his cabinet and largely followed departmental recommendations. Secretary of State Hughes towered over the others and had great freedom in running his department. Coolidge greatly admired Mellon, his Secretary of the Treasury, who not only was rich but shared the President's belief in the virtues of budget balancing, tax reductions, and debt retirement. Hoover, the ambitious Commerce Secretary, commanded Coolidge's respect but apparently not his liking.

Coolidge at first held a rather precarious position within his party. He had neither the confidence of the conservative Old Guard Republicans nor that of the progressive wing of the party. Moreover, the Harding scandals just coming fully to light caused him much embarrassment. It was by no means certain, therefore, that Coolidge would receive his party's nomination in 1924. Carefully maneuvering his way out of these dilemmas, Coolidge's first message to Congress concentrated on domestic affairs. It sounded neither a progressive nor a reactionary note. The message emphasized tax reductions and economy in government, and called for a constitutional amendment to restrict child labor and to permit the fixing of a minimum wage for women employees. He submitted the lowest budget since before the war with surplus revenue to be applied to the national debt. As Coolidge stated, "I have in mind that the taxpayers are the stockholders in the business corporation of the United States, and if this business is showing a surplus of receipts the taxpayer should share therein. . . ." Coolidge moved cautiously to investigate the Harding scandals. Fortunately, the Teapot Dome affair seemed to implicate several prominent Democrats as well as Republicans — some critics charged former Navy Secretary Daniels with being involved in the removal of the naval oil reserves from the national domain and it became known that McAdoo, a leading potential Democratic nominee for the presidency, had accepted (innocently) a legal retainer from oilman Doheny. Denby resigned from the Navy Department and Coolidge dismissed Daugherty and cancelled the fraudulent oil leases. Coolidge thus emerged untarnished and in a greatly strengthened political position. By his use of patronage Coolidge weakened the Old Guard and dominated the 1924 Republican convention. A dull affair, the convention had the distinction of being the first to be broadcast by radio. By then prosperity had returned to the country, and accompanied by his vice presidential running mate, Charles G. Dawes, Coolidge campaigned on the slogan "Keep Cool with Coolidge." Dawes, a Chicago banker who had favored a number of progressive reforms, had made a notable reputation as an efficient manager and economizer during World War I and as first Director of the Budget. A colorful character, press and public delighted in his underslung pipe and his favorite oath, "Hell and Maria."

Democrats gathered in Madison Square Garden for fourteen days of public brawling, a donnybrook of a national convention. New York City had to delegate additional police to keep order among delegates and spectators. The faction-ridden party was split between the eastern urban machines that backed New York's Governor Alfred E. Smith and the rural-oriented West and South, Protestant and dry, that supported William Gibbs McAdoo. The Ku Klux Klan became a divisive issue and a specific platform condemnation of it, backed by the eastern wing but opposed by many rural delegates from the South and West, went down to a narrow defeat. After 96 ballots neither Smith nor McAdoo could obtain the two-thirds majority necessary for nomination. The prize went on the 103rd ballot to a compromise candidate, the conservative and colorless John W. Davis of West Virginia. The addition to the ticket of Charles W. Bryan of Nebraska, brother of William Jennings Bryan, as the vice-presidential nominee, failed to mollify more liberally inclined Democrats. Davis, a former Solicitor General of the United States and Ambassador to Great Britain, had close Wall Street connections and failed to appeal to farmers, labor, or progressive elements.

Meanwhile, a revival of progressivism developed to voice the discontent of farmers and laborers with their minimal share in the prosperity of the Twenties. Wisconsin's maverick Republican Senator Robert M. LaFollette became its chief spokesman. A nominating convention was called in 1924, with delegates representing labor, farmers, and independents and socialists. At LaFollette's request, the convention rigidly excluded the Communists. The convention nominated LaFollette for the presidency, with Democratic Senator Burton K. Wheeler of Montana in the second place. The delegates agreed not to establish a formal third party in order not to damage progressives running for congressional and state offices on major party tickets. The platform, advanced in contrast to those of the two major parties but hardly daring or new, condemned monopoly and advocated public ownership of railroads and water power sites, abolition of anti-labor court injunctions, the election of federal judges, and protection of the right to collective bargaining. The Socialist Party endorsed LaFollette's candidacy, as did the A.F.L.

The election aroused comparatively little popular interest, half the eligible voters not bothering to go to the polls despite the recent enfranchisement of women. No significant differences separated the positions of the Republican and Democratic parties, and both tended to focus their attack on the LaFollette Progressives. Dawes, bearing most of the Republican campaign burden, repeatedly denounced LaFollette and made an especial effort to identify his followers with the Communists and other radicals, despite LaFollette's repudiation of Communist support. Elderly and in poor health, LaFollette suffered severe handicaps from lack of funds and the absence of local party organization. The Republicans, claiming credit for the return of prosperity, freely spent an estimated $4 million; the Democrats expended about $900,000, and the Progressives only a little over $200,000. Coolidge and Dawes scored a smashing victory, polling 15¼ million votes to Davis' 8 1/3 million and LaFollette's nearly 5 million votes. Coolidge carried the electoral votes of 35 states to Davis' 11 and LaFollette's 1 (Wisconsin). Davis received only 28.7 percent of the popular vote. Republicans also won solid control of Congress.

Policies favorable to business seemed even more marked after 1924 than before, reflecting the effective control conservative Republicans had in Congress and the White House. Coolidge exalted fiscal economy in government, declaring in his inaugural that "Economy is idealism in its most practical form." By the revenue act of 1926 the Republicans sharply reduced the maximum income surtax and estate taxes and eliminated gift taxes, although they made a few concessions to the small taxpayer. Despite tax reductions, the Treasury ran a surplus which it used to reduce the national debt from $24 billion in 1920 to $16 billion by 1930. Coolidge continued Harding's practice of appointing business-oriented men to the regulatory agencies. The Federal Trade Commission, for example, did try to prevent fraudulent advertising and misbranding but it did little to curb holding companies and other monopolistic devices. The

"I sympathize deeply with you Madame, but I cannot associate with you."
Rollin Kirby, Library of Congress, 1923.

President basked in business admiration and often invited prominent industrialists and financiers to the White House. His administration adhered to an easy credit policy to encourage the already booming prosperity. By 1928, however, even Coolidge felt disturbed by the fevered speculation on the stock market but he would not voice a public warning nor take other action to curb the excesses. Only an actual emergency, he felt, would justify presidential action.

Agriculture conspicuously failed to share in the apparent affluence of the decade. In many ways agriculture had made great progress, marked by new farming methods, machinery, improved seed, and fertilizer that greatly increased acreage production. Wartime prices had been good, land values boomed, and investments and acreage in cultivation grew. But as production continued to increase after the Armistice, prices fell precipitously. Foreign markets contracted after World War I and at home the supplanting of the grain-consuming horse with the gas-burning internal combustion engines in automobiles, trucks, and tractors and a national dietary change toward less starchy or fattening foods, reduced the demand for staples. Tradition-bound farmers responded to falling prices by raising more of the same commodity, thus furthering the decline. Most farmers found themselves caught in a cruel squeeze between the rising costs of manufactured goods and sagging farm prices. The total value of farm goods declined from $21.5 billion in 1919 to $11.8 billion in 1929. That decline resulted in increasing poverty, bankruptcies and mortgage foreclosures, more farm tenancy, and agitation for federal relief.

The Farm Bloc of members of Congress representing largely rural constituencies had been able in the early 1920's to obtain some favorable legislation for agriculture. The 1921 and 1922 tariff acts, at least in theory, had conferred benefits on farmers, the 1921 Packers and Stockyards Act prohibited monopolistic practices by the meat packers, the Capper-Volstead Act in 1922 freed marketing cooperatives from the anti-trust laws, and grain exchanges came under federal regulation in 1921 and 1922. But plans for more direct federal aid, although commanding large support in Congress, could not get by the roadblock of conservative presidents.

Pro-farmer spokesmen advanced a scheme known as McNary-Haugenism as a panacea for farm problems. Nurtured by George N. Peek and Hugh S. Johnson of the Moline Plow Company, the plan called for a two-price system. The government would purchase the surpluses of certain staple crops at a price based upon the world market price plus the tariff rate charged against such imports and sell them abroad for the going rate; meanwhile that portion consumed domestically supposedly would rise to the higher level paid by the government, which would compensate itself for the difference by levying a special tax on the producer or the distributor. The Coolidge administration adamantly refused to approve the McNary-Haugen bill in any of its several forms, denouncing it as inherently unworkable and as a type of objectionable class or paternalistic legislation improper for government. Coolidge vetoed such bills in 1927 and 1928. Instead, in addition to endorsing tariff protection, he encouraged farmers to curtail production and to form cooperatives as authorized by the 1922 Capper-Volstead Act — excellent advice, but manifestly beyond the capacities of most farmers.

The Election of 1928

In 1927 Coolidge, at his vacation retreat in South Dakota's Black Hills, suddenly and enigmatically announced that he would not seek a second elected term. The announcement aroused much debate about his motives and true purposes, some suspecting at first that he was merely feigning reluctance and wanted to be drafted to run again. But apparently Coolidge meant just what he said. He felt physically and emotionally weary of the labors and irritations of the presidency. He also, it seems, feared that prosperity might not continue much longer and thought if that happened more vigorous executive leadership would be required. In any case, his statement left the path open for the candidacy of Herbert Hoover. It was fitting that the decade of the Twenties, inordinately admiring the ideal of engineering efficiency, should end with the Great Engineer in the White House.

Hoover's life is the story of the self-made man. Born in West Branch, Iowa in 1874, Hoover suffered the loss of both his devout Quaker parents during his childhood. He entered Stanford University in its first class, studying geology and after graduation working for a wealthy Western miner. At age 23 he went to Australia as a mine scout for a London firm, already well-advanced on a mining career that took him across much of the world and made him a millionaire with a fortune of perhaps $4 million by 1913. During World War I he achieved worldwide fame, first as director of Belgian relief, then as Food Administrator in the Wilson administration, and subsequently in postwar relief activities in Europe. A movement developed to give him the Democratic nomination for the presidency in 1920 until he announced he was a Republican. He accepted an appointment from Harding as Secretary of Commerce, after securing a promise that he would have a role in all important economic policies. To take this new position Hoover declined an offer of a Guggenheim partnership with a guaranteed minimal salary of $500,000 per year. In the Commerce Department he enhanced his reputation both as a great humanitarian in the disaster and relief areas and as the efficient engineer in government encouraging greater productivity by American industry.

Hoover summed up his political philosophy in his *American Individualism*, published in 1922. He had an abiding faith in the individualism and democracy which he believed had made America great — equality of economic opportunity for all and freedom from political or economic domination, protected by a government encouraging cooperation for maximum production. The individual should combine social responsibility with opportunity and freedom, to promote both the individual and the common good. Government, therefore, should umpire the economy and encourage cooperation; government should not compete with private enterprise. Any extension of government beyond that point would undermine the all-essential quality of "rugged individualism" or initiative. He professed to favor collective bargaining though he in fact supported the open shop, a manifest contradiction, and he encouraged private unemployment, disability, and old-age insurance plans. Hoover believed in business-labor cooperation and business self-regulation and he encouraged formation of trade associations for those purposes. He considered overzealous use of the anti-trust laws as unwise and unnecessary.

With the withdrawal of Coolidge from the race, Hoover easily eclipsed his rivals and secured the Republican presidential nomination in 1928. Although viewed as an amateur by professional politicians, Hoover had genuine popularity with the nation at large. His nomination also represented a victory for business and industry and the business world contributed handsomely to the costs of his campaign. The platform in 1928 praised Coolidge prosperity, lauded the tariff, promised to enforce prohibition, and opposed any program putting the government into agriculture or business.

The Democratic Convention could not deny Al Smith the prize he had vainly sought in 1924. The big-city machines were determined to run Smith, the Happy Warrior as Franklin D. Roosevelt had called him in the 1924 nominating speech, and the rural South and Midwest had to accede reluctantly. The convention chose a Protestant dry, Senator Joseph T. Robinson of Arkansas, for the vice presidency, in order to balance the Catholic and "wet" Smith. The platform, not particularly daring or inspiring, promised among other things tariff reform, collective bargaining and restriction of court injunctions for labor, enforcement of the anti-trust laws, farm relief, and an "honest effort" at enforcing prohibition.

Smith's nomination symbolized an important urban revolution in American politics. Born in 1873 in a New York City tenement house, Al Smith had dropped out of school and worked in a fish market before entering politics. He made his way up through the Tammany Hall machine and served as sheriff and in the state assembly. Elected Governor of New York in 1918, he held that office, except for a two-year interval, continuously to 1928. An astute but principled politician, Smith never developed a large political vision, despite his numerous reform achievements relating to such issues as better health and safety laws and his sympathy with the urban lower classes. Yet his nomination in 1928 represented the surge to political consciousness of the urban masses of immigrants and their descendants, the ethnic and religious minorities on the lower end of the economic and social scale.

Smith's defeat by Hoover, understandably if incorrectly, often has been attributed to the religious issue. In the campaign the confident Hoover dealt in generalities while Smith endorsed farm relief and the repeal of prohibition. Despite the Democratic candidate's spirited defense of religious freedom, large numbers of Protestants apparently feared that a victory for Smith would destroy the barrier between church and state, impair the public school system, and, some warned, would enable the Pope to dominate the White House. Probably even more importantly, the campaign revealed rural hostility to city "wets" and dislike of Smith's East Side New York accent that came so gratingly over the radio. Methodist Bishop A. W. Leonard called for "Anglo-Saxon unity, against foreigners . . . who trample on our flag," and proclaimed himself "100 percent, Anglo Saxon. . . . We are the keepers of the Constitution, of the flag and of American citizenship." A fundamentalist spokesman railed at city immorality with its "card playing, cocktail drinking . . . divorce . . . dancing, evolution . . . and modernism," all of which Smith seemed to symbolize. Some progressive Democrats also reacted adversely to Smith's choice of General Motor's John J. Raskob as campaign manager, in a largely futile bid for business support. The election results gave Hoover a smashing victory of nearly 21½ million votes. Yet Smith had run better than Cox and Davis had earlier, polling 15 million votes or 40 percent of the popular total. Undoubtedly his religion and his urban back-ground cost him support in the rural South and West, but these same factors gained votes for him in the large cities and industrial states. In 1920 and 1924, the Republicans had carried decisively the twelve largest cities in the United States but in 1928 Smith reversed that situation and narrowly won these cities – a trend the Democrats continued and expanded in the Thirties. Moreover, the Democrats during this decade also gained steadily in congressional elections. The Democratic party thus had begun a transformation away from ruralism and Bryanism toward an urban base and urban-oriented interests and policies.

Smith probably had run better than any other Democratic candidate could have in 1928. He was defeated primarily by a combination of Hoover's great popularity and the still booming prosperity of the decade. The Republicans had carried 40 states, several in the upper and border South, and won control of Congress. Yet Republican analysts should have been greatly disturbed by the urban trend toward Smith and the Democrats.

Middle Road to Internationalism

The American government in the Twenties tried to develop middle-road policies somewhere between the isolationism of the past and Wilsonian inter-nationalism. Policy-makers had little other choice, granted the realities of Amer-ica's great economic power, its interests in foreign markets and stability, and its decisive role in the First World War. The Harding administration and its suc-cessors marked out a middle path of limited cooperation with the League, participation in the movement for arms limitations and peace, and a vigorous expansion of private American finance and trade abroad, all without binding political commitments or treaty obligations. In short, Republican leaders sought a world safe for America and its economic-political interests, without the potentially troubling obligations symbolized by Wilson's League of Nations. Foreign policy thus complemented the domestic policy of cooperation with business. The Senate reinforced this cautious approach by attaching to treaties its reservations or "understandings" that the United States did not thereby assume any enforcement obligations.

A majority of Americans had reverted to at least a mild isolationism by the mid-1920's, if indeed they had ever felt otherwise. Most had come to regard intervention in the First World War as a mistake. Isolationist currents ran particularly strong in rural areas and, because of rural over-representation, in Congress as well; most of the great newspaper chains, such as the Hearst and Munsey papers, were also isolationist. Senator Borah of Idaho, after 1924 Chairman of the Senate Committee on Foreign Relations, became the self-appointed Congressional watchdog for the isolationists. The "Idaho Lion," tall, massive of frame, and white maned, has been described as a noble man of ideals and principle but lamentably naive and ignorant, particularly about foreign affairs. He believed that the nation's duty consisted of avoiding foreign entanglements while setting a moral example to the world. He viewed the League as an immoral trap, a plot of the bankers and the European allies to entrap the United States and ensure their power and investments. Yet Borah did espouse disarmament conferences, the outlawry of war, and recognition of the Soviet Union.

Wilsonian internationalists continued to try to educate their fellow citizens in the nation's duties to the cause of world peace and stability. Internationalist groups, some pro-League while others concentrated on membership in the World Court or the movement for arms reduction, included among others the World Peace Foundation, the Carnegie Endowment for International Peace, the National Council for Prevention of War, and the Women's International League for Peace and Freedom. Millionaire Edward W. Bok gave a Bok Peace Award of $50,000 in 1924 to the best plan for joining the World Court and cooperating in a limited way with the League. The Foreign Policy Association carried on broad-scale educational work in international affairs. The Council on Foreign Relations, established in New York in 1921 and later broadened to include committees in major cities across the country, published *Foreign Affairs* quarterly and concentrated on promoting an interest in international affairs among the more influential members of the community. Internationalism scored particular success among secondary and college teachers and students. Many liberal internationalists focused their attentions upon membership in the World Court and responsible participation in the disarmament movement. Unfortunately for their cause, however, internationalists did not agree on a program, could not capture control of either major political party during the 1920's and had to contend with a hostile Congress.

When World War I ended, the United States, Great Britain, and Japan stood on the threshold of a naval arms race. The 1916 Naval Act provided for a vast increase of 156 American vessels, including 39 battleships and 12 battle cruisers. Obviously these plans would compel both the British and Japanese governments to make heavy expenditures in an effort to keep up. But in fact, after the Armistice the public and Congress made it clear they were against a costly arms race. Members of peace groups especially expressed dismay and advocated the calling of a conference to resolve the problem. Congress, having defeated the League, now pressured the President to adopt a program to promote peace without binding obligations. In 1921 Senator Borah introduced a resolution in Congress for a 50 percent reduction in naval building and the calling of a conference of the three major naval powers. Although he resented the Senate's intrusion into foreign policy and apparently preferred to continue naval construction until achieving parity with Britain, Harding gave way before the growing public clamor and issued invitations to a conference in Washington, to include also Far Eastern problems at the insistence of the British. To ensure the conference's success the administration appointed senators from both major political parties to the delegation. Harding left out the unpredictable Borah, however, in the group he named to assist Hughes: Lodge, Root and Democrat Oscar Underwood.

Invitations went to Great Britain, Japan, France, Italy, China and three other powers particularly interested in Far Eastern problems. Japan, fearful of losing recent gains in China, agreed to come because nearly half its annual budget involved military expenditures. Britain, while its leaders spoke bravely of maintaining naval supremacy at all costs, faced harsh economic facts that made it willing to accept naval equality with the United States. Soviet Russia wanted to attend the conference, but the American government refused to invite a government it did not recognize.

The Washington Conference marked the first time that a major international conference had ever met in the United States, a fitting tribute to American status as the greatest economic and potentially military power in the world. Secretary of State Hughes, dignified and grey-bearded, boldly seized the initiative in his opening statement to the body on November 12, 1921: "The time has come . . . not for general resolutions or mutual advice, but for action." He then stunned the assembled diplomats and naval experts, who had expected the usual generalities, with his proposal for a sweeping program halting capital ship construction for ten years and scrapping vast amounts of existing tonnage. According to Hughes, the United States should scrap 15 capital ships then under construction (some were over 80 percent completed), and 15 older battleships or a total of 845,740 tons of vessels; Britain similarly should junk 19 older capital warships of 583,375 tons and abandon plans for four new battleships, while Japan, the third ranking naval power, should give up 15 ships planned or under construction and ten older vessels for a total displacement of 448,928 tons. The British and Japanese naval experts were staggered by Hughes' proposal that sank more battleships "than all the admirals of the world had destroyed in a cycle of centuries." That ardent proponent of peace, William Jennings Bryan, present as an observer, listened to Hughes with tears coursing down his face. The American public and Congress reacted with an enthusiastic and overwhelming approval. One church minister summed up the mood of the hour when he called Hughes' speech "one of the greatest events in history."

Because his proposals aroused overwhelming popular support throughout the world and neither Britain nor Japan cared for a costly naval race, Hughes obtained most of his objectives. The Five Power Pact provided for a ten-year construction halt of capital vessels except for replacement of obsolete units, limited battleships to no more than 35,000 tons and 16 inch guns each, and established a 5:5:3 ratio in battleships and aircraft carriers for the United States, Great Britain, and Japan, with 1.75 ratios for France and Italy. Because France insisted upon a larger submarine tonnage, lesser craft remained unregulated. Japan received compensation for its smaller ratio by pledges that the United States would not increase fortifications west of Hawaii nor would Great Britain east of Singapore and north of Australia. The Anglo-Japanese Alliance was ended, replaced by the Four Power Pact between Great Britain, France, Japan, and the United States that declared mutual respect for each others' possessions in the Pacific and promised consultation if problems arose endangering the peace and stability of the area. In the Nine Power Pact, these four powers plus China and four others solemnly pledged to uphold the independence and integrity of China and to observe the principles of the Open Door. In related arrangements Japan agreed to return Shantung to China and to evacuate Siberia and the United States obtained cable rights on the Japanese mandated island of Yap.

The Senate approved these treaties – strongly endorsed by the press, internationalists, and peace groups – but attached a reservation to the Four Power Pact that made it clear that the American government assumed no obligation to uphold these commitments by force or by alliance. That action of course made this and other treaties signed in the Twenties worthless when subsequently challenged by aggressors. Although Republicans hailed the Washington pacts as the "greatest peace document[s] ever drawn," the Washington settlement obviously fell far short of membership in the League of Nations. However, it ended the capital ship arms race and promoted stability in the Pacific for a decade.

Critics then and later argued that because of the factors of distance and two-ocean or more responsibilities for the United States and Britain, the settlement in effect conceded Japan's naval predominance in the far Pacific. Yet the United States gave up little that it actually had. Even if the government had tried to achieve the planned expansion of the navy, Congress might well have refused to appropriate the funds – during the 1920's it was to fail to build the navy even to the treaty limits – and of course America's rivals would have had to counter-build. At most, therefore, the United States at the conference only traded a potential superiority for a naval and political settlement that saved it money, stabilized the Pacific, improved relations with Japan, and apparently protected China. On the other hand, perhaps the most unfortunate consequence of the conference was that it encouraged Americans in the easy belief that vital national interests and peace could be ensured without the assumption of binding commitments and obligations.

It proved almost impossible to extend meaningful limitations to lesser naval vessels. A conference at Geneva in 1927 failed to reach agreement on cruisers, primarily because Britain wanted more smaller vessels (6" gun cruisers) to guard its overseas empire while America wanted fewer but larger ships with longer cruising range (10,000 ton craft with 8" guns) to compensate for inadequate bases overseas. The threat from Congress of a construction race in cruisers — it authorized 15 heavy cruisers and an aircraft carrier in 1929 — and Hoover's diplomacy cleared the way for the London Naval Conference in 1930. The United States obtained full parity with Britain, but Japan was compelled to abide by the 5:5:3 ratio for capital ships while being compensated by a 10:10:7 formula for light cruisers and parity in submarines. The addition of an escape clause in case either of the three major powers felt threatened by a nonsignatory raised serious questions about the value of the agreement.

The movement to outlaw war illustrated the bright optimism about world peace that prevailed in the United States and Europe during the Twenties. Internationalists viewed it as a way of linking the United States indirectly to the League and its concept of collective security, but moralists, pacifists, and isolationists rallied to it because of its simplicity and lack of obligation. A Chicago lawyer, Salmon O. Levinson, Professor James T. Shotwell and President Nicholas Murray Butler, both of Columbia University, took a leading part in arousing popular interest in the scheme. They won Borah's invaluable support; he called the resulting pact "the only kind of a treaty the United States could sign" with the rest of the world. Borah and most Americans viewed outlawry as a simple and universal solution, resting solely upon world moral opinion for enforcement.

Aristide Briand, the French Foreign Minister, fired the opening diplomatic volley in 1927 when he appealed publicly for a Franco-American treaty outlawing war between the two countries. Apparently Briand hoped to tie a security hungry France more closely to the United States. President Coolidge and Secretary of State Frank B. Kellogg — the latter dubbed "Nervous Nellie" by reporters because of his fear of the isolationists in Congress — resented Briand's unorthodox public diplomacy and at first they ignored his suggestion. Because of growing public pressures, however, they decided to turn the tables on Briand by proposing a multi-national treaty to ban war. Although many diplomats were sceptical, world opinion rallied behind Kellogg's proposal. Fifteen nations signed the Kellogg-Briand Pact or Pact of Paris in August, 1928 and eventually 64 nations ratified the pact. Signatories solemnly promised to renounce aggressive and to rely upon peaceful processes to settle international problems; no provisions were made for enforcement. The Senate granted its approval by a vote of 85 to 1, along with an interpretation reserving the right to self-defense and the preservation of the Monroe Doctrine, and disavowing any obligation to uphold the treaty against violators. Not all Senators voted enthusiastically for the pact. Carter Glass of Virginia called it not "worth a postage stamp in the direction of accomplishing permanent international peace." Although millions here and abroad hailed it as a notable achievement for peace, the Pact of Paris seems at best an innocuous international gesture. In another sense it proved disastrous because it encouraged the misleading assumption that peace and security could be obtained without costs and obligations.

Any lingering doubts that President Harding and Secretary Hughes — the latter had favored membership in a league emphasizing judicial rather than political measures for peace — had of joining some type of world association quickly foundered before isolationist opposition in the Senate. Harding assured a cheering Congress on April 12, 1921 that in the "existing League of Nations, world-governing with its super powers, this Republic will have no part." The State Department concluded a separate peace treaty with Germany in 1921 reserving privileges under the Treaty of Versailles but none of its obligations. Despite the opposition of ex-President Wilson and many Democratic Senators, who viewed such a separate peace as cowardly, the Senate approved the Treaty of Berlin.

The Harding administration at first declined even to answer League correspondence; when criticism finally drove it to reply it was only informally and indirectly. Nor would the United States permit international agencies to which it belonged to come under League sponsorship. By mid-1922, however, the administration began to view the League with more tolerance. Coolidge told Congress in 1923 that while membership in the League was a closed question, the United States would cooperate with other nations in humanitarian efforts. The State Department began to send observers and later official representatives to attend technical and specialized conferences dealing with matters such as copyrights, pornography, prostitution, health, and suppression of the opium traffic. In other words, while America would not join the League in enforcing peace, it would cooperate in non-political international affairs. Thus the State Department rejected several attempts to tie the United States indirectly to collective security, such as the League's 1923 Draft Treaty of Mutual Assistance and the 1924 Geneva Protocol for the Pacific Settlement of International Disputes (which called for economic sanctions against aggressors). Under President Hoover the United States greatly increased its involvement in League activities, even to the extent of some cooperation with the League Council during the Manchurian crisis in 1931-32.

Peace groups and internationalists wanted the United States to join the World Court. They argued that Americans had been in the forefront of the movement for arbitration and international adjudication and that the World Court in a very real sense represented an American creation. Many supporters of the World Court also saw it as a first step toward closer relations with the League. Harding and Hughes endorsed membership in the court and by the mid-20's both major political parties favored it. Although most Americans apparently agreed, the isolationist bloc in the Senate managed to defeat the project. One irreconcilable opponent referred derisively to the Court's judges and asked rhetorically, "Who are these who would place above the American flag the bastard banner of internationalism?" After lengthy hearings and compromises, in 1926 the Senate finally approved joining but it attached reservations that were unacceptable to members of the Court. Another try in 1935 failed by 7 votes to obtain the necessary two-thirds majority in the Senate. The internationalists had won over the majority of Americans but they could not overcome the die-hard isolationists in the Senate.

Unfortunately all the cooperation with the League, the movement to join the World Court, and participation in arms limitation conferences fell short of the full participation and assumption of League responsibilities that might possibly have prevented the outbreak of World War II. Events in the Thirties soon demonstrated the futility of this middle-road foreign policy to serve America's best interests.

Economic Foreign Policy

European governments in 1920 owed the American government about $10 1/3 billion for wartime and post-armistice loans, most of it spent in the United States for war purchases. Despite the pleas of the war-weakened Allies, the American government, from the Wilson administration on, insisted that the loans were straight-forward financial arrangements to be repaid in full with interest. As Coolidge reportedly remarked, "they hired the money, didn't they?" Washington therefore rejected proposals for cancellation or sharp reduction as America's contribution to the general war effort. Moreover the United States officially denied European debtor claims that their ability to repay depended upon Germany meeting her reparations obligations. Despite European resistance and ill will — one French cartoon portrayed the United States as Uncle Shylock — the American government forced funding agreements upon the debtor countries providing for full repayment of the principle over a period of 62 years. Britain agreed to repay her debt of nearly $4.3 billion at an average rate of 3.3 percent interest, while the interest rate on Italy's $1.6 billion was reduced to 0.4 percent in view of her financially straitened condition. France proved most reluctant to sign an agreement for her debt of $3.4 billion, coming to terms at an interest rate of 1.6 percent in 1926 only after economic pressure in the form of an embargo against private loans to France. Yet America's war debt policy should be viewed as more short-sighted than grasping.

America had emerged from the war as the leading industrial and financial power in the world. Its industrial production by the late 1920's amounted to 46 percent of the world's total. The United States largely replaced Europe as the supplier of outside capital to Latin America and the Far East, while its imports from Europe declined sharply. By 1928 the combined governmental and private debts owed America reached a total of $21 billion. New York City had become the financial capital of the world, while American firms penetrated foreign tariff walls through branch factories and subsidiaries overseas. American exports also captured markets previously dominated by Europe, as for example Latin America. The State Department tried with limited success to guide overseas investments and loans but investors attracted to risky foreign ventures by high interest rates frequently ignored its advice. In Germany large sums flowed in from America for purchases of what turned out to be unsound provincial and municipal governmental bond issues. By the mid-Twenties, American economic and diplomatic leadership had helped establish an apparently stable open-door world. Unfortunately, that world order had serious defects: too many unsound American investments abroad, not enough investments in the development of economically backward countries, and insufficient trade between the industrialized nations.

Despite the fact that the United States had become a creditor nation on both the governmental and private levels, Republicans with a "debtor complex" insisted upon returning to a high protective tariff. As Harding put it in one of his characteristically muddled comments, "We should adopt a protective tariff of such a character as will help the struggling industries of Europe to get on their feet." The 1922 Fordney-McCumber Tariff, as noted earlier, sharply increased rates on numerous imports. The beginning of the Great Depression led to a further hike in tariff rates under the Hawley-Smoot Tariff of 1930 from the previous average of 25.9 percent to 50.02 percent on dutiable imports. President Hoover ignored the warnings of over a thousand economists and signed the highest tariff measure in American history. European countries, already running an adverse balance of trade with America and also feeling the effects of the depression, retaliated by erecting tariff walls against American goods. By 1932 the combined effects of the depression and tariff wars had reduced American foreign trade to the level of 1905.

American protectionism thus made it harder for Europe to recover from the war. Yet the State Department recognized some responsibility to promote European readjustment. Despite a formal refusal to acknowledge any connection between war debts and reparations, the State Department encouraged private American bankers to join Europeans in formulating the Dawes Plan in 1924 to lend Germany money and enable it to resume reparations payments – Charles G. Dawes headed the group and American bankers supplied over half of this loan. As a result of the Dawes Plan, France withdrew from occupation of the Ruhr and Germany seemed on the road to economic and political stability. Again in 1930, the American Owen D. Young headed another unofficial commission to reduce Germany's reparations debt from the original $33 billion to $9 billion. In 1931, as the economic depression spread around the globe, President Hoover initiated a one-year moratorium on all inter-governmental debts. He hoped the breathing spell would promote world economic recovery (and shore up questionable American loans in Germany), but the only long term result was to end virtually all payments on the war debts. The Allies and Germany then met at Lausanne and agreed to cancel virtually all reparations if the United States would sharply pare the war debts — Hoover declined, as American public opinion demanded. After the moratorium expired, all debtors but Finland defaulted on debt payments and soon even stopped payments of interest. The American public, caught in the toils of the depression, reacted with bitterness, resentments that have surfaced as late as 1967-68 when France's President Charles DeGaulle seemed to be attacking the stability of the American dollar and its gold reserve.

Ironically, the war debts paid to the United States almost equalled private American loans to Germany and Germany's payments to the Allies. About $2¼ billion had been invested in Germany, while reparation payments amounted to about $2 billion. This unsound chain broke down with the depression and the cessation of the flow of private American funds abroad. In retrospect, the United States would have been wiser to have cancelled or sharply reduced the war debts which would have aided Europe's recovery and the reabsorption of a democratic Germany into a peaceful world.

Republican foreign policies appeared to be successful as the Twenties drew to an end. They had curbed the naval arms race, stabilized the Pacific, and Europe apparently had recovered from the First World War. The United States enjoyed prosperity and its interests abroad seemed adequately safeguarded in a stable world order, all without paying a price of entanglement and obligations. This illusion of prosperity and a cost-free security speedily collapsed with the economic debacle that began in America in 1929 and soon engulfed most of the world. The great stockmarket crash and the depression it heralded quickly dispelled optimism about prosperity and international stability. In the next decade new foreign perils gradually compelled the United States painfully to swing back toward Wilsonian internationalism, while at home the puncturing of the prosperity balloon forced government to move from cooperation with business to direct intervention in the economy.

6

The Great Depression

PROSPERITY seemed a fact of life to many Americans by 1929. The stock market soared to astronomical highs as Herbert Hoover, the Great Engineer of the new business era of the Twenties, prepared to enter the White House. *Time* magazine honored Walter P. Chrysler, the manufacturer of the Plymouth and DeSoto automobiles and builder of the then world's largest skyscraper in New York City, as "Man of the Year." A new magazine, *Fortune*, emerged on the promise of the "generally accepted commonplace that America's great achievement has been Business." Calvin Coolidge, despite some private qualms, in his last State of the Union message succinctly expressed the national mood of self-congratulation:

> No Congress of the United States ever assembled, on surveying the State of the Union, has met with a more pleasing prospect than that which appears at the present time. In the domestic field there is tranquility and contentment . . . and the highest record of years of prosperity. . . . [We can] regard the present with satisfaction and anticipate the future with optimism.

Rarely have hopes been higher or so speedily and cruelly disappointed. By the end of 1929 the most disastrous stock market crash in history had occurred and years of bleak, grinding depression faced the American people. Revered prophets of the Twenties, businessmen, economic soothsayers, and politicians, almost overnight became figures of scorn and ridicule. Time-cherished values and traditions of free enterprise and economic opportunity suddenly acquired a hollow cynical ring, as people frantically sought panaceas for the stunning economic blight. More than ever before in American history, the multitudes trapped in an apparently inexplicable economic debacle looked to Washington for rescue. Government, reluctantly under Herbert Hoover and more readily during the era of the New Deal, felt compelled to prod, regulate, and tinker with the economy in desperate attempts to halt the downward spiral and to stimulate recovery. The interventionist welfare state emerged, as so-called *laissez-faire* policies of the past were abandoned for those of at least a partly planned and managed society.

Boom and Bust

The urge to get rich quick was a logical, if distorted, reflection of the mood of the Twenties. Hopes of obtaining wealth without effort and without serious risks seemed almost universal, as the frenzied booms in real estate and the stock market revealed. Prior to 1924 the stock market had been comparatively restrained and the dividends paid on most stocks corresponded reasonably to their market prices. The real bull market got underway in the latter part of that year. The average of the *New York Times* selected list of industrial stocks rose from 106 at the beginning of 1924 to 245 by the end of 1927. This did not indicate speculation, defenders of the market claimed, but only a delayed catching up of stock prices with increased corporate earnings. In 1928 the rise in stock prices became even steeper, prices advancing as much as twenty points a day. The *New York Times* average reached 331 or a gain of 86 points during the year. Some stocks that had never paid a dividend rose even more spectacularly. One scholar, Dixon Wecter, concluded that 90 percent of the stock market transactions reflected gambling rather than long-term investments.

Buying on margin, where a purchaser pays only part of the cost of the stock and a broker lends the remainder, increased rapidly. Banks and insurance companies, attracted by the high interest rates for "call money" used in margin transactions, diverted funds from capital investments and construction to the stock market. Such funds jumped from about $1 billion in 1924 to nearly $8½ billion prior to the crash in 1929. Money also poured in from all over the world, attracted by the high returns of the American market. Prices advanced to new highs in 1929, with little if any relationship to the actual earning power or worth of the stocks. Investment trusts multiplied, offering portfolios of stocks to those too inexperienced or cautious to invest directly. Local stock exchanges flourished across the country and many banks set up special facilities for investors. By the summer of the first year of the Hoover administration, the *New York Times* average recorded a high of 449, up 110 points in three months.

The crash came with stunning force. A few voices had warned of the dangers of such wild gambling but most spokesmen continued optimistically to predict even greater gains. The Federal Reserve Board, acting cautiously to avoid precipitating a crash, cautioned member banks in 1929 not to lend money for speculation and raised the discount rate to 6 percent, but without a noticeable effect. In September and early October, the market began to fluctuate uneasily. On October 23, thousands of speculators suddenly lost confidence and tried to dispose of their holdings. Panic struck on the next day, "Black Thursday," when brokers sold nearly thirteen million shares of stocks and prices fell disastrously. Rumors attracted crowds outside the stock exchange, drawn by reports that eleven speculators had jumped to their deaths in despair. The crowd waited for another to jump, but he turned out to be a repairman atop one of the nearby buildings (contrary to popular belief, the suicide rate declined, rather than rose, during the stock market crash and the depression). Inside the exchange, many frantic sellers found it impossible to find buyers for their holdings. Brokers, facing ruin, sold out margin buyers with heavy losses.

At noon on October 24, a group of bankers representing J. P. Morgan and Company and several major New York banks met to try to stem the tide. They pledged a pool, estimated to have been as much as $240 million, to halt the decline. Thomas W. Lamont of the Morgan firm spoke for the group: "There has been a little distress selling on the Stock Exchange," but "It is the consensus of the group that many of the quotations on the Stock Exchange do not fairly represent the situation. . . ." Widely hailed as saviors, the financiers acted in part to save their own skins by stabilizing the market and gaining time to get out without heavy losses. Richard Whitney, the agent of these "Lords of Creation," then entered the stock exchange and dramatically placed large purchase orders for major stocks at above the current bidding price. The gesture had only a temporary effect, for all across the nation thousands of stockholders frantically dumped their holdings.

The bottom fell out on Tuesday, October 29, the worst single day in the history of the market. Brokers sold nearly sixteen and a half million shares and the tickertape ran hopelessly behind as more sellers than buyers appeared. Prices continued to decline, within a few weeks wiping out paper values of nearly $30 billion. Despite optimistic statements by President Hoover, Treasury Secretary Mellon, and industrialists such as John D. Rockefeller, the collapse continued. By the end of the year, the *New York Times* average had fallen to 224 from the previous high of 452. Investment trust stocks became nearly worthless and even such giants as American Telephone and Telegraph fell from 310¼ to 193¼. The downward spiral continued throughout the next two years, until the *New York Times* average stood at an all time low in mid-1932 of 58 points. An estimated $74 billion in stock values had been lost.

Signs of an economic recession existed even before the stock market crash. Residential construction had fallen a billion dollars below the 1928 rate, consumer spending slowed, unsold business inventories rose sharply, and industrial production fell off with an increase in unemployment. Businessmen and consumers found credit tight and costly, and the rate of industrial plant growth declined. In addition, agriculture and certain other industries had never experienced prosperity throughout the decade.

After the crash, the economic cycle dipped even lower. Production dropped as factories responded to reduced consumption by laying off employees

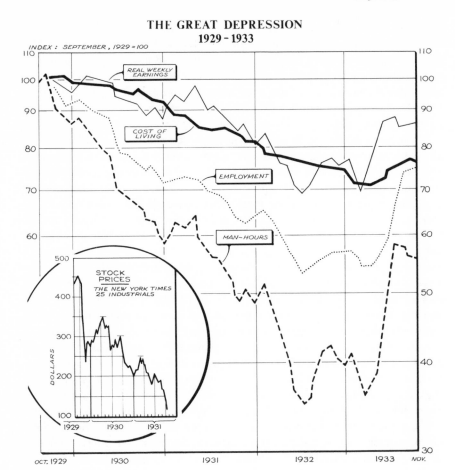

THE GREAT DEPRESSION
1929 - 1933

INDEX : SEPTEMBER, 1929 = 100

REAL WEEKLY EARNINGS

COST OF LIVING

EMPLOYMENT

MAN-HOURS

STOCK PRICES
THE NEW YORK TIMES 25 INDUSTRIALS

DOLLARS

OCT. 1929   1930   1931   1932   1933   NOV.

and curtailing operations, leading to still lower consumer demand and more layoffs in an ever-worsening spiral. By 1932 industrial production had fallen to less than half the pre-crash level, and the annual national income had dropped from $82 billion in 1928 to $40 billion. Bankers found themselves hard hit as debtors defaulted, real estate loans lost value, and speculative ventures collapsed. Loss of public trust and unsound practices resulted in numerous bank failures, especially among the smaller state banks unaffiliated with the Federal Reserve System.

Unemployment steadily grew. From an average of about two million in the Coolidge era, unemployment rose to three million in the spring of 1930, nearly four million by the end of that year, and almost seven million in late 1931. By 1932 between twelve and fifteen million Americans lacked jobs. Even those still employed often experienced sharp reductions in wages or were on part-time work. Farm prices, already depressingly low, fell 64 percent below the 1929 level. Some farmers burned corn for fuel, since they had unsold supplies and coal was relatively expensive. Farm income dropped proportionately, with the inevitable results of more indebtedness, mortgage foreclosures (a fourth of all farmers lost their farms), farm tenancy, and grinding poverty. Professional groups also felt the squeeze in lowered income and mounting debts.

The social effects of the depression were deep and destructive. As economist John Kenneth Galbraith notes, it raised serious questions for many, and especially for youth, about the old verities that thrift, hard work, and diligence would inevitably be rewarded by prosperity. The diligent as well as the improvident alike experienced the same fate. Relief and charity weakened habits of self-reliance and prolonged joblessness caused despair and fear. Security rather than advancement or daring enterprise seemed to have become the new universal goal.

Local relief and philanthropy proved hopelessly incapable of meeting the staggering burden of unemployment. Philadelphia had 300,000 people out of work by 1932, in contrast to the normal figure of 40,000; 55,000 families were on relief, receiving $4.23 a week which it was estimated provided only two-thirds of a minimum healthy diet. New York City found it necessary because of lack of revenue to reduce the weekly relief allowance to $2.39 a family and even then could provide for only half of the needy, while the Toledo, Ohio, commissary could spend only slightly above two cents per meal for those in want. In the larger cities, groups of ragged men, women, and children scavenged garbage dumps for scraps of food or clothing. In Chicago, according to one reporter, "Around the truck which was unloading garbage and other refuse, were about thirty-five men, women, and children. As soon as the truck pulled away from the pile, all of them started digging with sticks, some with their hands, grabbing bits of food and vegetables." So-called "Hoover-villes" or makeshift settlements festered around the larger cities, where homeless families dwelt in worn-out cars, tin shacks or caves. Hundreds of single men and women slept in the parks even during inclement weather, while others sought warmth and food in the jails. New "industries" sprang up, such as apple selling on the streets or shoeshine "boys" of all ages and backgrounds. Illustrating the desperate mood of the unemployed, Soviet Russia advertised in 1931 for 6000 skilled workers to go to Russia and was flooded with over 100,000 applications.

Youth was especially hard-hit. A survey in New York City in 1932 revealed that 20 percent of the children suffered from malnutrition — starvation in a land of plenty. Teachers in Chicago fed 11,000 hungry school children from their own meager resources. Hundreds of thousands of jobless youth of both sexes took to the road and drifted aimlessly across the country in search of opportunity, hitch-hiking or riding the rails on freight trains. Whole families packed their belongings and set off in ramshackle cars, attracted by rumors of jobs in California or elsewhere. Teachers received sharp salary cuts, and their salary was often in arrears. Chicago, whose teachers went unpaid for six months, issued promissory notes or script as tax revenues fell off. A number of schools closed their doors, particularly in rural areas and in the South. Georgia, for example, closed 1318 schools with a total enrollment of over 170,000 pupils.

The literature of the depression more nearly resembled that of the muck-raking era than the hedonism and debunking of the 1920's. Writers again became absorbed by social issues rather than with problems of individual fulfillment. There was a reawakening of national self-consciousness, as authors in volumes or articles bearing such titles as "My America," "Tragic America," or "The American Earthquake," analyzed the nation and the emergency it confronted. Erskine Caldwell's *Tobacco Road*, a ribald novel about the plight of the rural poor, became a popular Broadway play. John Steinbeck, in *The Grapes of Wrath*, described the forlorn migration of "Okies" and "Arkies," refugees from farm poverty and the dust bowl, many of whom sought a new life in the golden state of California only to encounter new disappointments. In *Native Son*, the gifted Negro writer Richard Wright related the obstacles facing a young Negro boy emigrating to the North. James T. Farrell wrote a trilogy on young Studs Lonigan growing to manhood in depression-ridden Chicago. A brilliant writer, Thomas Wolfe wrote in an autobiographical vein about boyhood in North Carolina and life in the North in *Look Homeward, Angel, Of Time and the River*, and *You Can't Go Home Again*. As the decade wore on and problems of the depression became compounded with dangers of fascism and war, Ernest Hemingway wrote of the Spanish Civil War in *For Whom the Bell Tolls*, and Sinclair Lewis in *It Can't Happen Here* warned of the menace of totalitarianism.

It seemed to many observers in the early 1930's that the United States faced an imminent revolution. Hunger riots occurred in several cities, mobs smashing and pilfering stores and warehouses in search of food and clothing. On May 1, 1930, as President Hoover was assuring the U.S. Chamber of Commerce of imminent recovery, a group of the jobless, organized by the Communists, demonstrated before the White House until dispersed by police with tear gas. In New York City, 35,000 people tried to march on the city hall. Detroit, the automotive capital, had such vast unemployment that William Z. Foster and the Communist Party picked it as the target for a major effort at unionization and increased party influence. Three thousand unemployed advanced from the city in an orderly procession on Henry Ford's River Rouge plant at Dearborn to deliver a petition, only to be turned back by police fire that killed four and wounded several. A funeral procession for the martyrs carried banners proclaiming that "Ford Gives Bullets for Bread." Desperate farmers forcibly prevented or interfered with mortgage foreclosure sales. In the mid-west, "farmers holiday" movements led by Milo Reno of Iowa tried to prevent the delivery of food to the cities until prices were raised. A group of about 20,000 war veterans, known as the Bonus Expeditionary Force because they sought full and advanced payment of the bonus for war services, camped with their families on the outskirts of Washington. Chanting

> Mellon pulled the whistle,
> Hoover rang the bell,
> Wall Street gave the signal
> and the country went to hell!

veterans forced Congress to debate the bonus bill. Passed by the House, administration pressure defeated the bonus in the Senate. Although the veterans were orderly and only a handful were communists, President Hoover refused to talk with them and regarded them as revolutionary. Finally, after the police panicked during a melée, he ordered the army under General Douglas MacArthur to evict the B.E.F. from its encampments. The dashing and bemedaled general carried out the task with tanks and with troops armed with bayonets and tear gas, chasing away the forlorn refugees and burning their tents and shacks. Hoover was to pay in lost popularity for his needless fright.

The Communist Party gleefully hailed the depression as proof of the bankruptcy of the capitalist system and eagerly anticipated revolution. The communists sent organizers to various cities to win over the jobless, organized protest meetings and marchers, and in 1931 called for a National Hunger March on Washington. Despite the despair of the times, the Communist Party garnered only a small number of converts. Intellectuals, disillusioned by the crassness of the 1920's and the economic debacle of the 1930's, seemed attracted to the cause rather than workers. Michael Gold edited the *New Masses*, a Communist revival in 1927 of the old radical *Masses* of the Progressive era, and printed much crude "proletarian" literature. A number of able writers either joined the Communist Party or contributed to the *New Masses*: John Dos Passos, Granville Hicks, Theodore Dreiser, Erskine Caldwell, and others. The aging muckraker and radical, Lincoln Steffens, in his *Autobiography* (1931) reiterated his earlier conviction that progressive reforms had not been enough; the capitalist system must be replaced and business nationalized as the communists had done in Russia. As he commented, "All roads in our day lead to Moscow." John Chamberlain's *Farewell to Reform* (1932) agreed that time had revealed the futility of progressivism and liberalism. Yet, despite an apparently unparalleled opportunity, by 1932 the Communist Party only had about 12,000 members. Obviously most Americans felt alienated by the revolutionary jargon of the communists and still clung to faith in law and order and the private property system. Even the small number of intellectuals won over tended to become speedily disillusioned by the dogmatism of the party and the brutal fanaticism of Joseph Stalin's dictatorship in Soviet Russia.

The causes and cure of the Great Depression were endlessly debated. Economist William T. Foster attributed the collapse to oversavings, reducing ability to consume goods. He contended that recovery would come only from heavier private and especially governmental spending. John Maynard Keynes, the brilliant British economist, agreed in his *Treatise on Money* (1930) that the depression was "a crisis of abundance" resulting from underconsumption. In this and subsequent writings, especially *The General Theory of Employment, Interest, and Money* (1936), Keynes advocated massive government spending via public works and other projects to create purchasing power and revive the economy. Keynesianism meant more than mere deficit spending; it called for government to plan for full employment and consumption. A Utah banker, Marriner Eccles, reached similar conclusions about the need for federal spending. Gardiner C. Means and Adolf A. Berle, Jr., authors of *The Modern Corporation* (1932), and Rexford Guy Tugwell concluded that the vast growth of corporate power and *de facto* price fixing made meaningless older assumptions about a free market and required a large measure of public planning of the economy and government spending to balance production with consumption.

In the words of the *New Republic*, many critics saw the depression as a great opportunity for the "democratization of industry." The experiences of World War I seemed particularly appropriate, for then, as philosopher John Dewey pointed out, all the belligerent countries had emphasized production for need and use rather than merely for profit. Gerard Swope of General Electric proposed a World War I type of Liberty Bond drive to raise money for large-scale governmental spending; subsequently he advocated the "Swope Plan" for a national economic council to supervise a network of private trade associations that would stabilize production, employment, and prices. McAdoo, formerly Secretary of the Treasury in the Wilson administration, called for a Peace Industries Board, resembling the old War Industries Board, to mobilize the economy in the new crisis. Whether advocating more business self-government, federal planning, or heavy pump-priming spending by Washington, all these voices agreed upon the necessity for greater governmental effort. Startling though their proposals seemed to many, they actually were only logical extensions of the tendency toward greater rationalization and organization of the economy that had been underway since the turn of the century.

It is now generally agreed that the stock market crash, itself largely the result of a gambling speculative mania, contributed importantly to the Great Depression. If the basic economy had been healthier, economist Galbraith points out, the collapse of the boom in stocks probably would have been less acutely felt. Since the reverse was true, the Wall Street debacle triggered a spiral of other collapses in the economy. Examining these underlying factors, it must be borne in mind that much of the prosperity of the 1920's had been founded on consumer industries rather than on heavy industry. Production of basic necessities such as food tended to be surpassed in importance by the production of durable or semi-durable goods, formerly considered luxuries, and by the growth of distributive and service industries. By their very nature, consumption of such goods and services could be sharply curtailed in times of economic distress, whether individual or national. Consequently the maldistribution of income in the decade, when industry retained too much of the gains of increased productivity as profits and passed on a disproportionately small share in the form of higher wages and lower prices, meant a sharp limitation in the ability of the average American to consume an ever-growing flood of goods and services. A Brookings Institute study estimated that 60 percent of American families received less than the $2000 annual income necessary to buy the minimum essentials. Industry simply produced far more than consumers easily could buy under prevailing wages and prices, even when aided by the new system of installment or credit purchasing. Production outstripped consumption, with the inevitable results of gluts of unsold goods, factory cut-backs, unemployment, and a further reduction of consumer purchasing power that touched off more rounds of retrenchment.

Other contributing factors involved a precarious corporate structure of holding companies piled on top of holding companies; a weak banking system marked by unsound credit practices and speculative loans and inadequate state or federal regulation; technological unemployment and the absence of unemployment compensation; and the diversion of profits and dividends from plant expansion or construction to stock market speculation. A series of national business administrations had failed to deal adequately with depressed agriculture or to enforce existing regulatory laws and had encouraged inflation and cheap money during most of the decade. World conditions undoubtedly contributed, though the depression came first to America and was felt more severely here. Foreign trade was unhealthy and a vast burden of inter-governmental and private international debts existed, made worse by the high tariff and war debt policies of the American government.

Hoover and the Great Depression

Few men have entered the presidency with brighter prospects than Herbert Hoover in March of 1929. Famed for his past services to the nation and mankind, the Great Engineer in politics confidently anticipated consolidation of the business "New Era." Four years later he left office, deeply embittered and near exhaustion from his ceaseless labors to cope with the depression, reviled as few other presidents in American history. Why, in view of his great talents, did he fail in this crisis?

Hoover's personal philosophy seems the primary explanation. Because of his own experiences, Hoover firmly believed in an "American system" based on individualism, economic opportunity, and private enterprise, with the government's role restricted to that of an umpire to regulate and encourage the economy. As he said during the 1928 campaign:

> It is as if we set a race. We, through free and universal education,
> provide the training of the runners; we give to them an equal start;
> we provide in the government the umpire of fairness in the race. The
> winner is he who shows the most conscientious training, the greatest
> ability, and the greatest character.

A skilled administrator, Hoover was not an effective political leader. Shy
and ultra-sensitive to criticism, he detested politics and could not project a
dynamic public image during the depression. Contrary to a widely-held opinion,
however, Hoover early recognized that a severe depression had hit America, even
if like some others he failed to perceive just how grave and prolonged it would
be. In past economic crises, recovery had set in by the operation of so-called
natural laws. Decreased production had permitted surpluses to be absorbed, and
declining costs in labor and raw materials had allowed the prices of goods to also
fall with a consequent revival of economic activity, aided by foreign markets and
a growing population. These processes, owing to a fairly stable population in the
1930's and to a worldwide depression, operated poorly if at all in the current
crisis.

Hoover realized that government must be more active in trying to quicken
the economy. Unlike the hands-off attitude of his predecessors during past
slumps, he involved the federal government as never before in anti-depression
measures. Especially in the last two years of his administration, he clearly
foreshadowed some of the approaches of Franklin D. Roosevelt's New Deal. Yet
he changed too slowly, when the times demanded rapid and even desperate
measures. Above all, he clung stubbornly to his belief that while the national
government must help the people to recover, the public would have to bear the
major burden and should not expect miracles. A prisoner of his earlier experiences and of Republican policies, he relied too much upon voluntary effort,
cooperation, and persuasion. He viewed direct federal aid as dangerous, for it
might weaken private initiative and responsibility and lead to federal control of
the economy. America had been built on the principle of individual self-help and
local responsibility, he firmly believed, and to weaken that by federal actions
would endanger the very qualities that had made the nation great.

Hoover called a special session of Congress, prior to the 1929 crash, to
cope with the farm problem and the tariff. Congress authorized the creation of a
Federal Farm Board with a revolving fund of one-half billion dollars to encourage farmers to plan production and marketing, especially through the formation
of nationally organized cooperatives. According to this self-help theory, farmers
could be educated voluntarily to restrain production in order to raise market
prices. With the encouragement of the Farm Board, farmers formed national
cooperative associations or corporations for the producers of grain, wool,
cotton, livestock, fruits and vegetables, and other commodities. Using pool
selling, loans on products stored for later sale, and other devices, the Farm Board
hoped to provide for more orderly marketing and improving prices. As a

temporary device to remove surpluses and generate a price rise, the cotton and grain stabilization corporations lent funds and then purchased those crops on the open market. At Hoover's insistence, the Farm Board could not impose production controls and farmers continued overproduction of cotton and wheat, despite Farm Board recommendations for restraint and the plowing under of cotton. The stabilization corporations accumulated huge unsalable stocks before admitting failure and abandoning their efforts in 1931 to prop up prices. As the depression deepened, wheat prices skidded to fifty-seven cents a bushel in 1931 and cotton sold for five cents a pound by 1932.

After the Wall Street debacle, President Hoover realized that the country faced more than a mere financial panic. Publicly, he exuded confidence. In October, he stated that "the fundamental business of the country . . . is on a sound and prosperous basis," and in November he declared that "any lack of confidence in the economic future or the basic strength of business . . . is foolish." Privately, however, the President decided not to follow Treasury Secretary Mellon's classic formula of letting the depression run what he described as its natural course until a bottom was reached and recovery began. Instead the President hoped to use governmental persuasion to cushion the shock and generate a more rapid revival of the economy. He called a series of conferences in Washington of businessmen, industrialists, agricultural spokesmen, and labor leaders, and obtained promises to maintain wage rates and continue capital investments. The conferences and optimistic statements illustrated Hoover's faith in encouraging cooperation between various groups in the private economy. Unfortunately as the depression deepened, the promises he obtained from business leaders could not or were not kept. The Federal Reserve Board relaxed credit and the Farm Board tried to raise agricultural prices. Hoover proposed to expand federal public works and urged the states to a similar program. The Hawley-Smoot Tariff of 1930 increased duties on agricultural and industrial imports, but proved to be a false hope as a weapon against the depression. Congress also enacted a tax cut in 1929 to stimulate the economy. Since taxes already had been very low, the reduction had negligible results.

At Hoover's suggestion, Julius H. Barnes of the United States Chamber of Commerce invited important businessmen in a National Business Survey Conference to discover and remove the key barriers in the economy in order to restore prosperity. The organization faded away by 1931, obviously a failure. The simple fact, to be repeatedly demonstrated during the depression, was that businessmen and farmers were too individualistic to take collective measures to raise wages and guide production. When the pinch became tighter most businessmen forgot about cooperation and adopted measures to protect themselves — wage slashes, layoffs, and production reductions — ensuring further declines in the economy, For example, a National Credit Corporation formed by bankers in response to administration suggestions, to enable stronger banks to strengthen essentially sound but temporarily endangered banks failed because the larger banks were unwilling to take the risk. At no time did President Hoover recommend any fundamental reform of the nation's economic machinery, though reform seemed necessary to many critics in the areas of stockmarket operations, banking, and the corporate structure.

To generate confidence and to minimize the hoarding of money, Hoover and his administration issued an unending stream of optimistic statements. Unfortunately, the President fell victim to his own optimism. Repeatedly he misinterpreted slight upward fluctuations in a generally downward economic spiral to reassure the country. Thus on May 1, 1930 Hoover proclaimed to the U.S. Chamber of Commerce, "we have now passed the worst and with continued unity of effort we shall rapidly recover." The spring upsurge, however, quickly passed and the depression continued. Had the economy been sounder, his methods might have succeeded as similar ones had in the 1921 slump. Unfortunately he let pass a crucial period when a relatively small increase in federal spending might have restored a balance.

Hoover refused to admit the failure of his indirect methods, despite further declines in the economy and growing popular criticism. The 1930 mid-term elections, though not a Democratic sweep, registered large gains for the opposition party. The Democratic National Committee was largely successful in fixing the responsibility for the depression on Hoover. The results of the election gave the Democrats a narrow control in the House of Representatives and a forty-seven to forty-eight balance in the Senate. Because of growing insurgency among western Republicans, Hoover faced an increasingly hostile Congress during the last two years of his term. Yet he resisted pressures for massive federal spending and stubbornly maintained that his recovery measures met the needs of the country.

A new danger disturbed the President. Declining federal revenues threatened to result in a huge public debt and possible abandonment of the gold standard. Falling revenues and the amount of deficit spending that Hoover reluctantly accepted increased the national debt from slightly over $16 billion in 1930 to $19½ billion in 1932. The deficit for 1931 alone neared $1 billion. To counter the deficit, Hoover slashed outlays for public works in order to avoid throwing the budget further out of balance. As the depression grew worse, Hoover blamed everything but the American economic system. Earlier he had condemned domestic overspeculation as the cause of the crash, but now he pointed to world conditions as the culprit. When the Creditanstalt Bank in Vienna collapsed, triggering similar financial debacles across much of the continent, Europeans dumped American securities resulting in a heavy flow of gold from America to Europe. To stem the tide, the Federal Reserve Board raised the rediscount rate from 1.5 percent to 3.5 percent saving the gold reserve but making credit tighter for businessmen. In still another attempt to cope with the world depression, Hoover in 1931 proclaimed a moratorium on inter-governmental debt payments in the vain hope of stemming the collapse abroad.

Although state and local and private relief agencies proved obviously inadequate, Hoover stubbornly clung to the conviction that they could meet the problem of unemployment. Even years later he was reluctant to admit the magnitude of unemployment. In his memoirs he explained the large-scale phenomenon of apple-selling on the streets as a shrewd scheme by the apple growers: "Many persons left their jobs for the more profitable one of selling apples." He did appoint an Emergency Committee for Employment, subsequently reconstituted as the President's Organization on Unemployment Relief, to stimulate voluntary and local charity. The first director, Colonel Arthur Woods, concluded that more was required on the part of the federal government and soon resigned. His replacement, Walter S. Gifford of American Telephone and Telegraph, fully concurred with the President's views. With much ballyhoo Gifford launched "a great spiritual experience" to remedy joblessness by persuading more people to employ one another. Testifying before Congress, Gifford insisted upon the soundness of the administration's policy and he condemned all proposals for federal relief. Business leaders claimed there would be recovery if government did not interfere by direct relief. They proposed (courtesy of J. P. Morgan) a "block system" whereby residents in an area would pledge weekly contributions for relief, and another plan for the collection of restaurant leftovers of food to be distributed to the poor.

In Hoover's mind, direct federal relief would destroy individual initiative and self-respect, weaken local government and voluntary charity, and result in a dangerous federal paternalism. Brushing aside unpleasant facts, Hoover repeatedly declared that all the needy were being taken care of. Far from there being any starvation, he assured the nation, the national health standards in fact had improved. Yet agonized appeals continued to flood into Washington for measures to prevent misery and suffering. When one group called on him at the White House in mid-1931 to urge direct federal action, Hoover confidently declared that the depression was over: "Gentlemen, you have come six weeks too late."

Hoover did consent to federal loans to buy seeds and tools for farmers stricken by the great drought in the Southwest's Dust Bowl in 1931, but he balked at a proposal to feed the farmers and their families or to extend direct relief to the unemployed. In the Senate, Robert F. Wagner of New York, who sympathized with the lowly and the unfortunate perhaps because he had been poor, led the fight for more accurate statistics on joblessness, proposed the expansion of public works, and backed other relief measures. The President, however, adamantly opposed such proposals. "Never before," he said on vetoing a relief bill, "has so dangerous a suggestion been seriously made in this country." The President reluctantly signed into law in 1932 the Norris-La Guardia Anti-Injunction Act, sought by organized labor to curb anti-strike court injunctions, but he vetoed a bill to strengthen the Federal Employment Service established in

1907. Hoover's defeat in 1932 can be attributed in large degree to his refusal to use federal resources in direct relief of the unemployed and needy.

The administration did act more boldly in two areas, if only in accordance with Hoover's philosophy. A federal Home Loan Bank Act was passed in 1932 to strengthen building and loan associations. Unfortunately thousands of home owners had already lost their homes — 273,000 in 1932 alone. The Reconstruction Finance Corporation, established in early 1932 and based on the War Finance Corporation of World War I, represented a more imaginative measure. Congress authorized the R.F.C. to lend money to banks, insurance companies, railroads, and agricultural credit associations. Although one critic derisively dismissed the R.F.C. as a "millionaire's dole," Hoover intended it to restore confidence in the nation's financial structure. He hoped in fact that its mere creation would be enough so that actual lending could be kept to a minimum. Unfortunately, R.F.C.'s first director, Charles G. Dawes, stirred up a tirade of denunciations when it became known that shortly after he had resigned from the R.F.C. that agency had loaned Dawes' own bank, the Central Republic Bank and Trust Company in Chicago, $90 million in a vain effort to shore it up. Hoover correctly defended the loan as proper but it seemed to many to demonstrate the willingness of the administration to help only big business. Yet despite such criticisms, the R.F.C. strengthened otherwise sound institutions and was a direct precursor to the New Deal's lending policy. Hoover reluctantly accepted subsequent legislation for the R.F.C. to lend up to $300 million to the states for relief purposes. The nearly bankrupt states, however, responded unenthusiastically because they preferred gifts. The R.F.C. and the states used loans so sparingly that only a few million dollars were actually advanced. The New Deal was to expand vastly the scope of the R.F.C.

By 1932, Hoover's philosophy of voluntaryism and self-help, with government confining its role largely to encouragement, had failed to overcome the crisis. Yet as Albert U. Romasco has pointed out, President Hoover had made a valiant effort within the limits of that approach and if he had not thus pioneered little would have been learned about how government should cope with a severe depression.

Depression Politics

Hoover was tired of coping with the depression but he sought to vindicate his policies by running for re-election in 1932, and he won renomination, though without any great enthusiasm by his party. Many progressive-minded Republicans either responded apathetically or deserted to the Democrats. Increasingly the rigid and self-righteous President became the target of widespread criticism and abuse. Cruel jokes circulated that he was indeed the world's greatest engineer, having "drained, ditched and damned" the entire country within the

"It seems there wasn't any depression at all!"
Fitzpatrick in the *St. Louis Post-Dispatch.*

span of a few years. One popular joke had Hoover asking Andrew Mellon for a nickel to telephone a friend, and the latter replied, "Here's a dime; call all your friends." Hoover's very name became an epithet, a symbol for despair and misery: "Hoover wagons" were old broken-down cars, "Hoover blankets" referred to newspapers used to cover forlorn men sleeping in the parks at night, and lean jackrabbits were re-christened "Hoover hogs."

Opening his campaign in Iowa, Hoover encountered protest picketers carrying placards. One sign read, "In Hoover We Trusted; Now We Are Busted." People booed him in Philadelphia and Salt Lake City, and he was jeered at in Detroit by several thousand veterans, unemployed, and some communists who surrounded his train. The hapless President reassured the nation that no "deserving American fireside" would experience cold or hunger that winter, small comfort to the millions of presumably "undeserving" who did.

Franklin D. Roosevelt, one of the most charismatic figures in American political history, held the front-runner position among Democrats in 1932. Born in 1882 into the aristocratic Roosevelt family at Hyde Park, New York, young Franklin grew up imbued with a sense of duty and service to family and the community. After education at Groton and Harvard, where his grades were gentlemanly but not outstanding, Franklin briefly went into law before he decided to emulate his famous cousin, Theodore Roosevelt, by entering politics. He married Eleanor Roosevelt, Theodore's niece, in 1905. A sensitive woman with an unhappy childhood, and deeply sympathetic with the less fortunate of this world, Eleanor had an incalculable influence in the development of her husband's social conscience and his interest in reform. Roosevelt received an excellent political education while serving in the New York State Senate. For the first time aware of the plight of the lower classes, he began to reveal attitudes and convictions regarding labor and agriculture that subsequently shaped the New Deal. He also learned invaluable political lessons about party regularity and he perceived firsthand that machine politicians, such as Al Smith, could also be men of honesty dedicated to public service. During the Wilson administration, he served ably as Assistant Secretary of the Navy under Josephus Daniels. An advocate of a big navy and knowledgeable in nautical terminology, Roosevelt was far more popular with high naval officers than was Daniels. Daniels was fond of his young assistant and overlooked Roosevelt's mockery of his southern manners and speech; subsequently, in a reversal of roles, Daniels served as Roosevelt's Ambassador to Mexico during the New Deal era. In 1920 Roosevelt received the vice-presidential nomination on the ticket with Governor Cox of Ohio and campaigned energetically in a lost cause for the Democrats.

Stricken with infantile paralysis in 1921, Roosevelt courageously fought back to a partial recovery; he often visited Warm Springs, Georgia and founded a center there for the treatment of polio victims. Roosevelt remained actively interested in politics despite his illness. He formed a political friendship with New York's Al Smith and supported him in his bids for president in 1924 and 1928. At the 1924 convention, Roosevelt on crutches hailed Al Smith as the "Happy Warrior" of politics and made a moving impression on the delegates. After Smith obtained the nomination in 1928, Roosevelt ran for governor of New York. Elected despite the defeat of the national ticket Roosevelt battled for regional planning to help both the farmer and the state in general, getting a constitutional authorization in 1931 for state acquisition of abandoned farms for reforestation, and he backed other conservation measures. Roosevelt continued

Smith's program for public power development on the St. Lawrence River.

When the depression came, Roosevelt operated "a little left of center" in his efforts to cope with state problems of unemployment and relief. He established a Commission on the Stabilization of Employment within the state and approved the concept of unemployment insurance. He created a state emergency relief administration, under the direction of Harry Hopkins. But even Roosevelt, probably the most progressive state governor then on the national scene, at first showed a marked unenthusiasm about expanding public works, and he tried to finance relief by raising taxes until compelled to accept larger deficits. He had not yet envisioned the positive role government intervention could play in the economy. As his biographer, Frank Freidel, states, Roosevelt shared the conservative belief in an unhampered free enterprise system, yet he also had been influenced by the Progressive Era's humanitarian commitment to social justice. At any rate, he managed to create an image of himself as a dynamic political leader fighting the depression, in contrast to Hoover's do-nothing approach. Aided by able political advisers such as James Farley, Louis M. Howe (his private secretary), and speech-writer Samuel J. Rosenman, Roosevelt won reelection as Governor in 1930 by a heavy margin. Thereafter, his national political star was on the rise and he began to challenge the Republicans. In several addresses early in 1932 Roosevelt sharpened his attack on the Hoover policies. The emergency was worse than 1917, he declared, and it required similar planned effort to "build from the bottom up" and not to neglect the "forgotten man."

Roosevelt thus was in a good position to win the Democratic presidential nomination in 1932, though he first had to brush aside Smith who had sacrificed himself in the Republican year of 1928 and thought he deserved another chance. Despite primary election set-backs in Massachusetts and California (Smith won by a three to one margin in the Bay State and Roosevelt came in a poor second in California), the Roosevelt forces beat back Smith and such rivals as Governor "Alfalfa Bill" Murray of Oklahoma. Roosevelt won the nomination on the fourth ballot at the Democratic convention in Chicago. John N. Garner of Texas got the second place on the ticket.

Roosevelt set the tone of the campaign in his precedent-shattering appearance before the convention to accept the nomination. Dramatically flying to Chicago, he proclaimed to the assembled delegates and the nation, "Ours must be a party of liberal thought, of planned actions, of enlightened international outlook, and of the greatest good to the greatest number of our citizens." He then spoke in general terms of the necessity for government aid and encouragement for agriculture, business, and the unemployed. "I pledge you [the delegates at the convention], I pledge myself, to a new deal for the American people. . . . This is more than a political campaign; it is a call to arms. Give me your help, not to win votes alone, but to win in this crusade to restore America to its own people." His stirring promise of a New Deal captured the public's imagination and furnished a label for his subsequent administration.

Roosevelt was criticized then and later for giving vague speeches that failed to spell out the details of his plans for defeating the depression. The *New Republic*, for example, evaluated Roosevelt as a man of good intentions but without great intellectual or moral force. Commentator Walter Lippmann dismissed him as "a pleasant man who, without any important qualifications for the office, would like to be President." True, he did not present a clear-cut program to the electorate, but that usually has been the pattern in American presidential elections. Roosevelt sought to win an election and naturally wanted to alienate as few voters as possible. He found it far safer to condemn Hoover's policies than to specify his own. Moreover, Roosevelt as a practical politician did not indulge much in theorizing or dogmatic philosophy. Yet he should not be viewed as an opportunist in the crass sense, for he believed in certain principles of responsible democratic government and its obligations to promote the welfare of all its citizens. Roosevelt in office revealed a pragmatic and experimental approach, willing to borrow ideas and programs from diverse sources in the desperate battle to relieve suffering and restore national prosperity.

Roosevelt did indicate in a general way the course his administration subsequently followed. Aided by his "brains trust" — Felix Frankfurter of Harvard, and Raymond Moley, Adolf Berle, and Rexford Tugwell of Columbia — he outlined some of the essentials of the subsequent New Deal program in a series of major speeches. At Topeka, Kansas, Roosevelt indicated the need for a federal crop-control program to rescue the farmers. He talked of regulation and aid for the bankrupt railroads at Salt Lake City, the dangers of a high tariff at Seattle, and in Portland, Oregon, he called for federal dam and power projects. He made his most radical proposals before the Commonwealth Club in San Francisco. There the candidate spoke of the need for an economic bill of rights including a decent minimum living standard, economic order, and government planning. When Hoover attacked him for advocating collectivism, charging that the New Deal would enslave America, Roosevelt toned down his speeches and began to criticize the Republicans for an unbalanced budget and a growing national debt. Hoover's $2¾ billion deficit, he declared, represented "the most reckless and extravagant [one] . . . that I have been able to discover in the statistical record of any peacetime Government anywhere, anytime." While pledging himself to greater economy in government and a balanced budget, in which he sincerely believed, Roosevelt left a loophole that more federal funds would be expended if necessary to relieve dire need and avert starvation. An experimental approach, more governmental regulation and intervention in the economy, some economic and social planning — the welfare, interventionist state — came to epitomize the New Deal.

The elections resulted in a Democratic landslide. Having claimed credit for the prosperity of the 1920's, the Republicans now were caught by the depression in a trap of their own making. Most voters remained impervious to Hoover's warning, a few days before the balloting, that if Roosevelt won "the grass will grow in the streets of a hundred cities, a thousand towns; the weeds will overrun the fields of millions of farmers. . . . Their churches and school houses will decay." Roosevelt won the votes of nearly 23 million Americans, or 57.4 percent, to Hoover's 15¾ million votes and 39.6 percent of the popular total. Despite the obvious breakdown of the capitalist system, Socialist Norman Thomas only polled 881,951 votes, less proportionately than in 1912, and the Communist Party candidate, William Z. Foster, managed to attract slightly over 100,000 votes. Hoover carried only six states and was as badly defeated as Smith had been in 1928. As Hoover later wryly commented, "Democracy is not a polite employer. The only way out of elective office is to get sick or die or get kicked out." The Congress became overwhelmingly Democratic, as the party not only capitalized on the urban minorities of the great cities but even broke into traditional Republican strongholds in the agricultural mid-West. The political revolution symbolized by Al Smith in 1928, when the Democratic party first significantly benefited from the growing political consciousness of urban ethnic and religious minorities and organized labor, approached fulfillment.

Interregnum

Between November, 1932 and inaugural day in March, 1933 President Hoover found himself a lame duck chief executive as all eyes focused on the president-elect. The two met in the White House in late November, 1932, and their representatives held several conferences. Pleading the need to bolster business confidence, Hoover tried to persuade Roosevelt to continue Republican policies and not to embark on the experimental tack indicated in the recent campaign. Specifically he urged pledges not to tamper with the dollar nor to unbalance the budget (which Hoover already had unbalanced). When Roosevelt warily declined to assume responsibility or to commit himself prior to taking office, the embittered Hoover blamed him for the further deterioration of the economy and the banking panic that became acute in the early months of 1933.

Hoover left office convinced that his methods had turned the corner on the depression until Roosevelt's election had shattered business confidence by the threat of federal tinkering with an otherwise sound economic system. Later he repeated that conviction in his *Memoirs*: "If the New Dealers had carried out our policies instead of deliberately wrecking them and then trying to make America over into a collectivist system, we should have made complete recovery in eighteen months after 1932. . . ." Few historians and economists today concur with Hoover's analysis. Hoover deserved credit for struggling with the depression, and some of his measures were to be continued in greatly expanded form by the New Deal. But the crisis was too severe for his palliatives to succeed. The times required a less conventional and more responsive leadership, and that his successor supplied in abundance.

7

Roosevelt and the New Deal

INAUGURAL DAY, 1933 dawned cold and overcast in Washington. The prevailing mood across the nation, however, was one of hope. As the *New York Times* summed up: "No President . . . ever came to greater opportunities amid so great an outpouring of popular trust and hope." The economy was continuing its sickening and bewildering downward lurch amidst misery and ruin. The very existence of the republic seemed imperiled and the people looked to the new chief executive for leadership.

Roosevelt Takes Command

Franklin D. Roosevelt radiated confidence and determination. His inaugural address, vague on specific proposals but exuding hope and the promise of energetic action, galvanized the American people and renewed their spirit: "This great Nation will endure as it has endured, will revive and prosper. So, first of all, let me assert my firm belief that the only thing we have to fear is fear itself — nameless, unreasoning, unjustified terror which paralyzes needed efforts to convert retreat into advance." Although the outgoing Hoover visibly shuddered at what he regarded as the demagoguery of Roosevelt's inaugural remarks, the people were impressed.

In his first two weeks in office, President Roosevelt quickly dispelled the national mood of despair. Rising early on his first full day in the White House, Roosevelt was wheeled by his aides into his still bare study and the New Deal began. It was not so much what he did — at this stage his acts were rather conservative and orthodox — but that, in contrast to Hoover, Roosevelt seemed to be grappling decisively with the depression.

The new chief executive faced an immediate crisis in banking. The annual number of bank failures had increased from 167 in 1920 to 2294 in 1931, and to an incredible 4004 in 1933. Loss of confidence among depositors led to runs on many otherwise sound banks and to the hoarding of gold. By inaugural day, thirty-eight states had been forced either to close all banks or permitted only limited operations. Responding to desperate pleas from the financial world and anxious to protect hundreds of thousands of large and small depositors, Roosevelt on March 5 proclaimed a national bank holiday. All banks would be closed, to gain time to reopen sound institutions and liquidate others with minimum losses. Called into special session, Congress quickly passed the Emergency Banking Act, the House of Representatives voting by acclamation and without seeing a copy of the bill that authorized issuance of new federal currency and gave the President full authority over gold transactions. In this first week Roosevelt met the governors of the states in conference and assured them of federal help. Two days later he held his first press conference, where he abolished Hoover's requirement that all questions from reporters be submitted in written form. Then in his first "fireside chat," an informal radio report to the nation that he was to use repeatedly and effectively, Roosevelt announced the reopening of the sound banks and urged the return of withdrawn funds. In an impressive demonstration of confidence in the President, on the following day long lines formed across the country as recently frightened depositors returned their money to the banks.

Roosevelt's handling of the banking crisis revealed the essentially conservative nature of the early New Deal. In view of the public's loss of faith in the banking system and hatred of bankers, Roosevelt probably could have obtained congressional approval for truly drastic measures, even nationalization of the system. Instead he remained content with legislation to restore confidence and improve the banks by closer federal regulation, while still leaving them under private ownership and management. The Glass-Steagall Act of 1933 separated commercial from investment banking, increased the powers of the Federal Reserve Board to curb speculation by banks, and established the Federal Depositors Insurance Corporation to insure all deposits in Federal Reserve banks up to $2500. Another measure two years later reorganized the Board of Governors of the Federal Reserve System and further increased its regulatory authority over bank credits and reserves. These measures helped reduce the annual rate of bank failures to forty or less, and most of these were small banks outside the federal system.

At the President's request, Congress passed the Beer Act, legalizing the sale of light wines and beer. Repeal of Prohibition by the Twenty-first Amendment to the Constitution followed soon thereafter. Keeping his campaign promises to reduce federal expenditures and balance the budget, Roosevelt persuaded a rather reluctant Congress to approve the Economy Act. That act slashed about $500 million from veterans' benefits and the salaries of federal employees. These and other planned actions caused thousands of congratulatory telegrams to flood into the capital, while newspaper columnists and editors lavished praise on the new administration. Congress reflected the national mood of urgency by passing legislation hastily and almost without debate. The temper of Congress in fact seemed to favor even more drastic and sweeping action than the executive proposed. In the remainder of his first hundred days in office, Roosevelt obtained congressional approval for measure after measure with minimal debate and controversy. Congress enacted fifteen major bills and numerous lesser acts, a legislative record unsurpassed in American history.

First New Deal

It is traditional to view Roosevelt's administration as falling into two rather clear divisions or periods. The so-called First New Deal, 1933-1935, presumably concentrated on relief and recovery activities; the Second New Deal, from 1935 to 1938, emphasized broad social and economic reform intended to preclude future economic catastrophes and to promote a larger degree of social justice for all citizens. Historian Arthur M. Schlesinger, Jr., prefers a different set of interpretative labels: the "New Nationalism" for the first period, character-ized by greater emphasis on government planning, integration, and regulation of the economy; versus the return to "New Freedom" approaches in 1935, when the administration manifested greater suspicion toward big business and placed more reliance upon trust-busting and punitive measures to cope with abuses in business and finance. Both interpretations have much validity and are useful tools in understanding the thrust and nature of the New Deal. They should not be taken too rigidly, however, for concern with issues of relief, recovery, and reform remained a constant preoccupation of the administration until the outbreak of the Second World War. Moreover, President Roosevelt manifested a non-theoretical and undogmatic approach to politics and government. Far from being radically inclined, the President leaned toward economic orthodoxy and conservatism. The depression compelled him to experiment and improvise, to borrow ideas and programs from a variety of sources, but his personal prefer-ences remained to avoid truly revolutionary changes and to return the govern-ment to a balanced budget as soon as possible. In short, Roosevelt hoped to reform capitalism as a bulwark of American democracy.

Columnist Walter Lippmann once commented that the major difference between the Hoover and the Roosevelt administrations seemed to be the willing-ness of the New Deal to spend larger sums with less regret. That interpretation had validity for early New Deal relief activities, but not later when the adminis-tration placed greater emphasis upon conserving human skills and dignity while providing relief. Hoover also had run deficits in fighting the depression, but he had refused to involve the federal government in direct relief to the needy and unemployed. Critics had condemned his approach as too timid and many argued that conditions required direct pump-priming expenditures to revive mass consumer purchasing power. The existing system of private, local, and state relief by 1933 obviously proved incapable of coping with the problem. Although Roosevelt preferred a balanced budget (he made a distinction between the ordinary budget that would be balanced and the emergency one that required compensatory expenditures), he plunged into direct federal relief. The President continued to anticipate an early end to such outlays and a return to fiscal solvency and a reduction of the national debt. He never accepted the Keynesian argument for protracted and massive federal spending and did not venture beyond comparatively modest emergency measures. While he managed to relieve acute suffering, he failed to eradicate unemployment and restore full prosperity. These goals remained unachieved until World War II at last mobilized the national wealth and energies and increased the national debt by truly astronomical sums.

The New Deal contributed to the language a new glossary of alphabetical agencies, many of them created to cope with relief. Harry Hopkins, a highly controversial figure and a New York state relief director under Roosevelt, assumed the primary responsibility in this area. One observer once described the outwardly cynical and often profane Hopkins as having "the purity of St. Francis . . . combined with the sharp shrewdness of a race track tout." Hopkins viewed the essential challenge as how to administer relief not only to feed people but to preserve their skills and self-respect. While he accepted the immediate necessity for direct handouts, he sought with the President's approval to supplant the dole with work-relief as soon as possible. Congress in May, 1933 appropriated $500 million for relief through the states and local agencies, largely handled through Hopkins' Federal Emergency Relief Administration. Hopkins insisted that relief hand-outs be given to the needy in cash rather than script redeemable in food, and that relief include not only food but housing, clothing, and medical needs. The administration established the Civil Works Administration, a subsidiary of the F.E.R.A., in late 1933 as a makeshift effort to give emergency jobs to the unemployed during the winter of 1933-34 at a minimum wage eventually fixed at thirty cents an hour. By early 1934, Hopkins had expended close to $1 billion through the C.W.A. and provided temporary employment to over four million people. Convinced that such heavy expenditures had achieved little beyond emergency relief, Roosevelt terminated the C.W.A. in the spring of 1934. Other forms of aid continued, however, and over $2 billion had been spent for relief by the end of the year.

The administration launched a second major attack on relief in 1935. FDR asked for nearly $5 billion for a massive program of federal emergency employment, the largest single appropriation to that date in world history. Conservative critics preferred the less expensive dole and opposed the bill as an unwise extension of executive powers. Republican Senator Arthur H. Vandenburg of Michigan reflected the view of the minority in Congress: "This measure requires Congress to abdicate; it requires the country to lean on a dubious dream; it requires posterity to pay the bills. . . ." Many supporters, however, feared that not enough funds had been requested. Congress passed the measure after much debate. Roosevelt divided the funds between Hopkins' newly created Works Progress Administration and Secretary of the Interior Harold Ickes' Public Works Administration. Hopkins and Ickes were in a sharp rivalry for control and because Ickes' P.W.A. necessarily expended money more slowly on carefully planned public projects, to his great distress his funds tended to be diverted to the freer spending W.P.A.

Charges of worthless make-work projects of "boondoggling" to the contrary, W.P.A. represented a notable attempt not only to conserve skills and relieve unemployment but also to perform socially useful work. It paid "security wages" that were higher than the dole but sufficiently below private wages to provide incentive to seek regular employment. Normally, as Professor Kenneth Galbraith comments, in a private profit economy such as that in the United States genius and money are lavished on the private sector of the economy while the public sector is sadly neglected. Now during a national emergency, the W.P.A. and other New Deal agencies could perform invaluable work. By 1941, the W.P.A. had expended nearly $11 billion, employed a grand total of about 8 million people, and completed 250,000 projects. Some waste inevitably occurred, but the gigantic effort remained remarkably free from overt politicking, while performing much useful labor that normally would not have been undertaken. Relief agencies built around 600 landing aircraft fields; constructed 500,000 miles of roads; completed over 100,000 bridges or viaducts; built or repaired 110,000 public libraries, schools, auditoriums, and hospitals; and served 600 million school lunches. These deeds represented remarkable achievements in view of the fact that W.P.A. had to choose projects that could be completed quickly and that would not compete with private industry or regular and more substantial public works.

To utilize and improve existing skills, Hopkins established under his agency a Federal Theater Project that employed 13,000 people and staged plays for thirty million people, while the Music Project in its first fifteen months presented live concerts before audiences totalling fifty million. The Federal Writers Project produced numerous publications from historical projects to state and local guides. The Federal Art Project employed needy artists to beautify public buildings and stage educational art displays. Another agency, the National Youth Administration, provided part-time jobs for 600,000 college students and 1½ million high school students, and aided an even larger number of non-school youths in acquiring vocational training. A veritable cultural revolution occurred under New Deal auspices, encouraging creativity and making its achievements accessible to the people. An impressed English critic, no doubt exaggerating, exclaimed that "Art in America is being given its chance and there has been nothing like it since before the Reformation." Although denounced by conservatives as frivolous and havens for radicals, Hopkins' agencies undoubtedly reduced the appeal of the communists.

The New Deal created other agencies that combined goals of relief, recovery, and reform. President Roosevelt's personal brainchild, the Civilian Conservation Corps, organized under civilian direction with Army reserve officers in charge, removed thousands of jobless youths from the city streets and gave them useful employment in more healthful rural environments. Thought of as a sort of moral equivalent to war, uniformed C.C.C. youth fought fires, reseeded forests, and engaged in flood prevention work. In 1932 when some 273,000 home owners lost their homes through mortgage foreclosures, Hoover had approved a system of Federal Home Loan Banks to bolster building and loan associations. Since that offered little direct help, Congress approved a Home Owners' Loan Corporation in 1933 to lend money to refinance home mortgages and repairs. By 1936 H.O.L.C. had loaned over $3 billion and held one-sixth of the national home mortgage indebtedness. The administration obtained a Federal Housing Agency in 1934 to encourage new home building, followed by a U.S. Housing Authority in 1937 that advanced money for slum clearance and low cost housing projects. A modest success, about one-third of the housing projects benefitted low-income Negro families.

The Farm Credit Administration extended similar relief to threatened farmers. The Resettlement Administration under Rexford Tugwell established three "greenbelt towns" of 500 to 800 families each near Washington, Cincinnati, and Milwaukee, and tried to help rural people move from worn out farms to better land. Faced with conservative southern opposition, the Resettlement Administration never could obtain sufficient funds to reduce sharply farm tenancy. After two years, it had only purchased five million acres of land and resettled 4,441 families. A southern Tenant Farmers' Union tried to organize sharecroppers and complained that most of the federal rural aid went to the larger landowners. The Farm Security Administration replaced the Resettlement Administration in 1937, to lend money to tenants to buy farms and to improve the lot of migrant farm laborers. The Rural Electrification Administration advanced funds to cooperatives to build electric power transmission facilities, so that where only 580,000 farms had been electrified in 1929 the number increased to about 2 million by 1941. Among other effects, rural electrification created a whole new market for electrical equipment and appliances, a good example of how apparently competitive government programs often benefit the private economy. Ickes' P.W.A. from 1933 to 1939 built nearly two-thirds of the nation's new school buildings, county courthouses, and city facilities, one-third of the hospitals and public health service buildings, and a number of warships for the Navy including the aircraft carriers *Yorktown* and *Enterprise*.

The Tennessee Valley witnessed one of the boldest and most controversial experiments in planned recovery and reform. In 1933 Congress authorized creation of the Tennessee Valley Authority to operate the existing Wilson Dam at Muscle Shoals and to construct new dams to prevent floods, to manufacture fertilizer and explosives, and to generate and distribute electrical power in the area. The activities of the T.V.A. helped transform the lives of the people in seven southern states, freeing them from floods, supplying cheap power, and encouraging development of diversified agriculture and industry. By 1940 per capita income in the Valley had risen 73 percent over 1933. Despite criticisms of this type of governmental regional planning as socialistic, the vast experiment aroused world-wide interest and created industrial facilities that proved of enormous national value during World War II. Opponents, however, prevented other power projects, such as Bonneville Dam on the Columbia River and Grand Coulee in Washington, from undertaking a similar experimental approach.

The New Deal turned Hoover's Reconstruction Finance Corporation into one of the most successful ventures in the struggle for recovery from the depression. Under the direction of Jesse Jones of Texas, the R.F.C. loaned funds not only to the larger financial institutions, as under Hoover, but to needy railroads, medium and small businesses, farmer cooperatives, and rural electrification projects. By 1938 the R.F.C. had loaned $10 billion and had become the largest single source of credit and investment funds in the nation. Nearly all of the loans eventually were repaid in full.

FDR pinned his main hopes for a quick knockout victory over the depression on the National Industrial Recovery Act, passed by Congress in June, 1933. The idea, another example of the influence of the Progressive era on the New Deal, derived from the War Industries Board of World War I that had been remarkably successful in obtaining business and governmental cooperation during that great emergency. Now a new and equally great emergency seemed to require a similar mobilization. The National Recovery Administration, directed by the flamboyant General Hugh Johnson, undoubtedly constituted a departure from the *laissez faire* attitudes of the past. Yet it was not a radical one, for apart from World War I experiences, the N.R.A. had a precedent in the trade associations that had flourished during the Twenties. It went a step beyond, however, placing federal authority behind attempts to regulate production and prices. N.R.A. encouraged various industries to frame codes of fair competition, exempt from the anti-trust laws but subject to governmental approval. Business in effect agreed in these codes on minimum wages and maximum hours in exchange for federal help in stabilizing production and prices. Section 7(a) of the N.I.R.A. recognized the right of workers to organize and bargain collectively with employers, and prohibited compulsory company unions (employer unions established to offset independent national unions). Consumers theoretically had representation in the N.R.A., but never effectively.

N.R.A. initially had the support of most businessmen. The administration hoped it would promote friendly cooperation between business and labor by eliminating wasteful competition and stabilizing prices and wages. Despite the objections of a few industrialists such as Henry Ford, who charged a plot by his competitors and what he called the "bankers' international," Johnson obtained codes for the major industries. He also launched a nationwide campaign with parades and flashy appeals to sign up over two and a quarter million employers under the N.R.A. Blue Eagles (the Blue Eagle symbol was patterned after the Navajo thunderbird emblem). N.R.A. in fact drew up far too many codes, many for unimportant "industries"; the 800 codes even included the dog food industry, mopstick manufacturers, and the burlesque theater. Johnson relied upon persuasion and appeals to patriotism, rather than legal action, to enforce the codes against violators and chiselers. After the first flush of enthusiasm, it proved to be a losing struggle. Complaints swiftly multiplied. Businessmen objected to organized labor's aggressive use of Section 7(a) to unionize workers. Small businessmen and liberals complained that the codes were fascistic and facilitated the growth of big business and monopoly, while consumers reacted unhappily to production curbs and increases in prices. An investigation by a review board under Clarence Darrow confirmed many of the charges and caused President Roosevelt to restrict price fixing and the proliferation of codes for small industries. The administration soon eased out the quick-tempered and often rash Johnson, noted for heavy drinking and "shooting from the hip."

Although many observers viewed N.R.A. as a failure, President Roosevelt thought otherwise and was displeased when it was invalidated by the Supreme Court in 1935. N.R.A. had tended to reduce production and raise prices and costs, but it could take credit for increasing employment by an estimated two million, reducing child labor, and improving working conditions across the nation. Above all, N.R.A. helped restore the nation's confidence during the darkest days of the depression.

The first Agricultural Adjustment Act, adopted in May, 1933 constituted another long step toward the interventionist state and a planned economy. The desperate plight of farmers, resulting from over production and declining prices, worsened by the depression, seemed to require a new remedy. Henry A. Wallace, the Secretary of Agriculture, can perhaps be called a mystic and faddist – he once tried to live on a diet of corn meal and milk after the example of Caesar's troops in Gaul – but he had a profound knowledge of agriculture. Wallace saw his task as leveling off farm production to avoid over production and to achieve "parity" in farm income comparable to other groups in the economy. The A.A.A. went beyond the Hoover farm program to include not only price supports but curtailment of production. It levied a special tax on food processors to finance government purchases of surpluses, and set acreage and production limitations on cotton, wheat, corn, and hogs. The first year the A.A.A. slaughtered six million young pigs and 200,000 sows (salvageable meat was used to feed the needy) and plowed under ten million acres of cotton. Aided by a drought in 1934, the program sharply reduced production and farm income had risen by 50 percent at the end of Roosevelt's first term. Like the N.R.A., however, the A.A.A. and its successors benefitted the large producers, who could control the local agencies, more than small farmers, tenants, or sharecroppers.

Searching for still other ways to speed recovery, and under great pressure from inflationists, Roosevelt with Congress' authorization turned to money manipulation. The theories of Cornell's Professor George F. Warren and others that the price of gold controlled the general commodity price level persuaded FDR to experiment with the gold content of the dollar. Roosevelt incurred the wrath of the orthodox by taking the country off the gold standard and then by buying gold at rates above the current world market price, hoping to encourage foreign trade and raise domestic price levels. Al Smith echoed the sentiments of the traditionalists when he sneered at the new "baloney dollar." The President finally abandoned the experiment and under the Gold Reserve Act of 1934 fixed the reserve gold content of the dollar at 60 percent of the 1933 rate or $35 per ounce. In 1936 an agreement with Britain and France achieved stabilization of currency exchanges. To satisfy the silver interests and inflationists, the Treasury purchased silver at well above the world market price. The only appreciable effect, besides bringing prosperity to silver miners, endangered the silver based currencies of China, Mexico, and Peru. Conservatives were horrified — one professed to fear that the monetary experiments threatened the end of civilization.

Attacks from the Right and the Left

Up to 1934 Roosevelt had followed the "politics of consensus," asking and getting support from all groups including business. As the midterm elections loomed, his coalition began to break down under assaults from the right and the left of the political spectrum. However, he retained the support of farmers, labor, the unemployed, and the underprivileged, and the Democratic party in the 1934 elections substantially increased its control of Congress.

By 1934 a number of conservatives and businessmen had become highly disenchanted with the New Deal. The N.R.A. had proved a disappointment, the national debt had mushroomed, and new agencies such as the Securities and Exchange Commission and the Federal Communications Commission, supervising the radio, telephone, and telegraphic systems, seemed to presage even greater federal control. In August a group of alarmed conservatives founded the American Liberty League to battle the New Deal and expose its allegedly dangerous drift toward socialism. Led by such bitter anti-New Dealers as Al Smith, Raskob, John W. Davis, and some top industrialists from DuPont and General Motors, the Liberty League crusaded to preserve the free enterprise system. Its adherents believed firmly in the Social Darwinist *laissez faire* world expounded in the late nineteenth century by William Graham Sumner. Natural economic law governed the world and, left unmolested, would bring recovery as surely as it had brought the depression. They viewed the New Deal as trying to replace these economic laws with a planned socialist society.

"A Master of Both Instruments." Edwin Marcus in the *New York Times* November 18, 1934.

Many conservatives were outraged at the large number of academicians and experts used by the New Deal, the so-called "Brains Trust." The Chicago *Tribune* repeatedly printed a cartoon caricaturing a college teacher in academic gown offering ridiculous advice to people wiser than he. The Hearst and Scripps-Howard newspapers, among others, joined the outcry. The *Saturday Evening Post* shrilly declared, "it is our country and not a laboratory for a small group of professors to try out experiments." One New Deal intellectual, Tugwell, has wryly retorted that such criticisms of brains caused him to wonder by what other part of the human anatomy government should be guided. In fact the Brains Trusters differed greatly among themselves, from the orthodox Raymond Moley to the liberal Harry Hopkins. In any case they did not dominate Roosevelt for he used them as he saw fit.

The true explanation of conservative discontent of course went deeper than this. The depression had toppled the high priests of finance and industry from their exalted positions and, stunned by their loss of prestige, embittered businessmen sought a scapegoat and vented their spleen on the essentially conservative Roosevelt. The President viewed his administration as remarkably moderate in its efforts to avert national collapse and he reacted with hurt and anger to conservative attacks. He thought of himself as the savior, not the destroyer, of the capitalistic system. Roosevelt's "swing to the left" in 1935 in large part reflected a reaction to what he regarded as uncomprehending and unfair criticism.

Attacks came from the left as well. Soothsayers peddled easy panaceas to exploit social ills and grievances. In Louisiana, Senator Huey P. Long, called the "Kingfish" after a character in the popular Amos 'n Andy radio comedy act, seriously worried Roosevelt with his "share our wealth" program. FDR once referred to Long as "one of the two most dangerous men in the country," comparing him to Germany's Adolf Hitler; the other man, in his view, was General Douglas MacArthur, whom he thought an ideal leader for those citizens willing to discard democracy for strong-man rule. The seventh of nine children, Long had been born in a log cabin in the uplands of Louisiana. After education at Tulane he practiced law and entered politics as the defender of the popular interests against the entrenched railroad, oil, and utility interests that dominated Louisiana and gave it the reputation as one of the worst governed states in the union. An intelligent man despite his hillbilly attitude and his intentionally crude and offensive manners and flashy clothes, Long won the governorship in 1928, appealing to the poor "red-necked" farmers. He pushed through reforms in Louisiana and by ruthless methods built a powerful state machine. Long obtained from the legislature measures to build roads, schools, and hospitals, taxed the privileged industries, and smashed the former ruling oligarchy. Not a die-hard racist, Long conferred benefits on both poor whites and blacks through free schools and other programs. On the other hand, Long did little to raise wages or aid the unemployed or needy through welfare legislation.

After Long was elected to the U.S. Senate in 1930 he first supported Roosevelt, but he soon broke with the New Deal and tried to attract a national following of his own. He confidently predicted that he would win the White House in 1936. Aided by a fundamentalist revivalist minister, Gerald L. K. Smith, Long called for confiscating all large fortunes and redistributing the wealth. Each family should be guaranteed a minimum living wage, pensions for the elderly, and free college education for all who wanted it. By early 1935 Long claimed 27,000 Share-our-Wealth Clubs with a mailing list of 7½ million people. Meanwhile he made himself virtual dictator in Louisiana and ruled by force and intimidation, until assassinated in the corridor of the state capitol building in September, 1935 by the son of one of his opponents whom the Long machine was trying to ruin.

In California, already a mecca for the retired and the elderly, the sixty-seven year old Dr. Francis Townsend promoted a scheme to cure the depression by aiding the millions of needy oldsters. Known as the "Ham and Eggs" movement, Townsend's plan called for payment of $200 a month to each person over age sixty. Since the money would have to be spent in the month it was paid and would be financed by a 2 percent sales tax, the rapid turnover would generate vast purchasing power and restore prosperity. Although financial experts pronounced the scheme absolutely unworkable, Townsend had established 12,000 clubs by 1934 and enlisted millions of members. Meanwhile, the old socialist warrior, Upton Sinclair, had another cure for the depression. E.P.I.C., or End Poverty in California, advocated state operation of uncultivated farms and idle industry for the benefit of the jobless. Land colonies and workers' villages would produce for their own use rather than for profitable sale, and this socialist-syndicalist system would eventually spread across the nation to transform society and the economy. A strange movement known as Technocracy also emerged in California and elsewhere. Inspired by the writings of the unorthodox economist, Thorstein Veblen, its advocates called for discarding democracy and the capitalist system, and allowing the engineers to run the economy on the basis of full production where everybody "produces what he uses and uses what he produces." Father Charles Coughlin, the Roman Catholic radio priest of Detroit, proposed still another cure-all. He had turned against the New Deal in 1934 and founded his National Union for Social Justice. He preached a type of Christian fascism to his radio audience of between thirty and forty-five million listeners, flailing away at evil bankers and advocating nationalization of the banks and inflation of the currency. These groups cooperated very ineffectively in an effort to defeat FDR, forming the Union Party in 1936 and running William Lemke for the presidency.

A rash of strikes began in 1934, triggered by long standing grievances and the more favorable climate for unionization created by the Roosevelt administration. In the Twenties the American Federation of Labor, with its craft philosophy and oganization, had proved unequal to the challenge of unionizing the mass industries. Clinging to the traditional emphasis on voluntaryism and self-reliant unionism, some of the leaders of the A.F. of L. either opposed or were lukewarm at first to proposals for government support of collective bargaining, and federal unemployment insurance and old age pensions. However, Section 7(a) of the N.I.R.A. offered opportunities for smashing company unions and organizing semi-skilled industries such as steel, automobiles, and coal. The A.F. of L. wanted to recruit these workers not into one industrial union but into separate craft unions. John L. Lewis of the United Mine Workers, Sidney

Hillman of the Amalgamated Clothing Workers, David Dubinsky of the International Ladies' Garment Workers, and others in 1935 established a Committee for Industrial Organization for recruitment on an industry-wide basis. After sharp fights with older craft unions — Lewis actually exchanged blows with one craft leader at the A.F. of L. convention in 1935 — the Lewis faction split off from the A.F. of L. in 1936 and set up what became the Congress of Industrial Organizations. Using illegal sit-down strikes, workers unionized General Motors in 1937 and compelled the other automotive manufacturers to follow suit. A threatened strike brought U.S. Steel, most militantly anti-union of the mass industries, to terms. The lesser companies, known as "Little Steel," defeated unionization in a bitter strike in 1937. However, other industries fell into line and by 1939 the C.I.O. had become a major rival to the older A.F. of L. Union membership in general had grown prodigiously under the New Deal, numbering almost nine million by 1938 as compared to only three million in 1933.

"Swing to the Left"

Responding to pressures from the left and attacks from the right, Roosevelt's annual message to Congress in January, 1935 outlined a bold new approach. "In spite of our efforts and in spite of our talk," Roosevelt declared, "we have not weeded out the overpriviliged and we have not effectively lifted up the underprivileged." He called for measures to provide adequate housing, social security, and a decent living standard for all. Flaying obstructionism by big business and the wealthy, the President also advocated a new and more equitable tax policy to shift the burden of public expenditures to those better able to bear it. Two days later, Roosevelt asked Congress for billions of dollars for a massive assault on unemployment, to be waged primarily by Hopkins' W.P.A.

During the summer of 1935 Roosevelt cracked the whip over Congress and launched the Second New Deal. Advisers, such as Felix Frankfurter and Supreme Court Justice Louis Brandeis, argued that cooperation with big business had failed and that an all-out effort was necessary. A second Hundred Days ensued. The Wagner Labor Relations Act, accepted by Roosevelt as a replacement of Section 7(a) of the N.I.R.A., reaffirmed the right of labor to organize and bargain collectively with employers. Congress approved creation of a National Labor Relations Board to outlaw unfair labor practices and to conduct elections in industry to certify union bargaining agencies. The N.L.R.B. understandably enraged business leaders. This measure was supplemented in 1938 by the Fair Labor Standards Act banning child labor under sixteen and fixing a national minimum wage, at first at forty cents an hour, a maximum forty hour work week, and time and a half for overtime work. Although its terms were to go into effect over a period of years and a minimum wage of $16 per week was obviously inadequate, many businessmen and other employers, especially southerners in the low-wage South, roundly denounced the measure. Other measures launched slum clearance and public housing projects and strengthened the T.V.A. A furious battle was waged over the Utility Holding Company Act. Drafted by New Dealers Thomas C. Corcoran and Benjamin V. Cohen, the bill provided for federal regulation and coordination of utility companies to obtain greater efficiency, and contained a highly controversial "death sentence" clause allowing the Securities and Exchange Commission to dissolve holding companies that could not demonstrate that they contributed to the efficiency of the actual operating firms they controlled. The utility companies fought back, led by Wendell L. Wilkie of Commonwealth and Southern, flooding Congress with lobbyists and letters of protest. Congress finally passed a so-called compromise measure that was still very tough: the government would have to defend dissolution orders to utility holding companies.

Two other measures, the income tax and social security, aroused business and conservative hostility. Roosevelt told Congress and the nation that past tax laws had "done little to prevent an unjust concentration of wealth and economic power," and a new approach was needed that would promote "a wider distribution of wealth." The resultant Wealth Tax Act of 1935 increased the graduated income tax on the upper brackets to a maximum of 75 percent, and imposed higher inheritance, gift, and corporate income levies. Though denounced as a socialistic measure to redistribute wealth, the tax hike was rather moderate by later standards; in any case such taxes have failed to reduce significantly the share of wealth received by the upper-income groups. Studies in the 1970's reveal that while the overall living standard has advanced greatly since the depression, wealth remains concentrated in a few hands. In 1922 the top 2 percent of all families held 33 percent of the nation's private wealth, versus 32 percent in 1958; the top tenth of income recipients got around a third of the total income in 1910, versus 30 percent in 1960.

The Social Security Act of 1935 dealt with a problem that was of growing public concern. In 1861 only one of forty Americans was sixty-five years or over, but by 1940 the number had increased to one out of every fifteen and was mounting. This increase reflected a declining birth rate, the drastic slowing of immigration, and improved medical care. Most major industrial countries in Europe had recognized the problem long before and had adopted compulsory old-age insurance programs. The elderly particularly suffered from the depression, as they exhausted savings and private insurance and could not find employment. Yet conservatives denounced any government plan for aiding these unfortunates as socialistic and destructive of self-reliance. Introduced in Congress by Senator Wagner of New York, the Social Security Act provided old age insurance for those aged sixty-five and over, to be financed by taxes on wages and payrolls. Supporters added a system of federal-state unemployment compensation, plus aid to dependent mothers and children and the physically handicapped. Although the act had defects, especially in failing to provide for the elderly indigent already retired, it represented a notable landmark in catching up with the social problems of the twentieth century. As Roosevelt remarked at its formal signing, the Social Security Act did not remove all the dangers and risks of life, but it gave "some measure of protection to the average citizen."

The New Deal at High Tide

Ignoring Al Smith's disgruntled plea to pick "some genuine Democrat," the Democratic convention in 1936 renominated President Roosevelt by acclamation. The platform, which reflected the New Deal's turn against big business, pledged a vigorous enforcement of the anti-trust laws. The Republicans chose Governor Alfred M. Landon of Kansas; Frank Knox, owner and editor of the Chicago *Daily News* and a strong opponent of the New Deal, received second place on the ticket. The Republican platform realistically conceded many of the New Deal reforms, merely promising to administer them more efficiently and economically. The colorless Landon, often called a Kansas Coolidge, had moderately liberal views but he was embarrassed by support of the conservative Liberty League. Al Smith deserted the Democratic party to support Landon, calling the New Deal a "dismal, dull, dark, and dreary failure." Other dissident Democrats, among them Bainbridge Colby and John W. Davis, declared for Landon. To his great distress, Landon also found himself upstaged in the closing weeks of the campaign by Hoover's unwonted and increasingly bitter denunciations of the New Deal. Meanwhile the anti-New Deal Hearst newspapers printed a jingle,

> The Red New Deal with a Soviet Seal
> Endorsed by a Moscow Hand.
> The strange result of an alien cult
> In a liberty-loving land.

Hearst urged voters to choose Landon since the communists had denounced the Republican nominee. As for Roosevelt, Hearst stated: "Naturally the Communists flock to him. 'Every bird knows its own nest.' "

FDR waged a vigorous campaign. In his acceptance speech, he excoriated what he described as the "economic royalists," those special interests that sought to preserve their privileges and to block reform and regulation. In moving phrases he proclaimed that "This generation of Americans has a rendezvous with destiny." It was good politics, even though critics accused him of stirring up class hatreds. In subsequent speeches he emphasized the anti-big business orientation of the Second New Deal and the need to increase individual opportunity and freedom. With an efficient political organization directed by Postmaster General Farley, Roosevelt attracted the support of organized labor, farmers, the reliefers, and small businessmen. Most newspaper owners and editors opposed FDR but working reporters overwhelmingly favored him. Attesting to his successful undercutting of the radicals, the Union Party of Lemke ran poorly, polling only 882,479 votes instead of the 10 million or more predicted by Father Coughlin; the Socialist vote declined to less than 200,000, and the Communists fell to a low of 80,159 out of 44 million votes cast.

The black population outside the South had increased rapidly since World War I and comprised an important element in the urban vote. Traditionally Republican since the Civil War, even as late as 1932, northern Negroes voted Democratic in 1936 by heavy margins. The New Deal had won their support not only by non-discriminatory relief measures but also by appointing some blacks to political office. Mrs. Roosevelt was known to sympathize with blacks and FDR often consulted black leaders. No doubt the New Deal gave racial equality only token support, but it seemed a clear improvement over the past. Roosevelt thus carried by huge majorities the larger cities and eastern industrial states.

The final tally in 1936 revealed that Roosevelt had polled 27,751,597 million votes to Landon's 16,679,583 million, or 60.4 percent of the popular vote. FDR carried every state except Maine and Vermont. As Roosevelt quipped about his tidal wave triumph, it had been a baptism by total immersion in which the other fellow nearly drowned. The Democratic party had become the new majority party, exploiting an urban political revolution through its appeal to the city masses. Yet ironically 1936 marked the high water of the domestic New Deal, for Roosevelt subsequently encountered increasing resistance in his efforts to extend reform.

Defeat: The Court Packing Plan

The federal judiciary during Roosevelt's first term remained heavily Republican and conservative in tone. Only an estimated 28 percent of the 266 federal judges were Democrats. The Supreme Court contained four very conservative justices, George Sutherland, Willis Van Devanter, James C. McReynolds, and Pierce Butler; three more liberal justices, Harlan F. Stone, Louis Brandeis, and Benjamin N. Cardozo; while Justice Owen J. Roberts and Chief Justice Hughes apparently sought to preserve a balance between the two groups. The average age of the Justices was nearly seventy-two.

The federal judiciary at all levels seemed to be mounting an attack upon New Deal legislation, issuing 1600 injunctions against the government in 1935-36 alone. The administration watched anxiously as some of these cases moved up to the Supreme Court. A series of blows fell quickly as the Court ruled adversely on the "hot oil" case (a law banning interstate shipment of oil produced in violation of state quotas) and the Railroad Retirement Act. Then in May, 1935 the Court unanimously struck down the N.R.A. in the Schechter Poultry or "sick chicken" case. The Court majority ruled that the selling of poultry did not come under the interstate commerce powers of the federal government and that Congress unconstitutionally had delegated legislative powers to the executive. The Court invalidated the A.A.A. in 1936 by a vote of six to three, on the grounds that the processing tax constituted an improper delegation of legislative functions and an invasion of the reserved powers of the states. The justices also struck down the Guffey-Snyder Bituminous Coal Act in a five to four decision, and restricted the powers of the Securities and Exchange Commission in another decision. The Court, in a case directly affecting presidential powers, ruled that the chief executive could not remove members of such quasi-judicial bodies as the Federal Trade Commission. Clearly many of these decisions reflected not so much the requirements of the Constitution as the personal preferences and prejudices of the Justices. The deeply disappointed Roosevelt exclaimed to reporters, "We have been relegated to the horse-and-buggy definition" of the Constitution.

Apparently Roosevelt had decided to attack the Supreme Court even prior to his reelection in 1936. Meanwhile he sought to repair much of the damage done by the adverse decisions by obtaining stop-gap legislation from Congress. As noted earlier, the Wagner Act in 1935 saved the labor provision of the N.R.A. The Soil Conservation and Domestic Allotment Act of 1936 managed to curtail agricultural production through voluntary and compensated withdrawal of acreage for conservation purposes. In 1938 Congress enacted the second A.A.A. to limit production and achieve parity prices for crops via subsidies on a voluntary basis. Yet the administration feared that the Court might also strike down these and other measures. In his annual message in January, 1937, Roosevelt called for legislation to promote opportunity for all citizens as "the deeper purpose of democratic government." Again, in his second inaugural address, the President spoke of "one-third of a Nation ill-housed, ill-clad, ill-nourished," and declared that the goal of his second administration would be to eradicate these ills.

But would the Supreme Court abide by the election returns and accept new sweeping social measures? Or would these too be doomed by hidebound Justices? To forestall that possibility, Roosevelt in early 1937 suddenly sprang his "court packing" plan on a stunned Congress and nation. He believed that he had a popular mandate to achieve additional reform and he resolved not to let the "Nine Old Men" on the Court frustrate the national will. To do otherwise, he feared, would entail the risk that society might break down and collapse into anarchy or fascist reaction.

Roosevelt had committed a serious political blunder, probably the greatest of his career. He failed to consult congressional leaders prior to his decision and he underestimated the popular reverence for the Supreme Court as a body above politics. Instead of openly advocating a constitutional amendment to restrict the Court's powers, he presented Congress a scheme that claimed to be a reform to improve the efficiency of the judiciary. For each Supreme Court Justice reaching the age of seventy and not retiring, a new Justice could be appointed up to a total membership of fifteen; additional judges would also be appointed on the lower levels of the judiciary, and other measures would be adopted to quicken the processes of adjudication.

Chief executives since Jefferson's day had often fumed about the obstructionist role of the Supreme Court and had contemplated attempts to curb its review power. Yet conservatives condemned Roosevelt's plan as destroying the constitutional balance of the national government, bar associations denounced it, and so did a number of liberal supporters of the New Deal such as Senator Burton K. Wheeler of Montana. Voluntary organizations to "save the Constitution" sprang up across the nation and several state legislatures adopted resolutions against what Hoover labeled a court-packing scheme.

Too late to repair the damage, Roosevelt in a fireside talk tried frankly to explain his case to the people. His proposal, he declared, sought to "save the Constitution from the Court and the Court from itself." He unwisely refused compromises such as requiring a seven to two majority by the Court to invalidate federal laws or enlarging the Court by the addition of two more justices. Roosevelt was supremely confident after his reelection and determined to curtail the power of the Court. His case received a blow when Chief Justice Charles Evans Hughes publicly denied that the Court lagged in its work. Finally the Court undercut the President by reversing its recent trend. (Apparently the change was not a response to Roosevelt's attacks and had begun to take place before he announced the court scheme.) By a vote of five to four the high court upheld the Wagner Act in the Jones and Laughlin Steel case and thereby seemed to presage acceptance of other important New Deal laws. Justice Van Devanter also resigned under a new law permitting retirement at age seventy with full salary and Roosevelt had his first opportunity to fill a vacancy. Subsequently the Court also validated the Social Security Act. Yet Roosevelt persisted in the fight, despite an adverse majority report by the Senate Judiciary Committee. Finally, after his loyal floor leader, Senator Joseph T. Robinson of Arkansas, died of apparent overstrain, FDR had no choice but to retreat. Too many important members of his own party in Congress, many conservative southern Democrats but also a number of moderates and liberals, had opposed his plan. Although he took some comfort in the Court's more liberal turn – he had lost the battle but won the war, many said – Roosevelt had experienced his first serious defeat and blow to his myth of political invincibility that opened deep rifts within his own party. Yet, the Court fight at least speeded up the legitimatizing of the New Deal's vast expansion of federal powers and the changed role of government.

The Conservative Reaction

A conservative coalition of Republican and southern Democratic congressmen, largely from rural areas, began to take shape. Members of this loose bloc shared a preference for balanced budgets and states' rights and looked with suspicion on welfare programs and the rise of organized labor. Southern white conservatives especially disliked the equalitarian effect of New Deal legislation on the Negro in the South and feared for the southern way of life. Moreover, as Jeffersonian Democrats they disliked the burgeoning bureaucracy of the New Deal and its increasing orientation toward the urban masses after the 1936 elections. Many southern Democratic congressmen had given the New Deal only reluctant support in the past – on occasion not even that – and the Court fight emboldened them to move into more open opposition (Roosevelt's appointment of the liberal Senator Hugo Black of Alabama to Van Devanter's place added to their displeasure). The conservative coalition drew support from the public reaction against sit-down strikes and labor unrest during 1937, widely blamed on New Deal radicalism and "coddling" of the unions. Despite the new bloc's informality and lack of cohesion on all issues, it functioned well enough by 1939 to prevent further significant gains in New Deal legislation.

1937 proved a difficult year for FDR. Not only did he experience the Court defeat but Congress refused to endorse his plan for a sweeping reorganization of the executive branch. Roosevelt had proposed combining or subordinating a number of semi-independent executive agencies, the creation of two new cabinet-level departments, for Social Welfare and Public Works, and provisions for six presidential administrative assistants. Many thoughtful observers, including a number of political scientists, had long advocated such reforms. Hoover himself had favored such a reorganization when president. Yet conservatively inclined Republicans and southern Democrats resisted strenuously and charged presidential dictatorial ambitions. They blocked the measure in 1937 and 1938, although it finally obtained approval in 1939 in a much weakened version. Even so, the act marked a major advance in managing a modern complex governmental machine.

A sharp economic slump in 1937 added to Roosevelt's difficulties. The President, influenced by his fiscally more conservative advisers led by Henry Morgenthau, Jr., the Secretary of the Treasury, and by his own inclinations, had reduced deficit spending and slashed W.P.A. payrolls in 1936 in the mistaken belief that prosperity had returned. A recession promptly set in during the summer of 1937, causing farm prices to decline and unemployment to rise from about five to over nine and half million. Obviously the economy still required heavy federal spending and Roosevelt by 1938 felt compelled to override conservative opposition to secure approval for increased outlays by the W.P.A. New Deal measures had not cured the depression but only alleviated it. Probably only really massive federal expenditures, as urged by Keynes and others, would have worked, but Roosevelt was too orthodox to accept that solution.

Despite huge Democratic majorities in Congress, Roosevelt had encountered serious resistance to the program he had presented to Congress in 1937. Resolving to remould his party into a more liberal movement, he attempted in the 1938 primaries to purge certain conservative Democratic senators and representatives, mostly southerners such as Senators Walter George of Georgia and "Cotton Ed" Smith of South Carolina. The effort backfired as most of them survived; the new Congress, with a larger Republican minority, thus became even more conservative. The major parties remained as coalitions of divergent interests without clear philosophical and ideological differences. The New Deal virtually came to an end. After 1938 the emphasis shifted to digesting gains already made and to questions of foreign policy that seemed more imperative as the world plunged toward another global conflict.

The New Deal in Retrospect

Probably no chief executive since the days of Andrew Jackson aroused as much impassioned controversy as Franklin D. Roosevelt and his New Deal. Criticism varied from shrilly intemperate charges of dictatorship, socialism, or communism, to more reasonably expressed disapproval of centralization of federal authority at the expense of the states, impairment of self-reliance and initiative through welfare programs, and wasteful deficit spending and a huge public debt. Roosevelt personally became the butt of many ribald and cruel jokes about his health and family life. Some apoplectic critics could only refer to him as "that man." His wife Eleanor especially drew much abuse because of her clearly expressed sympathy for the lowly and oppressed of all races and her endorsement of liberal causes.

Of course Roosevelt also aroused deep affection and dedicated support, as the millions of votes he polled amply attested. Even twenty years after his death the Roosevelt name and political legacy remained powerful assets to the Democratic party. More importantly, he inaugurated profound changes in the role of government in society and the economy that have helped shape the course of subsequent American history.

Was the New Deal revolutionary or evolutionary? or essentially conservative? Oceans of ink have been used in attempts to answer these questions. Most historians today emphasize the continuity of the New Deal with the past. In their desperate battle against the depression, Roosevelt and his advisers drew freely from the ideas and programs of earlier years. The Populist and Progressive eras supplied a number of specific proposals for regulating the economy, aiding the farmer, developing natural resources, and protecting the worker and less fortunate members of society. The experiences of mobilization in World War I provided another fruitful source of ideas and programs. Even the prosperous years of the Twenties and the Hoover administration offered precedents for New Deal experiments and measures. In fact it is difficult to think of a single New Deal program that in some way had not been suggested or tried in the past. In this sense Roosevelt and his administration were not highly original. Most of his reforms flowed from existing circumstances and reflected public demands to cope with the deep social needs created or emphasized by the Great Depression. Or to express it differently, the New Deal represented the culmination of a half-century of historical change marking the rise of an organizational type of capitalism and the development of the regulatory interventionist state.

Roosevelt's greatest personal contributions probably lay in his dynamic personality and optimism, his sympathy with the underprivileged and distressed, and his willingness to experiment and use more fully the powers of government in long overdue efforts at relief and reform. Although a good politician, he was not the master politician often assumed as his defeats in the Court fight and his failure to remould the Democratic party in the 1938 congressional elections revealed. His administrative tactics also left much to be desired, characterized by dependence on conflicting conservative and liberal advisers and his reluctance to grant clear-cut delegations of power and responsibility. New Deal agencies overlapped one another in a crazy-quilt jungle of conflicting authority and personal rivalries. Moreover, all the New Deal pump-priming spending and relief measures failed to overcome the depression. In 1939, on the eve of World War II, millions of people were still unemployed despite the expenditure of billions of dollars through the W.P.A. and similar agencies. Roosevelt could never abandon his hope of returning to a balanced budget and could not bring himself to spend on the really gigantic scale necessary to eradicate the depression – that chance came with the national emergency created by the Second World War. Above all, he sought to preserve a modified capitalist structure, not to destroy it. And clearly, as a practical politician he aimed his programs primarily to benefit the great middle class. Thus although the New Deal helped a vast number of citizens, millions of blacks, slum dwellers, rural agricultural workers, and unemployed remained at the bottom of the economic ladder.

Yet even though the New Deal fell short of transforming American society, it still marked a bold new phase in our history. Its reforms when judged against the past remain impressive and enduring. The welfare-interventionist state had come to stay in America. New Deal reforms became a permanent part of the fabric of American life. In subsequent years, political debate raged not about whether gains such as Social Security, unemployment compensation, aid to agriculture, public power and conservation projects, and regulation of the economy should be kept, but about how to improve and better administer them. Thus the Republican candidate in 1952, Dwight D. Eisenhower, declared that "Never again shall we allow a depression in the United States." and he promised to mobilize the "full power" of government if necessary to that end. The New Deal marked an irreversible turning point in American life.

8

Prologue to the

Second World War

THE GREAT DEPRESSION not only represented a turning point in the domestic history of the United States, it also marked a watershed in its foreign relations. Threats to the nation's peace and security caused the Hoover administration to begin to move away from the less demanding neo-isolationist policies of the Twenties, and Roosevelt's New Deal completed the return to the collective security approach of the Wilson era.

The year 1931 marks the opening of a decade of economic misery and international crises. While the United States slid deeper into the slough of the Great Depression, the blight spread abroad, inflicting paralysis and despair on Europe and Asia. Only the rigidly controlled state economy of the Soviet Union remained relatively immune to the deadly disease that cursed the capitalist world. The depression not only inflicted incalculable loss and misery on millions of people across the globe, it wrecked the postwar system established at Versailles and Washington.

The collapse of the economic system seemed to tip the balance almost everywhere toward irrationalism, violence, and war. In Germany the frail democracy of the Weimar Republic crumbled as Adolf Hitler grasped dictatorial power; Italy already had succumbed to the posturing and jut-chinned Fascist dictator, Benito Mussolini; totalitarian parties on the left and right proliferated throughout Europe, even in the old democracies of Britain and France; and in the Far East, right wing, super-patriotic, and militaristic groups surged to the fore with their plans for solving Japan's problems through imperialism and conquest.

The Great Depression intensified isolationist sentiment in the United States. Trying desperately to achieve domestic recovery and fearful of another series of wars in Asia and Europe, most Americans seemed more than ever determined to erect an isolationist wall around their country. The neutrality laws adopted in the mid-Thirties served notice of that determination. A strange paralysis of will seemed to afflict not only the United States but also the great European democracies. Great Britain and France almost supinely observed the rise of totalitarian dictators who openly expressed their contempt for democracy and barely troubled to hide their plans to "rectify" the Versailles settlement. Only belatedly did the western democracies, the United States most tardily of all, recognize the peril and act to meet it.

Crisis in the Far East

The Far East had seemed to promise a new era of progress and stability during the Twenties. The great powers had curbed the arms race and agreed to preserve the territorial status quo in the Pacific at the Washington Conference. In Japan, moderates held power and pursued a policy of conciliation toward China and cooperation with the western powers. Meanwhile, at home they began to curb military expenditures and undertook a number of social reforms. Even China seemed to make progress toward unity and stability. China's failure to obtain the restoration of Shantung at Paris in 1919 had ignited the May Fourth Movement, a sharp surge of nationalist sentiment, particularly among students, aimed at throwing off the unequal treaties (fixed tariff and extraterritoriality) forced upon China by the great powers in the past. Chinese intellectuals and reformers determined to transform Chinese civilization and to modernize China so that she could protect her own interests in the Far East. The American government in general looked favorably upon this nationalist movement, hoping for a unified, strong, and friendly new China able to defend itself. Sun Yat-sen, with Soviet aid, revitalized the Kuomintang or nationalist movement in the early 1920's. Chiang Kai-shek emerged as his heir, broke with the Communists in 1927, and by 1929 he had succeeded, at least outwardly, in unifying his country. Time proved, however, that his power depended too heavily upon the warlords, the wealthy merchants, and large land holders, thereby preventing social reforms that might have forestalled the eventual seizing of power by the Chinese Communists.

Chiang Kai-shek's movement disturbed Japan and thereby the Pacific treaty system. The Chinese Nationalists struggled fiercely to cast off the unequal treaties and to "redeem" the lost provinces in Manchuria. Popular boycotts repeatedly broke out against western and Japanese business interests in China. But the principal crisis came in Manchuria, a fertile and strategically important frontier area that long had been a center of rivalry between China, Russia, and Japan. Legally belonging to China, Manchuria actually constituted a sort of undeveloped frontier area between the three powers, with Japan entrenched in the south and Russia in the center and north. The Nationalists began a drive to evict the other two competitors. Chiang Kai-shek's movement first attempted to compel Soviet Russia to surrender control of the Chinese Eastern Railway in Manchuria, but his forces met a firm rebuff in 1929. Not much fighting occurred in this brief border war, as Soviet troops invaded the area and Russian aviators frightened the ill-prepared and motley Chinese forces by dropping bags of sand and rotten cabbages on them. The State Department blunderingly tried to invoke the Pact of Paris until rebuffed by a Russian government with whom it had no formal diplomatic relations.

Undaunted by the Soviet check, the Chinese Nationalists also tried to undermine Japan's position in Manchuria, built around the Japanese-owned South Manchurian Railway. The Nationalists refused to recognize the validity of past Sino-Japanese treaties relating to Manchuria and carried on anti-Japanese propaganda and boycotts against Japanese goods and merchants in China and Manchuria. Moreover, the Nationalists planned to construct a rival railroad and port to undercut the Japanese in Manchuria. Many Japanese became alarmed and feared that the Foreign Office under Baron Shidehara followed too soft a policy to protect Japan's interests. Most Japanese viewed Manchuria as strategically and economically vital to the island empire, the center of about 90 percent of Japanese foreign investments, while to the north lay the threat of Russian communist power. Above all, the Japanese feared the emergence of a strong modern nation-state in China, able to challenge Japan's interests in China and her preeminent position in the Far East.

A group of Japanese militarists and nationalist organizations – such as the Black Dragon Society, the Cherry Blossom Society, and the Blood Brotherhood – eagerly awaited an opportunity to seize control and plot a new course for their nation. These militarists and super-patriots, drawn largely from the junior officers of the army, regarded themselves as reformers who would sweep away the alien trappings of western democracy. Japan seethed with change and discontent caused by rapid industrialization and urbanization, and the consequent uprooting of rural people and weakening of older traditions. The reactionary nationalist groups saw the Army alone as capable of destroying the stranglehold of big business and the politicians, and restoring Japan to her ancient ideals and virtues as one great national family under the divine emperor. Japan's true course, they propagandized, dictated reform at home and an aggressive foreign policy to assert leadership over all East Asia. Unfortunately western blunders helped undermine the moderates in Japan. Sensitive Japanese already resented Japan's small end of the 5:5:3 naval ratio fixed by the Five Power Pact. They were affronted further by other signs of western discrimination and condescension, such as tariff barriers against Japanese goods and the American Immigration Act of 1924 that excluded Japanese and other Orientals. The world-wide economic debacle of 1931 that hit Japan along with most of the world gave the militarists their chance.

Alarmed at Chinese Nationalist plans in Manchuria, the Japanese army struck suddenly. On the night of September 18, 1931, Japanese agents rigged a small explosion on the rail lines near Mukden. Claiming Chinese provocation, Japanese troops quickly moved out of the leased areas and seized the major cities and evicted Chinese soldiers and officials. By early 1932, most of Manchuria had fallen to Japanese control and they soon proclaimed the so-called independent state of Manchukuo. Emperor Hirohito and the civilian authorities at Tokyo did not approve the attack but were powerless to halt it. The Foreign Office made apologies and promises to the western powers, only to have them nullified by new aggressions by the military.

The Japanese militarists and super-nationalists combined successful conquest with a campaign of intimidation and assassination of moderate opponents at home. Extremists assassinated the Prime Minister in 1930 in protest against the London Naval Agreement; two years later another Prime Minister and a cabinet member met a similar fate; and in 1936 assassins narrowly missed the Prime Minister but killed his brother-in-law by mistake, along with several other officials. Meanwhile Japanese patriotic pride had been greatly stimulated by the easy victory in Manchuria, where an estimated 60,000 Japanese troops with little difficulty drove back Chinese forces of about 400,000 men. Moderate Japanese thus found their position undermined by the militarists. The militarists gradually took control of the Japanese government and adopted an aggressive course aimed at hegemony in the Far East. After Manchuria, the military began to subvert northern China from the rule of Chiang Kai-shek, pulled Japan out of the League of Nations in 1933, and after failing to obtain naval parity with England and America in 1934 had the government denounce the naval arms limitations treaties.

Chiang Kai-shek at first tried to follow a conciliatory course toward Japan, despite the loss of Manchuria, and conceded her special economic privileges in North China and Inner Mongolia. Growing anti-Japanese sentiment in China, however, particularly among students, compelled the Nationalist chief to adopt a firmer policy against further Japanese encroachments. The Japanese militarists determined to strike again, ignoring the depression-paralyzed western nations and a Soviet power then being weakened by Stalin's bloody purge of communist leaders. In July, 1937, after a clash in Peiping, the "China Incident" began, an all-out undeclared war intended to reduce China to a protectorate.

The Stimson Doctrine

Henry L. Stimson, Secretary of State under President Hoover, differed rather sharply with his chief over Far Eastern policy. Hoover had not known Stimson very well and decided on him for the State Department only after three other men had declined the post. Stimson, an old follower of Theodore Roosevelt and a former governor general of the Philippines, came from a stern mold.

Confident, moralistic, and with a Roman sense of duty, he conceived of world relations as governed by strict standards of moral principles and mutual respect. He sympathized with China, but more importantly he viewed Japanese aggression as threatening the entire post-World War system upon which rested world peace. Stimson believed that firmness and a show of force would compel Japan to observe its treaty obligations. In contrast, President Hoover was a "worrier" about domestic and foreign problems. Although not a narrow isolationist by any means, he was determined to limit America's foreign commitments and to keep the nation at peace. Moreover, coping with the depression monopolized his time and energies. The two men also differed in petty but annoying ways. Hoover, an early riser and hard worker, frequently felt irritated by Stimson's more relaxed pace and shorter working hours. Stimson, over 60 years of age, suffered from a variety of infirmities that kept him away from the State Department for days, and he was fond of golf and other relaxations.

Stimson was at first inclined to trust the Japanese civilian leaders to restrain the military. Like many observers, he overestimated the strength of the moderates and underestimated the determination of the army. By rebuffing a Chinese appeal to invoke the Pact of Paris in September, 1931 Stimson unwittingly encouraged continued aggression when a firmer policy might have been more effective. The Council of the League of Nations, though greatly embarrassed, also tended to rely upon the Japanese moderates to restore control and contented itself with a request for a mutual withdrawal of armed forces.

By early October, 1931, however, both Stimson and the major League powers realized that the Japanese Army was firmly in command. Carefully maneuvering in order to avoid unnecessarily weakening the Japanese moderates or permitting the League to saddle the United States with the responsibility for challenging Japan, Stimson suggested that the League Council invoke the Pact of Paris, with similar American action. When the League powers declined to act and instead suggested unilateral American measures, Stimson refused. Then the League Secretary General proposed that the League Council meet on the problem, with American participation, and Stimson with Hoover's approval agreed. He had won a diplomatic victory of sorts, though valuable time had been lost. A few days after the principal League powers reminded Japan and China that they had been signatories to the Kellogg-Briand international "kiss of peace," the United States dispatched a similar note. The Council fixed a deadline for the withdrawal of Japanese troops to their original positions, but Japan refused to comply. Subsequently the League's Lytton Commission investigated the Manchurian clash and in its report in 1933 fixed primary responsibility upon Japan, while acknowledging Chinese provocation. Japan thereupon denounced the report and walked out of the League.

Hoover reacted with alarm when possible sanctions against Japan came up for discussion. He would not cooperate with measures that might be adopted by the League. Yet the American attitude was not alone to blame for the failure to follow up condemnation of Japanese aggression. Neither Great Britain nor France felt greatly distressed by Japan's actions, especially as long as they occurred in areas remote from their own interests in the Far East. In fact, important elements in both countries tended to welcome Japanese rebukes to the disorderly Chinese government with its anti-foreign agitation and boycotts, and looked upon Japan as a salutary check to the power and designs of communist Russia in Asia. Some conservatives in England even talked of the need to revive the old Anglo-Japanese alliance, in preference to cooperation with the United States.

The President agreed with Stimson that the United States must formally condemn the Manchurian conquest. In identical notes to Japan and China on January 7, 1932 the American government refused to recognize any changes in China brought about by force and in violation of the Open Door Policy or the Pact of Paris. The British and French governments at the time failed to adhere to this "Stimson Doctrine," though they did so subsequently under the prodding of the smaller League powers. After the bloody "rape of Shanghai," when Japanese forces brutally bombed and attacked Shanghai early in 1932 in retaliation against anti-Japanese boycotts and riots, Stimson asked for British cooperation in a display of naval force and the invocation of the Nine Power Pact. Some authorities feel that decisive collective action at this point might have forced Japan to halt. Britain, however, distracted by the depression, left the responsibility primarily to the United States. Stimson interpreted the cautious response of the British Foreign Secretary, Sir John Simon, as a refusal and decided to act alone.

Stimson resorted to a public letter to Senator Borah of the Senate Foreign Relations Committee. In this letter, dated February 23, 1932, he reaffirmed the principles of the Open Door and invited other powers to adopt the non-recognition policy. He also intimated that because the Five Power Pact limiting naval armaments was closely linked to the Nine Power Pact the United States might regard the violation of one as nullifying the other. His threat of a resumption of the naval arms race had some effect, particularly when the Senate committee on naval affairs recommended passage of a $1 billion construction bill. Tokyo decided on a retreat and arranged a truce in Shanghai. Yet though disturbed, Japan's leaders soon perceived that an isolationist America, preoccupied with the depression, would not follow words with deeds.

At this point Stimson wanted to threaten Japan with still firmer action but he could not persuade President Hoover. Stanley K. Hornbeck of the State Department's Far Eastern Division argued that vigorous measures would avert an eventual war with Japan. Japan seemed particularly vulnerable to economic pressures, because of its large export trade with the United States and its heavy dependence on America for oil, scrap iron and steel, and other commodities vital to modern industry. Although Stimson had doubts about actually embargoing trade, he wanted at least to brandish that economic weapon. However, William

"Japanese Production of Notes." Berryman in the *Washington Evening Star.*

R. Castle, the Undersecretary of State, agreed with President Hoover that economic coercion or threats would probably lead to war rather than peace. Castle was not necessarily pro-Japanese; he simply saw Japanese predominance in the Far East as inevitable and possibly even beneficial in terms of stability.

The President felt so apprehensive that Stimson had to dissuade him from publicly undercutting his policy of pressure on Japan. The Secretary hoped that uncertainty in Tokyo about America's next step would have a restraining influence. Yet while he was absent in Europe on an official trip, Castle with Hoover's approval made two speeches revealing that the United States opposed trade boycotts and would not go beyond a moral rebuke of aggression. Upon his return to Washington, the furious Stimson tried to repair the damage and managed to persuade the President to leave the Pacific fleet at Pearl Harbor for the 1933 naval war games. He hoped thereby to continue pressure on the Tokyo authorities, but apparently all that he accomplished was to convince more Japanese that the United States was their chief opponent. Unquestionably, Hoover's position against forceful measures or even threats reflected majority sentiment in America. Most citizens approved non-recognition and sympathized with the Chinese victims of aggression, but they also wanted to avoid war with

Japan or any other great power bent on an expansionist course.

The United States obviously lacked sufficient naval power and popular will to restrain Japan. Moreover, its moral gestures affronted one of its best customers — American trade with China, despite the old illusion of a vast potential market, was very small while Japan was the third largest purchaser of American exports. American policy toward Japan's aggression in Manchuria reflected a high degree of moralistic outrage and traditional missionary-nourished sympathy with China. There was a realistic element also — Stimson feared that Japan had undermined the postwar settlement and if unchecked would stimulate aggression elsewhere. Yet if the United States felt it must condemn Japanese aggression, it should have been prepared to follow words with action. Its moral rebukes merely enraged the militarists and presented them with additional ammunition to persuade their people of American enmity, while leaving them free to pursue their conquests. Many Japanese regarded western condemnation as hypocritical at best. In the words of Yosuke Matsuoka, later Japan's foreign minister, "The Western Powers taught Japan the game of poker but after acquiring most of the chips they pronounced the game immoral and took up contract bridge."

Early New Deal Foreign Policy: Drift and Inconsistency

Roosevelt's early foreign policy has aroused much debate. Did he adhere essentially to the neo-isolationist course of his Republican predecessors, avoiding binding political commitments abroad? Or did he recognize American interests in a stable world and seek cooperation with other states to curb aggression and war? Roosevelt took a great interest in international affairs, as his private correspondence amply reveals, reflecting his education and his earlier service in the Wilson administration. But in practice, at least through 1936, he followed a course not greatly different from that of Hoover. Why? In part because domestic issues of recovery and reform absorbed most of his energies. Furthermore, these were years of mounting withdrawal sentiment in America. A practical politician, Roosevelt well realized the need for caution in foreign affairs in order to obtain the support of powerful liberal isolationists in Congress for his domestic legislation. He once remarked, "It's a terrible thing to look over your shoulder when you are trying to lead — and to find no one there." But equally important, despite his internationalist or Wilsonian orientation, FDR could not be completely impervious to the isolationist currents of his day — to some degree he too shared isolationist views and emotions. Consequently, FDR's first administration revealed drift and inconsistency, with isolationist and internationalist policies incongruously intermixed.

Cordell Hull, 61 years old when he took office, served longer than any other Secretary of State — 11 years and 9 months before he resigned at the end of 1944. A Tennessee politician and dedicated Wilsonian, Hull viewed world affairs from a Wilsonian perspective of idealistic and moral principles. He had a rather simple panacea for world troubles: freer trade, a revival of morality, and the application of international law. Hull's absorbing interest was to remove or reduce barriers to international trade. In other areas he lacked specific solutions and was inclined to deliver moral lectures to erring foreign governments. Hull indeed resembled the great leader he so revered — like Wilson, he had a pronounced penchant for expressing moral indignation. He made his most significant contributions to New Deal foreign policy in trade reciprocity and the Good Neighbor Policy. His naive view of power politics and his faith in moral exhortations poorly fitted him to deal with the threat of aggressions in Europe and the Far East. Hull, although never close to the President and highly suspicious of FDR's very able and sophisticated friend in the State Department, Undersecretary Sumner Welles, nevertheless played an important part in American foreign policy until Pearl Harbor. Thereafter, he found himself increasingly bypassed.

Roosevelt continued his predecessor's short-sighted course toward the League of Nations and the war debts question. During the 1932 election, FDR had conciliated William Randolph Hearst and other isolationist die-hards when he assured an audience that the present League had fallen away from Wilson's ideal and the United States had no place in it. He even failed to name an ambassador to the League, the least that many internationalists expected, and he left it up to Secretary of Labor Francis Perkins to get the United States into the International Labor Organization. After the moratorium, Hoover had shown some interest in scaling down the war debts owed to America. Roosevelt, realizing this would be highly unpopular in the United States, continued to insist upon full payment of the debts. When all the European debtors except Finland defaulted in whole or in part, he signed the 1934 Johnson Act prohibiting private or governmental loans to foreign governments in default. Subsequently in 1940 and 1941 he regretted thus tying his hands in foreign affairs.

The World Economic Conference that met in London in 1933 has frequently been cited as proof of FDR's isolationism during his first years in office. According to many historians, Roosevelt sacrificed international considerations to the needs of domestic recovery. In fact, most major powers followed narrowly nationalistic economic policies.

Roosevelt selected a strangely mixed lot for the American delegation. Hull, without a voice in the appointments, nominally led a group composed of free traders, protectionists, inflationists, planners, and hard-money men. Moreover, as an ardent advocate of lowered tariff barriers, Hull had little sympathy with the domestic planners in the N.R.A. and A.A.A. who sought to raise prices by curtailing production and restricting the entry of competitive foreign products. Senator Key Pittman, chairman of the Foreign Relations Committee of the Senate and a member of the delegation, apparently spent most of his time at the conference defending higher prices for silver and scandalizing London with his drunken sprees. Another delegate, a Texas banker, revealed ignorance of even the simplest facts of international affairs. An adviser, William C. Bullitt, became preoccupied with trying to discover hidden dictaphones in London and greatly annoyed the British with attempts to pry information from the secretary of the Prime Minister. Hull had hoped to achieve a reduction of tariffs at the conference, only to have the President decide against it for the present while the Secretary of State was enroute to London. He arrived, as he noted bitterly, with empty hands and nothing to offer but platitudes. Even the opening of the assemblage was delayed because the President was slow in approving Hull's speech — Europeans were annoyed at this discourtesy. To cap the confusion, New Dealer Raymond Moley arrived as FDR's messenger during the middle of the conference, capturing the headlines and overshadowing the enraged Hull. Little wonder that an amazed Prime Minister MacDonald asked an American observer how FDR could have chosen such a delegation.

With war debts and a permanent stabilization agreement ruled out by FDR, hopes at the conference centered on a temporary exchange arrangement. Just as an agreement had been reached, however, Roosevelt decided that it would be unwise to freeze commodity prices at their existing low level. Therefore on July 2 he sent the famous "bombshell" message vetoing even a temporary stabilization of currencies. Released on July 4 and widely hailed in America as a new Declaration of Independence from the international banking interests, Roosevelt's message expressed satisfaction that the "old fetishes" of the financiers were being supplanted by planned national currencies, and he piously rebuked the European nations for not balancing their budgets and living within their means. The hapless Hull managed to prolong the futile conference for a few more weeks before it adjourned amid a nearly universal chorus of denunciations of the United States.

Roosevelt no doubt committed a diplomatic blunder in his bombshell message, but he was not alone responsible for the debacle at London. The other major powers also maneuvered for national advantage, seeking currency rates that would favor their own commerce at the expense of others. Moreover, the powers showed little interest at the conference in tariff reductions or any other definite remedies. Roosevelt's mistakes lay in not having decided on a clear policy earlier, and in the unnecessary abruptness of his July message that allowed other governments to blame him for the failure of the conference. Yet in truth, the United States, the world's foremost economic power, had failed to show any leadership in developing a cooperative approach to international recovery. The fascist nations gleefully hailed the failure in London and drew a parallel between Roosevelt's emphasis on national solutions for recovery and their own methods. International trade after the London fiasco increasingly became a matter of bilateral governmental bartering rather than free private exchanges.

The World Disarmament Conference, convened in 1932, still limped along when FDR entered office. France demanded security before reductions, and Germany wanted equality with France. Hoover previously had attempted to make the conference a success, first by suggesting the abolition of all offensive weapons and then by proposing one-third reduction in all armaments. Roosevelt tried also, offering a package containing a pledge of non-aggression, overall arms reductions, and an American promise in case of crisis to consult with other powers; if the United States agreed on the designation of an aggressor, it would not interfere with any sanctions the League might impose. Roosevelt apparently dared not go further toward collective security. In any case, the disarmament conference ended in failure when Chancellor Adolf Hitler ordered the German delegates to walk out of the meeting and announced that Germany would withdraw from the League.

Hull finally obtained the tariff reductions that he had desired to revive international trade and promote a more peaceful world. By the Reciprocal Trades Agreement Act of 1934, regularly renewed in subsequent years, the executive could negotiate agreements with other countries, reducing existing tariff rates by as much as 50 percent. The State Department completed sixteen agreements within the first three years under the act, most of them with Latin America. By 1940, the number had increased to twenty-two. Apart from winning some good will abroad, and some quickening of trade, especially in Latin America, the Reciprocal Trade approach fell lamentably short of Hull's liberal dream. Too many other countries, especially the dictatorships, preferred protectionism or governmental bartering.

Recognition of the Soviet Union

President Roosevelt realistically decided that the time had arrived to recognize Soviet Russia. His Republican predecessors had continued Wilson's policy of non-recognition, reflecting moral disapproval of communist ideology, methods of government, and the Soviet's repudiation of foreign debts. While most Americans approved non-recognition, a number of liberals always had been inclined toward tolerance, or even endorsement, of the Soviet system as an experiment for the improvement of mankind. Several developments gradually softened opposition to recognition in America. Many Americans mistakenly viewed Lenin's New Economic Policy as indicating an abandonment of socialism and a return to the free enterprise system in Russia. After Lenin's death in 1924, Americans observed with some pleasure that he was replaced by an obscure Joseph Stalin instead of that well-known and feared advocate of world revolution, Leon Trotsky. Moreover, many American businessmen subscribed to the illusion that recognition would bring increased trade with Russia, especially after most European countries recognized the former outcast and renewed their economic relations. The Great Depression heightened the lure of trade, which

Soviet authorities cleverly exploited to facilitate diplomatic recognition. Moscow initially sought recognition primarily for reasons of prestige. The growth of the fascist threat in Europe and Japanese expansion in the Far East also made recognition attractive for the security it might provide.

By 1933 a number of large American firms, such as General Electric, Ford, and International Harvester, had entered the Russian market. In 1930 the United States briefly surpassed all competitors in exports to Soviet Russia. Stalin's first Five Year Plan, calling for increased mechanization of industry and agriculture, seemed to promise vast new opportunities for American exporters. They felt acute disappointment, therefore, when the volume subsequently fell off and Germany replaced the United States as Russia's foremost supplier. Business spokesmen and politicians such as Senators Hiram Johnson and Borah argued that recognition would greatly facilitate the growth of American trade with the Soviets. Of course, many Americans remained opposed to recognition on moral and religious grounds. Patriotic groups such as the American Legion and the Daughters of the American Revolution, members of Protestant and Roman Catholic Churches, the A.F.L., and the chambers of commerce provided the bulk of the opposition. As long as Hoover occupied the White House, these negative viewpoints prevailed. As the El Paso *Herald* sneered at proponents of recognition on trade grounds, "A dangerous Red is any Russian who appears in America without placing an order for machinery."

FDR favored formal diplomatic relations on the realistic grounds that whatever one thought of it the Soviet regime had existed for sixteen years; moreover, a restoration of official relations hopefully would bolster the status quo in the Pacific against Japan and would strengthen non-aggressive forces in Europe. After preliminary explorations, Soviet Foreign Commissar Maxim Litvinov arrived in Washington. He made it clear that Russia preferred unconditional recognition prior to negotiations on outstanding issues, in accordance with the pattern she had followed in establishing diplomatic relations with other countries. The American authorities, however, insisted on negotiations first. With Roosevelt taking a direct part in the conversations, recognition was completed on November 16, 1933. The arrangement established diplomatic relations, provided freedom of religious worship for Americans in Russia, and promised to halt Russian propaganda and subversion in the United States. Roosevelt and his advisers insisted upon the religious provision, primarily because the American people took such issues seriously and had long objected to Soviet Russia as a godless regime. Public opinion also required the promise that neither government would interfere "in any manner" in the internal affairs of the other, though some of the American negotiators may have taken the Soviet pledge seriously. Russia dropped its claims for compensation for damages during the American intervention in North Russia and Siberia and promised further negotiations on the question of debts. American claims totalled over $630 million, including about $187 million owed by the former provisional government in bond issues, private loans, and property confiscations. In their "gentlemen's agreement," Litvinov mentioned a possible settlement for $75 million, while Roosevelt referred to a figure of $150 million.

Most Americans approved the establishment of formal relations. Litvinov was honored at a farewell luncheon at the Waldorf-Astoria Hotel, attended by the representatives of such giant capitalistic firms as J. P. Morgan and the Pennsylvania Railroad. The President of International Business Machines even urged Americans to promote better relations in the future by refraining "from any criticism of the present form of Government adopted by Russia." Unfortunately for such enthusiasts, recognition of the Soviets proved a disappointment. Trade remained small, primarily because Russia lacked the necessary funds and private long-term credits were deemed too risky by businessmen and financiers. The hoped-for diplomatic benefits also proved illusory, the two powers failing to achieve any notable collaboration either in regard to Japan or Europe. The debt negotiations also ended in deadlock. Russia in effect refused to agree to any sum unless the United States provided double that amount in the form of long-term governmental loans or credits. Since such a settlement would merely increase Russian indebtedness to the United States, the State Department rejected it. The Soviets, needless to say, continued their propaganda and subversion in this country. When Secretary Hull protested the continuation of revolutionary activities, trumpeted at the seventh congress of the Comintern at Moscow in 1935, the Soviet government blandly disavowed the private and separate international communist apparatus that happened to be meeting on Russian soil. Litvinov reportedly had told an American communist when he made the agreement in 1933, "The letter [pledge] is a scrap of paper which will soon be forgotten." The State Department did not forget it, however, and lodged repeated protests. A growing number of Americans soon came to view recognition as a serious mistake.

The Good Neighbor

Long before the era of the New Deal, the American government had begun to cultivate better relations with Latin America. The Wilson administration and its Republican successors in the 1920's became aware of Latin American resentment of the Colossus of the North and tried to assuage it. Latin American critics cited a long list of Yankee "crimes" and blunders: the "rape of Panama"; armed interventions and military rule in the Caribbean; economic penetration and exploitation of Latin America; and the refusal of the United States to subject its actions to international restraints by joining the League of Nations. Above all, the Monroe Doctrine and its infamous Roosevelt Corollary — justifying preventive intervention in the Caribbean in the name of security — aroused hatred and fear among neighbors to the south. American businessmen, eager for new markets and investment opportunities, urged a more conciliatory course on the State Department. So did many other Americans, appalled at the often exaggerated accounts of harsh military rule by the marines in Haiti and the Dominican Republic. For these reasons, and because after 1918 the United States no longer felt insecure about the Panama Canal, the government began to abandon its benevolent imperialism.

The new era began during the last year of the Wilson administration. Secretary of State Bainbridge Colby announced America's intention to withdraw soon from Haiti and the Dominican Republic, and he made a brief but successful good will tour of South America in 1920-1921. The wooing became more ardent under his successors. The marines left the Dominican Republic in 1924, although the State Department retained financial controls until 1941. The Senate approved a treaty with Colombia in 1921 that paid her $25 million for the 1903 Panama affair, and cleared the way for eager Yanqui oil concessionaires to operate in that country. American forces decamped from Nicaragua in 1925, only to return the following year when revolutionary disturbances broke out between the Liberal faction supporting Juan B. Sacasa against the pro-American regime of Adolfo Díaz. Henry L. Stimson went to Nicaragua on a special mission in 1927 and arranged a political truce and new marine-supervised elections. The truce soon collapsed and American troops began to chase the "bandit" forces of Augusto Sandino. The marines remained until 1933 and the financial controls until 1944. The Clark Memorandum, released in 1930, disclaimed any valid connection between the hated Roosevelt Corollary and the Monroe Doctrine, although it did not repudiate interventionism on other grounds.

The Pan American movement, dating back to the first conference in 1889, drew new strength from Washington's conciliatory policies in the 1920's. Secretary of State Hughes ensured that the United States did not dominate the Fifth Pan American Conference that met at Santiago, Chile in 1923. The conference endorsed the Gondra Convention for cooling-off treaties on the Bryan model, which eight states including the United States eventually ratified. President Coolidge personally opened the Sixth Pan American Conference, held at Havana in 1928. Hughes, again heading the American delegation at this and a subsequent special conference, helped secure approval of an arbitration agreement along the lines of the Pact of Paris outlawing aggressive war.

Even relations with difficult Mexico improved in the Twenties. Article 27 of the 1917 Mexican Constitution, providing for national ownership of oil and mineral deposits, had caused sharp controversy between Washington and Mexico City. President Carranza threatened to apply these provisions retroactively to American holdings acquired before 1917. Moreover, the Carranza regime's anticlerical policies aroused much ill will among Roman Catholics in the United States. After Carranza's fall, Hughes negotiated the Bucareli settlement with his successor, Álvaro Obregón, in 1923. Obregón agreed not to apply Article 27 retroactively and promised compensation to foreign owners for land expropriated for Mexico's agrarian reforms.

Relations quickly soured when the next Mexican regime, under Plutarco Elías Calles, returned to Carranza's position and imposed severe restrictions on foreign oil properties. Foreigners could own land only if they renounced the protection of their governments and oil leases acquired before 1917 were to be limited to 15 years. Moreover, the Calles' regime fought the hierarchy of the Catholic Church by nationalizing Church property, closing convents and religious schools, and requiring priests to register with the state. Catholics in the United States naturally felt outraged and they urged diplomatic intervention. The larger American oil companies resisted the land and oil decrees and appealed to the State Department for protection. President Coolidge and Secretary of State Frank B. Kellogg (1925-29) at first reacted sharply, implying communist Russian influence in Mexico and the supplying of Mexican arms to Nicaraguan rebels. The two quickly adopted a more conciliatory approach, however, when Calles indicated a willingness to arbitrate and a U.S. Senate resolution endorsed a peaceful solution. Coolidge sent his old friend, Dwight Morrow, on a special mission to Mexico City, instructed only to "Keep us out of war with Mexico." Morrow speedily established rapport with Calles and the Mexican people. He arranged a good will visit by humorist Will Rogers and a special flight to Mexico City by America's air idol, Charles A. Lindbergh, fresh from his solo triumph across the Atlantic. These gestures helped ease the way to a face-saving arrangement reviving the Bucareli agreement. It proved to be only a temporary solution to the oil problem, but at least it silenced talk of intervention and restored a degree of harmony to Mexican-American relations.

President Hoover made such notable contributions to Pan Americanism that some historians credit him with originating the Good Neighbor policy. While President-elect, Hoover undertook a good will tour of Latin America in 1928 during which he tried to dispel distrust and several times used the phrase "good neighbor" in his speeches. In office he refrained from further armed interventions, despite revolutionary disturbances in Panama, removed American troops from Nicaragua in 1933, and promised withdrawal in Haiti. He also abandoned the moralistic Wilson recognition policy for a return to the traditional practice of recognizing *de facto* regimes regardless of how they came to power. Yet like his predecessors, Hoover refused to pledge that armed intervention would never again be used. Treaty arrangements with several Caribbean states sanctioned the right of intervention and he and his advisers felt the United States could not be certain that it might not again be necessary to intervene to protect foreign lives and property.

President Roosevelt in his inaugural address pledged a policy of the Good Neighbor toward all the world, but the phrase soon came to be applied exclusively to his policies in Latin America. His contributions to hemispheric harmony constituted virtually a new policy and entitled his administration to primary credit as the originator of the Good Neighbor policy. The policy paid handsome dividends in promoting the security and unity of the Western Hemisphere as the danger of another world war increased. Latin Americans hailed FDR as "el gran democrata," and many viewed his New Deal as a model for reform in their own countries. His accomplishments in Latin America and his role as leader of the western world during the Second World War, the spokesman for the aspirations of the common man everywhere, earned Roosevelt near deification in Latin America. Whatever the historical debate about the authorship of the Good Neighbor Policy, Latin Americans almost unanimously gave the credit to FDR.

The Good Neighbor policy is best defined as non-interventionism and the multi-lateralization of the Monroe Doctrine from a U.S. doctrine into a hemispheric defense responsibility. Further, it supplanted the high protectionism of the Republican era with reciprocal trade agreements, and was prepared to sacrifice when necessary private American economic interests in Latin America for the national interests of the United States. Cordell Hull delighted apprehensive Latin Americans at the Seventh Pan American Conference at Montevideo in 1933 when he voted for a resolution of non-intervention by armed force in the internal affairs of any Western Hemisphere state, except as sanctioned by international law. He reiterated this pledge without any reservation at the special Pan American Conference convened at Buenos Aires in 1936 that was personally opened by President Roosevelt. Latin Americans cheered these renunciations by the United States. A Mexican delegate at the Montevideo conference expressed the feelings of many when he exclaimed, "I wish to submit my profound conviction that there is in the White House an admirable, noble, and good man – a courageous man who knows the errors of the past but who feels that the errors really belong to the past."

In the interval between these two conferences, the marines left Haiti as Hoover had promised and in 1934 the State Department agreed to abrogate the so-called Platt Amendment with Cuba, a treaty that had given the United States the right to intervene in the island. The latter action came only after the United States twice perilously neared armed intervention during the overthrow of the Gerardo Machado dictatorship and its successor. Sumner Welles, American Ambassador to Cuba, had encouraged Machado's fall but he was greatly distressed when the next regime also was toppled and threatened armed intervention. Rejecting Welles' recommendation, an alarmed FDR and Hull perceived the danger that diplomatic interference might culminate in armed intervention. These experiences made Roosevelt willing to renounce forceful measures unconditionally.

Alarmed at the threat of war in Europe and by fascist activities in Latin America, the United States sought to multilateralize the Monroe Doctrine from a U.S. unilateral policy into a collective defense system for the Western Hemisphere. Argentina, traditionally a rival of the United States for leadership in the Western Hemisphere and a country increasingly under strong fascist influences itself, repeatedly blocked Washington's proposals for a binding commitment for mutual measures to repel outside aggression. Hull finally managed to obtain a loose declaration at the Eighth Pan American Conference held at Lima in 1938, for consultation and cooperation against subversion or external threats to the peace of the hemisphere. Canada, a fully self-governing dominion within the British Commonwealth, remained apart from the Pan American movement in order to preserve its nationality and its ties to England. In effect, however, Roosevelt brought Canada under the scope of the inter-American system when at Kingston, Ontario, in 1938 he declared that the United States could not see Canada threatened by conquest. After the outbreak of the Second World War, Canada and the United States concluded joint defensive arrangements. The United States thus prepared the way for closer collaboration during World War II and the creation of the Organization of American States after the war.

The Roosevelt administration revealed during these years that while it continued to be concerned with the legitimate economic interests of American citizens in Latin America, it would no longer act as a bond collector for Wall Street. In fact, when necessary, the administration prepared to sacrifice substantial private interests for the sake of better political relations with Latin America. When Bolivia expropriated Standard Oil Company holdings and Venezuela demanded increased royalties from American oil companies operating in that country, the State Department refrained from threats or retaliation and sought to arrange equitable settlements. Mexico proved more difficult, but there too the State Department successfully applied the new tactics. President Lázaro Cárdenas, a leftist reformer, expropriated foreign-owned lands and oil properties in 1938. Although an exasperated Hull inclined toward retaliation, Roosevelt, at the inspiration of Ambassador Josephus Daniels, arranged settlements that left American investors highly displeased but avoided a serious crisis between the two countries. American oil companies had to accept compensation of $24 million for holdings they evaluated at half a billion dollars. A subsequent Import-Export Bank loan from the United States helped Cárdenas' successor pay for even these reduced compensations.

Isolationism at High Tide

Isolationist sentiment became stronger and more pervasive in America in the mid-1930's. Economic distress at home, disillusionment with the 1917-1918 Great Crusade, and war clouds abroad, generated a growing conviction that the United States should shun foreign entanglements that might lead to war. As Senator Borah said in 1934, America was not and would not be isolated economically, "But in all matters political, in all commitments of any nature or kind, which may encroach in the slightest upon the free and unembarrassed action of our people, or which circumscribe their discretion and judgment, we have been free, we have been independent, we have been isolationist." Isolationism seemed particularly strong in the mid-West, though it was not limited to that region. The midwestern reaction was a reflection of large numbers of German and Scandinavian-Americans and geographical remoteness, but above all of agrarian radicalism. Farmers looked with distrust upon eastern big business and financial firms as exploiters of rural folk. Many agrarian isolationists believed that big businessmen and financiers had brought about intervention in the recent world war, from which they had profited at the farmers' expense. Of course isolationism appealed to other than agricultural groups. It drew support as well from urban reformers and idealists and cut across political lines. Isolationism gradually became more conservative as liberals swung toward internationalism in the last years of the decade.

Anti-war novels, articles, movies, and revisionist histories reflected and contributed to the popular mood of pacifism, disillusionment, and withdrawal. Peace movements proliferated and flourished and college students, like their counterparts in the late 1960's, demonstrated against war and demanded the expulsion of R.O.T.C. units from campuses. Novels by writers such as Erich Remarque — his *All Quiet on the Western Front* became a popular movie — Ernest Hemingway, and John Dos Passos depicted war as senseless and barbaric. Muckraking books by Helmuth C. Englebrecht, *Merchants of Death*, and George Seldes, *Iron, Blood and Profits*, strengthened the popular conviction that the common man fought so that bankers and munitions manufacturers might prosper. Some historians revised the previously accepted version that Germany had been solely responsible for the war in 1914 and for American involvement in 1917. Revisionist scholars sought not merely the truth about events in 1914-1917 but to influence current public discussions on foreign policy and to prevent intervention in another war injurious to liberal reform at home. Harry Elmer Barnes pioneered in revisionist studies during the mid-1920's. Barnes had been an ardent supporter of Wilsonian internationalism until disillusioned by the postwar settlement. His *Genesis of the World War* (1926) denied German "war guilt" and condemned American neutrality as so one-sided and pro-Ally that it led to an unnecessary and unwise intervention in the war. Among others, Walter Millis, *Road to War* (1935), a Book-of-the-Month Club selection, and C. C. Tansill, *America Goes to War* (1938), also indicted the one-sided nature of American neutrality in 1914-1917. To a very large degree, the revisionists won the intellectual community to their views and helped create that climate of public opinion that explains passage of the neutrality laws in the 1930's. A Gallup poll in April, 1937, for example, revealed that 64 percent of the public regarded American intervention in the First World War as a mistake. In that same year the Emergency Peace Crusade observed the 20th anniversary of the 1917 war entry with a "no foreign war crusade," and those senators and representatives who had voted against war in 1917 were lavishly praised.

The Nye Committee Hearings were symptomatic of the popular disillusion-

"Wilhelm and Adolf." Vaughan Shoemaker, *Chicago Daily News,* **1938.**

ment. Responding to demands for federal regulation of the arms industry, from groups such as the Women's International League for Peace and Freedom, the Senate in 1934 authorized a special inquiry into the munitions industry. The administration, caught off-guard, failed to block the selection of Republican Senator Gerald P. Nye of North Dakota, a rough-hewn arch-isolationist, to head the inquiry. FDR probably could have made a greater effort to remind the nation that the country had fought for more serious reasons than profits in the recent war, but he failed to do so. Apparently Roosevelt shared popular aversion to arms profiteers and he hoped to obtain controls over them. Nye's committee, heavily over-representative of rural isolationist viewpoints but also backed by urban pacifists and anti-big business liberals, staged a public circus in uncovering the huge profits made by eastern financiers and the munitions industry during the neutrality years. The committee's sensational releases helped convince many citizens that profit-hungry capitalists had dragged the United States into the World War. As Nye summed it up, "When Americans went into the fray, they little thought that they were there and fighting to save the skins of American bankers who . . . had two billions of dollars of loans to the Allies in jeopardy." The investigation seemed almost as much anti-big business in bias as anti-war, and it reflected the widespread view that greedy bankers and industrialists encouraged international strife. Americans seem periodically susceptible to "devil theories" of history, as the "military-industrial complex" stereotype of the late 1960's again indicates.

Ironically, Roosevelt himself suggested neutrality legislation to the Nye Committee in 1935 to bar American citizens from traveling on belligerent ships. A threatened conflict between Italy and Ethiopia offered the occasion. FDR apparently hoped to avoid the risks of being involved in a future war by issues of neutral rights; American policy, freed of the burden that had plagued President Wilson, then could be based on more fundamental national interests. Roosevelt hoped that any ban against the arms trade would permit him to discriminate between aggressive and defensive nations, but he encountered a threatened filibuster by the pacifist and isolationist bloc in Congress. He accepted a substitute measure, prepared by Senators Pittman and Borah, that provided for a mandatory arms embargo. Upon a presidential proclamation of the existence of a foreign war, the sale or transportation of munitions to belligerent countries would be prohibited, and at the executive's discretion citizens could be warned not to take passage on belligerent vessels. FDR, to Hull's disappointment, signed the measure because it was due to expire in six months and he hoped at that time to obtain a more satisfactory law. Apparently he also thought that application of the 1935 Neutrality Act would hurt Italy in case of war with Ethiopia.

When Congress passed the Neutrality Act, Europe seemed once more on the threshold of a major war. As noted earlier, Fascism, a peculiar blend of idealism, romantic nationalism, conservatism, and militarism, had come to power in Italy in 1922. Led by their "Duce," Benito Mussolini, the Fascists achieved some worthwhile reforms and social stability but at the price of a totalitarian dictatorship. Mussolini in general remained pacific in foreign policy until the Great Depression and the rise of Adolf Hitler in Germany began to undermine the Versailles settlement. Hitler adeptly exploited popular resentment of the Versailles Treaty, mass unemployment and economic distress, and the weaknesses of the postwar democracy in Germany. His National Socialist or Nazi Party espoused policies similar to Italian Fascism and took power in early 1933, only a few weeks before Roosevelt's inauguration in the United States. Using violence and intimidation, Hitler fastened a brutal dictatorship on the German people. He began to rearm Germany, threatened to use force to rectify the 1919

THE AXIS IN EUROPE, 1936 ᵀᴼ SEPT. 1, 1939

settlement, and launched violently anti-Jewish persecutions within the Third Reich. The American Ambassador, William E. Dodd, warned the President and the State Department about Hitler's plans for conquest, while the anti-Semitic

Nuremberg Laws fully revealed the evil nature of the Nazi regime. A growing exodus of German Jews fled to the United States, among them the noted physicist Albert Einstein. (It should be noted, however, that the administration and Congress, owing to apathy and prejudice, failed to relax the immigration laws to permit large numbers of Jews to seek haven in America.) Yet until Mussolini's Ethiopian venture revealed the supineness of Great Britain and France, Hitler acted fairly cautiously in foreign affairs.

When Mussolini invaded Ethiopia in the fall of 1935, the League Council condemned the attack and invoked economic sanctions prohibiting loans and the export of arms and war materials to Italy. The alarmed British and French governments, however, anxious not to drive Italy into Hitler's arms, carefully left oil, vital to Mussolini's war machine, off the list of sanctions. This appeasement of dictatorship also led to a still-born attempt at compromise, the Hoare-Laval plan for giving Mussolini two-thirds of Ethiopia, but public wrath in Britain and France caused its repudiation. Meanwhile, Mussolini's legions, armed with advanced weapons and using poison gas, completed the conquest of primitive Ethiopia, the first victim to appeasement.

Roosevelt and Hull deemed it politically unwise to cooperate openly with League sanctions, but they invoked the Neutrality Law even though Mussolini had not formally declared war. Unfortunately, and contrary to the administration's expectations, this action had little effect on Italy, which did not need to import arms, while hurting Ethiopia who did. The administration then called for a moral embargo against oil shipments to Italy, urging American firms not to increase supplies to Mussolini's war machine. The administration found it difficult to enforce the moral embargo, however, and its action failed to encourage the League to adopt sterner sanctions. Britain and France thereby missed a promising opportunity to involve the American government more closely with League efforts to defend the peace. Their timidity encouraged Hitler to reoccupy and fortify the Rhineland, to restore conscription, and to launch a large naval and military aviation program in defiance of the Versailles Treaty. Conclusion of the Rome-Berlin Axis in 1936 solidified the new alignment of fascist powers against the western democracies, supplemented in the same year by German and Italian anti-Comintern pacts with Japan.

Congress approved the second Neutrality Act in February, 1936, while Mussolini digested his Ethiopian conquest. The act prohibited loans as well as sales of arms to belligerents and directed the President to extend the ban to new belligerents entering a war, an obvious warning of non-cooperation with League members that might be drawn into hostilities through sanctions against aggressors. The isolationist tenor of American sentiment and policy became even clearer when the Spanish Civil War broke out in the summer of 1936. Despite a non-intervention agreement among the major European powers, Germany and Italy actively supported the arch-conservative and fascist-tinged rebel forces of General Francisco Franco against the Spanish republican armies. Many American liberals and intellectuals sympathized deeply with Republican Spain and several thousand American volunteers fought for the Republic in the Abraham Lincoln Battalion and other units. Although the communists were active in organizing pro-Loyalist committees in America, most American sympathizers simply admired the heroic resistance of the Republicans and viewed the civil war as a crucial struggle between democracy and fascism. Conversely, a minority of American conservatives and Roman Catholic spokesmen saw Franco as a bulwark against atheism, socialism, and communism in Spain. The majority of Americans, however, tended to be apathetic or neutral about the civil war. A poll classified 12 percent of the public pro-Franco, 22 percent pro-Loyalists, and the remainder either neutral or without an opinion.

The Roosevelt administration gave full support to Anglo-French efforts to isolate the Spanish Civil War. Although normally a recognized government is permitted to import arms despite internal disturbances, Roosevelt and Hull treated the conflict virtually as one between two sovereign states. They proclaimed a moral embargo against shipment of war material to either the rebels or the legal government in Spain. Subsequently Congress formally extended the neutrality law to apply to the civil war. The Loyalists alone suffered from the Anglo-French and American attempts to isolate the conflict, for Germany and especially Italy cynically violated their non-intervention pledges to supply Franco with arms and "volunteer" troops. President Roosevelt was to contemplate raising the embargo against the Loyalists, but he desisted because of domestic opposition and the obvious hopelessness of the republican cause.

The third Neutrality Act, enacted in 1937, marked the final stage in the effort to immunize America from war. Although FDR still desired more flexible provisions to permit him to discriminate between aggressors and their victims, he was deeply involved in the court packing fight and left the responsibility primarily to Senator Pittman of Nevada, the Chairman of the Senate Committee on Foreign Relations. Pittman, not an ardent internationalist and anxious to preserve the independent role of his committee, repeatedly advised the administration to move cautiously in seeking modifications in the neutrality laws. The 1937 act renewed the ban on arms sales and loans to belligerents and prohibited travel on belligerent passenger and merchant vessels whenever the President should proclaim the existence of a foreign war. At the executive's discretion, the exportation of non-military goods to belligerents could also be prohibited during any war in the next two years unless done on a "cash and carry" basis. In a sense the new measure represented a compromise, benefitting the Axis powers in case of war with an arms embargo and yet offering the western democracies, who would control the seas, the opportunity to purchase vital raw materials for cash and to transport them away in their own ships. "Cash and carry" also reflected an agrarian bias against eastern industrialists and financiers, and a determination to keep open profitable markets for farm products in Europe.

The President found his freedom of maneuver sharply restricted by the neutrality law. Arms and loan bans would have to be applied to aggressive and peaceful states alike. Underlying this act and the earlier neutrality laws were highly debatable assumptions that no basic moral issues were involved in the struggles taking place abroad, no fundamental American national interests were at stake, and that the nation could be secure in its hemisphere regardless of external developments. For the sake of isolation and peace, Congress had abandoned the nation's traditional policy of defending neutral trading rights on the high seas. As several commentators quipped, the neutrality acts appeared to be an attempt by Congress to legislate the United States *post facto* out of World War I. The whole episode seemed to reveal not that people do not learn from history but that too often they learn the wrong lessons.

Roosevelt and Collective Security

Events moved inexorably toward a second world war. In July, 1937, in the "China Incident," Japan launched a campaign to bend China to her will, an effort that bogged down her armies in China, drenched the country in blood, and eventually culminated in war with the United States. In March, 1938 Hitler entered Vienna and annexed Austria to the Third Reich, in violation of the Versailles Treaty. Flushed with easy triumphs, the Fuehrer next turned his attention to the Sudeten Germans living in Czechoslovakia and threatened war if these people were not returned to the Reich. The British and French governments lacked the will to defend the Versailles settlement and the Italo-Ethiopian War had discredited the League. British Prime Minister Neville Chamberlain, under the delusion that he was dealing with rational men, still hoped to appease the dictators. Politicians in England and France, unnerved by memories of the staggering casualties of World War I and apologetic for the "harsh" Versailles Treaty, deluded themselves that concessions to the "legitimate" grievances of Germany would appease the Nazis and avert a new war. Chamberlain and the French Premier, Edouard Daladier, journeyed to Munich in the fall of 1938 and bought "peace in our time" by sacrificing Czechoslovakia. The Nazi dictator quickly broke his promises. After digesting the Sudetenland, he seized the remainder of Czechoslovakia early in 1939. Not to be outdone, Mussolini invaded tiny Albania in April of 1939. Only then, as Hitler turned his attention to the German population in the Polish Corridor and Danzig, did Britain and France resolve to resist even if it meant war.

Prior to 1937, Roosevelt and Hull had not followed a consistent foreign policy. Not only had the administration accepted crippling neutrality legislation without putting up prolonged resistance, but FDR himself sometimes sounded an isolationist note in public. The Democratic platform in 1936 reassured the electorate that the country would not be pulled into war by political or commercial entanglements. During the campaign, Roosevelt declared his resolve to insulate America from foreign conflicts and remarked, "I hate war. I have passed unnumbered hours, I shall pass unnumbered hours, thinking and planning how war may be kept from the Nation."

The China war and the crises in Europe caused Roosevelt to take a more decided internationalist course. He hoped somehow to prevent a general war but, if that failed, to strengthen peace-loving states against their assailants. When Japan launched the "China Incident" in 1937, his concern involved more than sympathy with China; it seemed to him that the forces of order and security everywhere stood on the defensive. Japan's aggressions comprised only one aspect of this assault against world peace and decency. FDR did not invoke the neutrality laws in Japan's undeclared war, because he wanted to give China whatever aid possible.

In his "Quarantine Speech" in Chicago, on October 5, 1937, President Roosevelt tried to alert the American people and to prepare them for a more responsible foreign policy. Speaking in the heartland of isolationist America, he indicated that the nation's security depended on cooperation with other peaceful states: "Let no one imagine that America will escape, that America may expect mercy, that this hemisphere will not be attacked." After proclaiming the principle that international gangsters should be segregated as society quarantines the carriers of dangerous diseases, Roosevelt declared, "We are determined to stay out of war . . . but we cannot *insure* ourselves against the disastrous effects of war and the danger of involvement; we cannot have complete protection in a world of disorder in which confidence and security have broken down."

The Chicago address aroused favorable response across the country, but it also ignited isolationist criticism and charges of war-mongering. Some alarmed isolationists even muttered threats of impeachment. It soon became apparent, however, that the President had no clear policy changes in mind. He may have contemplated some kind of collective neutrality whereby, without adopting economic or military sanctions, peaceful states would morally condemn aggressive powers. In subsequent remarks to reporters, however, he beat a hasty retreat and denied even the intention of passing moral condemnation on the aggressors. In retrospect it seems clear that FDR burnt his fingers at Chicago and thereafter felt more apprehensive than probably he should have about the strength of isolationism in America.

The League of Nations condemned Japan's aggression in China as a violation of the Kellogg-Briand and Nine Power Pacts, and suggested a conference of signatories of the Nine Power Pact. Shortly before the United States and the other signers, plus Russia, met at Brussels in November of 1937, Roosevelt made it clear that he did not favor vigorous measures against Japan; apparently he saw the role of the conference simply as bringing moral pressure to bear. Japan declined to attend and only Russia advocated strong measures. Britain and France left the initiative to the United States, while Roosevelt and Hull recoiled from economic sanctions against Japan. Consequently the confer-

THE JAPANESE EMPIRE, 1939

ence achieved nothing beyond a pious reaffirmation of treaty principles. The
Brussels Conference was not only a fiasco but a disaster. The fact that it met
encouraged China to continue resistance in the hope of substantial aid, while its
failure emboldened Japan's leaders to persist in their course.

The *Panay* incident in December, 1937, further revealed the reluctance of
the United States to risk conflict with Japan. Japanese warplanes deliberately
attacked the American gunboat *Panay* and three Standard Oil Company tankers
on the Yangtze River and strafed survivors in the water. Yet unlike the *Maine*
incident in 1898, most Americans reacted mildly and wanted to withdraw all our
ships and men from the area to avoid future incidents. The government accepted
Japanese apologies and reparations. The incident also quickened congressional
support for the so-called Ludlow Amendment to the Constitution, prohibiting
war except in case of actual invasion or with majority approval in a national
referendum. The administration had to exert strong pressure, including a letter
from the President that was read in the House of Representatives, to block the
bill from coming to the floor for formal debate and action.

Encouraged by slowly increasing public support for a stronger course, the
State Department began to deal more firmly with Japan. The Two-Ocean Naval
Act of 1938 vastly increased naval construction – even isolationists accepted the
need for greater hemispheric defense. Meanwhile Japan, heretofore apologetic
for many of her acts, openly proclaimed in late 1938 a "New Order" for East
Asia; no longer would she give even lip-service to the principles of the Open
Door in China. Hull strongly objected to the "New Order" and reasserted
American rights in China and the Far East. The administration gave Chiang
Kai-shek a small loan in 1938 to bolster China's currency and its morale, and
slapped a moral embargo against the sale and shipment of aircraft to Japan. FDR
ordered the Pacific Fleet moved temporarily to Pearl Harbor, a graphic reminder
to Tokyo of American power and will to resist. Finally, the State Department
opened the way for economic retaliation on July 26, 1939 when it gave notice
terminating the Japanese-American commercial treaty of 1911.

War between the United States and Japan was not yet inevitable, although
clearly the two countries followed sharply diverging courses. From the stand-
point of practical interests, American policy has been viewed as highly unrealistic. The American economic stake in China, as noted before, fell far short of its
trade with Japan. Moreover, Japan clearly ranked as the strongest power in East
Asia. Would Washington have been wiser merely to lodge formal protests against
the aggressions in China while patiently working for greater moderation by
Japan? Or, if that failed, to have acquiesced in fact to Japanese control of China
as inevitable? From the later perspective of the Cold War and the Japanese-
American Security Treaty, our policy in the 1930's has seemed questionable to
some scholars. Roosevelt and Hull, however, not gifted with our hindsight,
believed that aggression must be opposed lest it spread everywhere. In short,
they saw Japan's attack upon China as part of the general breakdown in world

security and peace. Moreover, the American leaders thought that a greater display of firmness offered a chance of restraining Japan. Even after the European war erupted in 1939, FDR and Hull continued to hope that hostilities could be avoided with Japan, while they concentrated American attention upon Hitler's conquest of Europe. They did not view Japan as an immediate threat to American security until Tokyo concluded the Tripartite Alliance with the Axis powers in September, 1940.

The Waning of Isolationism

Public opinion splintered under the impact of foreign events. Isolationists and non-interventionists feared involvement in war and were increasingly suspicious of FDR's leadership, as the Ludlow Amendment indicated. The internationalists, however, felt a growing apprehension about the Axis threat in Europe and Japanese militarism in Asia, and they supported the administration's movement toward collective security. Many previously pacifist or isolationist liberals began to shift into the internationalist camp. Some professed to fear the dangers of fascism at home, where anti-Semites rallied behind fascist organizations such as William Dudley Pelley's Silver Shirts, the German-American Bund, and the Christian Front. The formation of the House Committee on Un-American Activities in 1938 also disturbed thoughtful citizens. Headed by Representative Martin Dies of Texas, the committee tended to ignore right-wing activities and concentrated on ferreting out communist infiltration and front organizations. The Dies Committee permitted witnesses at its hearings to make unsubstantiated and reckless charges of communism against individuals who often had no opportunity for rebuttal. Some 640 organizations were denounced as controlled or infiltrated by the communists.

Communism had become more respectable during a time of crisis when Soviet Russia had joined the Western democracies in opposition to fascist aggression. In the United States, Earl Browder, who replaced William Z. Foster as General Secretary of the American Communist Party, pursued the Popular Front strategy, playing down revolutionary jargon and urging a coalition of all democratic forces to oppose fascism. A number of organizations, such as the American League Against Fascism, apparently had been founded by the communists as front organizations to rally intellectuals and other groups. Browder boasted of his Revolutionary War ancestry and described communism as merely twentieth-century Americanism. The Communist Party successfully penetrated various peace and youth groups and some C.I.O. labor unions. A few also found places in the executive government, but none in key policy-making positions and their importance has often been grossly exaggerated.

Roosevelt played only a small and indirect role in the Czechoslovakian crisis. He cabled Hitler twice in behalf of peace and approved Prime Minister

Chamberlain's request that Mussolini use his influence to avert hostilities. Americans greeted the Munich settlement with profound relief that war had been avoided. Thus the American government and people at this time obviously favored appeasement of the Nazi Fuehrer. As Hitler violated his pledges and anti-Jewish outrages multiplied in Germany Roosevelt publicly voiced disapproval. He recalled the American Ambassador after the violent *Kristallnacht* in Germany — a wave of anti-Jewish riots and stringent repressive measures that followed the assassination of a German diplomat in Paris by a Jew.

Hitler fully reciprocated American dislike and recalled his ambassador. He viewed the United States as a racially mongrelized society that could not even cope with the economic depression. America need not be taken seriously, he told his intimates in 1938, because it was too impotent to fight and would not go beyond meaningless moral gestures in international affairs. The German military shared his opinion. Using "racial arithmetic," Hitler concluded that the polyglot United States was held together only by the glue of 20 million superior Anglo-Saxons or 60 million of valuable racial stock; therefore, Germany with its larger population of Aryans was far more powerful. The neutrality laws strengthened his contempt. Yet after war broke out, he wisely concentrated on Europe and left America to the tender ministrations of Japan.

In the light of Hitler's "restraint" toward the United States prior to December, 1941, how seriously did he menace American interests? Some revisionist historians have argued that a Nazi conquest of most of Europe would not have endangered the United States. In an immediate sense, such criticisms may be sound — probably Hitler would have been too exhausted to have turned upon the western hemisphere for some years. Yet he did contemplate expansion into Latin America, and obviously if triumphant in Europe he would have increased German penetration. American leaders feared that successful aggression spawned more aggression and that it would be potentially dangerous to live isolated within an Axis-dominated world.

By 1939 President Roosevelt clearly recognized the bankruptcy of isolationism. He warned Congress and the nation of the serious crisis facing the world and advocated measures short of war to restrain aggression. In mid-April, 1939 he appealed to Hitler and Mussolini to reassure thirty-one countries that they would not be attacked. Hitler rebuffed him in a satirical speech to the Reichstag, his puppet legislature, while Mussolini failed to respond. FDR and Hull attempted without success to persuade Congress to repeal the Neutrality Law or at least to modify it so that the executive would not have to apply an arms embargo against countries attacked by the dictators. Although unstated, the administration implied that in case of war between the western democracies and the totalitarian states, America's own interests required a victory by the democracies. The isolationists refused to relent, however, and Senator Borah confidently predicted that there would be no war in Europe in 1939.

Contrary to Senator Borah's prediction, Hitler was about to unleash the

Wehrmacht against Poland and the western democracies. On August 23, 1939 the world was shocked at news of the signing of the Nazi-Soviet Pact in Moscow, a perfidious deal made while Anglo-French military talks with Russia were still underway. With the danger of a major two-front war eliminated, Hitler felt free to pursue his Polish venture despite Anglo-French opposition. On September 1 the *Luftwaffe* rained destruction on Poland; two days later, Great Britain and France fulfilled their promises to the Poles and declared war on Nazi Germany.

The twenty-year armistice had expired; World War II had begun. But while isolationism remained powerful in America, the shock of recent events had weakened it badly. Various polls since 1937 had indicated that most Americans viewed Nazi Germany as morally wrong and that in case of a major war they favored supplying arms to the western democracies despite the neutrality laws. Now as war raged in Poland, another Gallup poll indicated that 84 percent of the American people desired an Allied victory and 76 percent, despite an overwhelming desire to remain at peace, expected America to become involved sooner or later. Although over two years more elapsed before the United States entered the war, public opinion had begun to adjust to that prospect by the fall of 1939.

9

Retrospect, 1914-1939

TWENTY-FIVE YEARS had elapsed since America watched in shocked dismay as Europe plunged into war in 1914. Now another great conflict had begun, and citizens with a sense of history could foresee that the United States once more would be involved. A pessimistic observer might conclude that little had changed in that quarter of a century, except for the worse.

Yet the America of 1939 was vastly different from that of 1914. It was not merely that an age of innocence, of confidence in unbroken progress and peace, had passed. The nation had grown in population from about 95 million to nearly 131 million people, despite the restriction of immigration in the Twenties and its virtual cessation during the depression years. The industrial infrastructure had grown prodigiously during World War I and the 1920's, and had survived the depression intact – it was to reveal its incredible productive potential in the Second World War. Overseas investments and trade, with all the vicissitudes of the intervening years, had increased from $2½ billion in 1914 to nearly $11 billion by 1940, graphic evidence that the United States ranked first in the capitalist world. The nation also had made great strides in improving public health and education. Even the trials of the depression had served for most citizens to strengthen faith in the democratic system and its ability to cope with the challenges of modern industrial life.

Two of the most significant developments in American life during this quarter-century involved the rationalization of business and the development of the machinery of the regulatory interventionist state. The impulse of business to organize into larger structures and to rationalize production and sales, underway in the late nineteenth century, greatly quickened during the Progressive Era and in the Twenties. Huge corporations emerged, trade associations formed to stabilize production and curtail often destructive competition, industrial research and scientific management sought greater efficiency and productivity, and advertising and salesmanship enlarged the market for an ever-increasing flow of goods and services. The 1929 crash and the Great Depression, however, revealed the inability of the business world to solve satisfactorily the problem of distribution. The existing system failed to pass enough of the savings from more efficient production on to the consuming public in the form of higher wages and lower prices. Hence the unique phenomena in the Thirties of over-production and under-consumption, and of suffering in the midst of plenty.

Governmental intervention in the private economy on a far larger scale than ever before provided the response to these problems. The regulatory state had been developing since 1887 and 1890, when Congress had enacted the Interstate Commerce Act and the Sherman Anti-Trust Act. The Progressive Era enlarged the regulatory function: conservation of natural resources, improved regulation of the railroads, acts to protect consumers and to prohibit harmful business practices, and reorganization of the nation's currency and banking system. World War I temporarily brought an even larger economic role for the federal government as it managed the nation's transportation system and guided production and distribution. In the postwar decade the national Republican administrations de-emphasized regulation while using government to aid, stimulate, and cooperate with business. While the achievements of that "new era" were substantial, they were not sufficient to avoid the coming of the Great Depression. Hoover's methods of voluntaryism having proved to be unavailing against the depression, Roosevelt's New Deal reverted to the techniques and approaches utilized so efficiently during the war of 1917-1919. A degree of government planning for production and distribution ensued, most notably in the N.R.A. and the A.A.A. For the first time, the federal government moved massively into the field of direct relief for the unemployed and the needy. Other measures indicated at least a partial awareness that the problems of an industrialized and urbanized America could no longer be left solely to the individual or to private groups. Wages and hours laws, unemployment insurance, social security, public housing projects, farm resettlement and soil conservation, adventures in social engineering such as the T.V.A., these and other measures undoubtedly fell short of all that might have been accomplished but at least a notable beginning had been made toward modernizing America's social and economic institutions. Whatever remained to be done, one fact seemed clear by 1939: the United States would never return to the so-called *laissez faire* role of government in the past.

The processes of industrialization that had created these domestic problems also played a prominent part in America's rise to great world power and its belated acceptance of the responsibilities that entailed. Economic growth had led to a search for foreign markets; that and a heightened sense of national power and destiny had plunged the United States into overseas empire and entanglement in world political currents before the Progressive Era had begun. Leaders such as Theodore Roosevelt and Woodrow Wilson began to perceive

America's vital interests in foreign affairs and the fact that as a great world power its actions or failures to act necessarily affected the world scene. The First World War dramatically revealed the nation's stake in a stable world. Yet the causes of America's entry into war in 1917 were sufficiently unclear to the public that a majority of citizens apparently failed to understand those interests or to perceive the necessity of a more responsible postwar role for their country. Reaction and disillusionment, consequently, became almost inevitable after the Great Crusade of 1917. Yet Republican and Democratic administrations in the postwar years could not withdraw the nation from world affairs; instead they walked a tight-wire between isolationist sentiment at home and obligations and interests abroad. It required the cumulative impact of a series of foreign aggressions, crises, and war in the 1930's before isolationist sentiment in America began to diminish and the government could adopt more realistic policies to defend what it regarded as the nation's vital interests. Although not completed until 1941, that educational process had well begun by September, 1939.

Suggestions for Further Reading

The following books and articles, acknowledging the author's sources, are intended as a guide for the student and not as an exhaustive listing.

I. The Wilson Era, 1914-1921:

Any serious study of the origins and philosophy of Progressivism, as well as the New Deal, should begin with Richard Hofstadter's *The Age of Reform: From Bryan to F.D.R.* (New York, 1955); and Eric F. Goldman's *Rendezvous With Destiny* (New York, 1952). Robert H. Wiebe, *The Search for Order, 1877-1920* (New York, 1967), is a recent reappraisal of the period and provides a suggestive departure for interpreting the Twenties as well. Brief but provocative essays on Bryan, Theodore Roosevelt, Wilson, Hoover, and Franklin D. Roosevelt, are in Hofstadter's *The American Political Tradition and The Men Who Made It* (New York, 1949). For more specialized works on Progressivism, see David W. Noble, *The Paradox of Progressive Thought* (Minneapolis, 1958); Edward C. Moore, *American Pragmatism: Peirce, James, and Dewey* (New York, 1961); Christopher Lasch, *The New Radicalism in America, 1888-1963* (New York, 1965); Henry F. May, *The End of American Innocence* (New York, 1959); and Morton White, *Social Thought in America* (Boston, 1949). Also see Louis Hartz, *The Liberal Tradition in America* (New York, 1954); and Arthur Ekrich, Jr., *The Decline of American Liberalism* (New York, 1956). Arthur S. Link, *Woodrow Wilson and the Progressive Era, 1910-1917* (New York, 1954), succinctly interweaves Wilson's New Freedom policies at home and abroad. Stimulating broad surveys are by William E. Leuchtenburg, *The Perils of Prosperity, 1914-1932* (Chicago, 1958); and by David A. Shannon, *Between the Wars, 1919-1941* (Boston, 1964). Samuel P. Hays, *The Response to Industrialism: 1885-1914* (Chicago, 1957) and "The Politics of Reform in Municipal Government in the Progressive Era," *Pacific Northwest Quarterly*, LV (1964), 157-169, Robert H. Wiebe, *Businessmen and Reform: A Study of the Progressive Movement* (Cambridge, Mass., 1962), and Forest McDonald's *The Torch is Passed* (Reading, Mass., 1968), offer correctives to older interpretations and stress the role of business leaders in reform. In this connection also see the articles by Howard W. Allen, "Geography and Politics: Voting on Reform in the United States Senate, 1911-1916," *Journal of Southern History*, XXVII (1961), 216-228; and William T. Kerr, Jr., "The Progressives of Washington, 1910-1912," *Pacific Northwest Quarterly*, LV (1964), 16-27. Greater emphasis upon the conservative business nature of Progressive reform is found in *The Triumph of Conservatism: A Reinterpretation of American History, 1900-1916* (New York, 1963), by Gabriel Kolko. Michael Rogin, "Progressivism and the California Electorate," *Journal of American History*, LV (1968), 297-314, points out that progressivism in that state may have been led by middle and upper-class leaders but its base rested upon immigrant and labor votes. Jonathan Daniels' *The Time between the Wars: Armistice to Pearl Harbor* (New York, 1966), a volume in the Mainstream of America Series, is a colorfully written impressionistic account of the two postwar decades. Also see the caustic and witty comments of that acute if biased observer, Alice Roosevelt Longworth, *Crowded Hours* (New York, 1933).

There are numerous biographical studies of President Wilson. Ray Stannard Baker's semi-official volumes on *Woodrow Wilson: Life and Letters* (Garden City, N.Y., 1935-1939, 8 vols.), and *Woodrow Wilson and World Settlement* (Garden City, N.Y., 1922, 3 vols.), are rich in documentary materials and are still useful. They are being superseded by the monumental biography written by Professor Link, of which five volumes have been published to date: *Wilson: The Road to the White House* (Princeton, 1947); *Wilson: The New Freedom* (Princeton, 1956), treating domestic and foreign policy in 1913 and 1914; *Wilson: The Struggle for Neutrality, 1914-1915* (Princeton, 1960); *Wilson: Confusions and Crises, 1915-1916* (Princeton, 1964); and *Wilson: Campaigns for Progressivism and Peace, 1916-1917* (Princeton, 1965), that ends with entry into the World War. Two very short biographies provide good studies of the man and his times: John M. Blum, *Woodrow Wilson and the Politics of Morality* (Boston, 1956); and John A. Garraty, *Woodrow Wilson, A Great Life in Brief* (New York, 1956). Sigmund Freud and William C. Bullitt, *Thomas Woodrow Wilson* (Boston, 1967), have attempted a psychological analysis of that complex man, but the reader will find a sounder historical, and probably psychological account, in the volume by A. L. and J. L. George, *Woodrow Wilson and Colonel House* (New York, 1956). Arthur Walworth's two-volume biography of *Woodrow Wilson* (New York, 1958), is useful but adulatory. Charles Seymour, *The Intimate Papers of Colonel House* (Boston, 1926-1938, 4 vols.), treats Wilson's principal adviser. For an analysis of recent literature on the Wilson era, see Richard L. Watson, Jr., "Woodrow Wilson and His Interpreters, 1947-1957," *Mississippi Valley Historical Review*, XLIV (1957), 207-236.

Wilsonian foreign policy has also been extensively studied. A recent general account is by Julius W. Pratt, *Challenge and Rejection, 1900-1921* (New York, 1967). Link's *Wilson the Diplomatist* (Baltimore, 1957), examines Wilson's major foreign policies in a series of essays; also see the biography by Link, cited before. For general accounts of both foreign and domestic events, see *American Democracy and the World War* (Boston, 1936, 3 vols.), by Frederic L. Paxson; and *The Great Crusade and After, 1914-1928* (New York, 1931), by Preston W. Slosson. Daniel M. Smith, *The Great Departure* (New York, 1965), concentrates on the period of the United States and the World War, 1914-1921. Norman A. Graebner has edited *An Uncertain Tradition: American Secretaries of State in the Twentieth Century* (New York, 1961), that contains essays by Richard Challener and Daniel M. Smith on Wilson's first two Secretaries, Bryan and Lansing; for Bainbridge Colby, see Smith, *Aftermath of War* (Philadelphia, 1970). Paolo E. Coletta has published a sound and detailed biography of the Great Commoner: *William Jennings Bryan* (Lincoln, Nebraska, 1964-1970, 3 vols.). Ross Gregory, *Walter Hines Page: Ambassador to the Court of St. James's* (Lexington, Ky., 1970), analyzes Page's pro-Ally views in a prize-winning study. For books that focus on geographical areas, consult the relevant chapters in Samuel Flagg Bemis, *The Latin American Policy of the United States* (New York, 1943); Dana G. Munro, *Intervention and Dollar Diplomacy in the Caribbean, 1900-1921* (Princeton, 1964); Burton F. Beers, *Vain Endeavor, Robert Lansing's*

Attempts to End the American-Japanese Rivalry (Durham, N.C., 1962); and Roy W. Curry, *Woodrow Wilson and Far Eastern Policy, 1913-1921* (New York, 1967). *The Vanity of Power: American Isolationism and the First World War, 1914-1917* (Westport, Conn., 1969), by John Milton Cooper, Jr., depicts Bryan's role in the birth of self-conscious isolationism.

For guides to the historical debate on the causes of American involvement in World War I, the student should examine Richard W. Leopold, "The Problem of American Intervention, 1917: An Historical Retrospect," *World Politics*, II (1950), 405-425; and Daniel M. Smith, "National Interest and American Intervention, 1917: An Historiographical Appraisal," *Journal of American History*, LII (1965), 5-24. During the 1920's and 1930's, the debate revolved around revisionism: see Warren I. Cohen's stimulating study, *The American Revisionists: the Lessons of Intervention in World War I* (Chicago, 1967). C. Hartley Grattan, *Why We Fought* (New York, 1929), wrote an early scholarly revisionist study of American involvement that emphasized the unneutrality of Wilson's policies. *Road to War* (Boston, 1935), by newspaperman Walter Millis, gives much attention to public opinion. Edwin Borchard and W. P. Lage, *Neutrality for the United States* (New Haven, 1937); and Alice M. Morrissey, *The American Defense of Neutral Rights, 1914-1917* (Cambridge, 1939), are highly critical of administration interpretations of international law and neutral practice. The most thoroughly researched revisionist study, though he professed no particular view in his preface, is by Charles C. Tansill, *America Goes to War* (Boston, 1938). H. C. Peterson, *Propaganda for War* (Norman, Okla., 1939), writes from the revisionist point of view; see too James M. Read, *Atrocity Propaganda, 1914-1919* (New Haven, 1941). Charles Seymour rejects the revisionists arguments and attributes the causes of intervention primarily to Germany's ruthless submarine warfare: *American Diplomacy During the World War* (Baltimore, 1934), and *American Neutrality, 1914-1917* (New Haven, 1935). Studies of the 1917 intervention written since the end of the Second World War have given more attention to the world setting of American foreign relations, and have been more aware of various psychological, economic, and strategic factors bearing on policy. Among the best are the previously cited works by A. S. Link; Edward H. Buehrig, *Woodrow Wilson and the Balance of Power* (Bloomington, Ind., 1955); and Ernest R. May, *The World War and American Isolation, 1914-1917* (Cambridge, 1959). Barbara W. Tuchman, *The Zimmermann Telegram* (New York, 1958), emphasizes the effects on public opinion of that maladroit German effort. Lloyd C. Gardner, "American Foreign Policy, 1900-1921: A Second Look at the Realist Critique of American Diplomacy," in Barton J. Bernstein, ed., *Towards A New Past: Dissenting Essays in American History* (New York, 1968), 202-231, provides an interpretation from the viewpoint of "New Left" historians. Gardner depicts Wilsonian internationalism as a "thick rhetoric of morality" covering a drive to exert world economic and political influence. See too William Appleman Williams, *The Tragedy of American Diplomacy* (New York, 1959).

The most recent study of wartime politics is by Seward W. Livermore, *Politics is Adjourned: Woodrow Wilson and the War Congress, 1916-1918* (Middletown, Conn., 1966). Domestic social and economic developments are covered in the previously cited books by Slosson and Paxson. Also see K. Austin Kerr, "Decision for Federal Control: Wilson, McAdoo, and the Railroads, 1917," *Journal of American History*, LIV (1967), 550-560. On problems of mobilization, finance, and the military, consult Harvey A. DeWeerd, *President Wilson*

Fights His War (New York, 1968); Charles Gilbert, *American Financing of World War I* (Westport, Conn., 1970); and Edward M. Coffman, *The War to End Wars: The American Military Experience in World War I* (New York, 1968). On wartime propaganda, see George T. Blakey, *Historians on the Homefront: American Propagandists for the Great War* (Lexington, Ky., 1970). The wartime climate of repression is fully treated by Gilbert C. Fite and H. C. Peterson, *Opponents of War, 1917-1918* (Madison, 1957); and Harry N. Scheiber, *The Wilson Administration and Civil Liberties* (Ithaca, N.Y., 1960). Ruhl J. Bartlett, *The League to Enforce Peace* (Chapel Hill, 1944); Laurence W. Martin, *Peace Without Victory: Woodrow Wilson and the British Liberals* (New Haven, 1958); and Lawrence E. Gelfand, *The Inquiry: American Preparations for Peace* (New Haven, 1963), describe the formulation of plans for the peace. Arno J. Mayer, *Wilson vs. Lenin* (New Haven, 1959), offers an analysis of the ideological conflict between the two great prophets of the modern world. An excellent recent study by N. Gordon Levin, Jr., *Woodrow Wilson and World Politics: America's Response to War and Revolution* (New York, 1968), interprets the President's policy from 1917 to 1919 as directed against the outdated imperialism of the past and against Bolshevism. Wilsonian diplomacy toward Russia and the subject nationalities of eastern Europe has been extensively studied. William A. Williams, *American-Russian Relations, 1781-1947* (New York, 1952), emphasizes an anti-Bolshevik motive to the American decision to intervene in Siberia and northern Russia; Betty Miller Unterberger, *America's Siberian Expedition* (Durham, 1956), views it as intended primarily to check Japanese expansionism; while George F. Kennan's two volumes of a projected three volume work on *Soviet-American Relations, 1917-1920 (Russia Leaves the War*, and *The Decision to Intervene*, Princeton, 1956, 1958), tend to stress military factors and Allied pressure. See Christopher Lasch, "American Intervention in Siberia: A Reinterpretation," *Political Science Quarterly*, LXXVII (1962), 205-223. For American reactions to the Bolshevik coup, consult Peter G. Filene, *Americans and the Soviet Experiment, 1917-1933* (Cambridge, Mass., 1967). Louis L. Gerson, *Woodrow Wilson and the Rebirth of Poland* (New Haven, 1953); and Victor S. Mamatey, *The United States and East Central Europe, 1914-1918* (Princeton, 1957), are the standard works on those two topics. *The Immigrant's Influence on Wilson's Peace Policies* (Lexington, Ky., 1967), edited by Joseph P. O'Grady, contains well-researched essays on the activities of various minority groups in behalf of their motherlands. Relations with America's fellow belligerents are handled by Arthur Willert, *The Road to Safety, A Study in Anglo-American Relations* (London, 1952); W. B. Fowler, *British-American Relations, 1917-1918* (Princeton, 1968); and David F. Trask, *The United States in the Supreme War Council* (Middletown, Conn., 1961). H. R. Rudin's *Armistice, 1918* (New Haven, 1944), covers the negotiations leading to the German decision to capitulate.

Paul Birdsall's *Versailles Twenty Years After* (New York, 1941), is still the best single volume study of the peace conference as a whole. For American policy, see Thomas A. Bailey, *Woodrow Wilson and the Lost Peace* (New York, 1944). *Anglo-American Relations at the Paris Peace Conference of 1919* (Princeton, 1961), by Seth P. Tillman, is an excellent work. Two older and highly critical accounts by junior level British participants should be consulted for the flavor of the debate on the Versailles Treaty: John Maynard Keynes, *The Economic Consequences of the Peace* (New York, 1920); and Harold Nicolson, *Peacemaking, 1919* (Boston, 1933). Standard works on their subjects are René Albrecht-Carrié, *Italy at the Paris Peace Conference* (New York, 1938); Ivo J.

Lederer, *Yugoslavia at the Paris Peace Conference* (New Haven, 1963); and Sherman D. Spector, *Rumania at the Paris Peace Conference* (New York, 1962). Russian problems have received a long overdue detailed discussion by John M. Thompson, *Russia, Bolshevism, and the Versailles Peace* (Princeton, 1966). Arno J. Mayer, *Politics and Diplomacy of Peacemaking* (New York, 1967), emphasizes efforts at the Paris Conference to destroy or contain Bolshevism. Two articles are indispensable to an understanding of the League of Nations issue: George Curry, "Woodrow Wilson, Jan Smuts, and the Versailles Settlement," *American Historical Review*, LXVI (1961), 968-986; and Kurt Wimer, "Woodrow Wilson's Plan to Enter the League of Nations through an Executive Agreement," *Western Political Quarterly*, XI (1958), 800-812.

The battle for Senate approval of the Versailles Treaty is handled in T. A. Bailey's interpretative *Woodrow Wilson and the Great Betrayal* (New York, 1945), that sees the President rather than Lodge as the culprit in the case. The Massachusetts' Senator's motives are analyzed by John A. Garraty, *Henry Cabot Lodge* (New York, 1953). Other prominent figures are covered by P. C. Jessup, *Elihu Root* (New York, 1938, 2 vols.); Richard W. Leopold, *Elihu Root and the Conservative Tradition* (Boston, 1954); Belle C. and Fola La Follette, *Robert M. La Follette* (New York, 1953, 2 vols.); Henry F. Pringle, *Life and Times of William Howard Taft* (New York, 1939, 2 vols.); and Marion C. McKenna, *Borah* (Ann Arbor, 1961). Sondra R. Herman, *Eleven Against War* (Stanford, 1969), analyzes concepts about international law and world organization held by American thinkers, 1898-1921. Warren F. Kuehl, *Seeking World Order: The United States and International Organization to 1920* (Nashville, 1969), points out that Wilson's commitment to collective security diverged from the mainstream of American internationalist thought. Ralph Stone, *The Irreconciliables: The Fight Against the League of Nations* (Lexington, Ky., 1970), depicts Wilson as playing into the hands of the Irreconciliables. For the effects of Wilson's illness on the Treaty fight, see Edwin A. Weinstein, "Woodrow Wilson's Neurological Illness," *Journal of American History*, LVII (1970), 324-351. Selig Adler, *The Isolationist Impulse: Its Twentieth Century Reaction* (New York, 1957), graphically portrays the constellation of forces arrayed against the treaty. Three articles by Kurt Wimer analyze Wilsonian political strategy: "Woodrow Wilson's Plan for a Vote of Confidence," *Pennsylvania History*, XXVIII (1961), 279-293; "Woodrow Wilson and a Third Nomination," *ibid.*, XXIX (1962), 193-211; and "Woodrow Wilson Tries Conciliation: An Effort that Failed," *The Historian*, XXV (1963), 419-438. The best account of the 1920 election is by Wesley Bagby, *The Road to Normalcy* (Baltimore, 1962).

II. The Twenties:

The best source to begin a re-examination of the Twenties is found in a very provocative article by Henry F. May, "Shifting Perspectives on the 1920's," *Mississippi Valley Historical Review*, XLIII (1956), 405-427. A recent evaluation from the traditional point of view is by John D. Hicks, *Republican Ascendancy, 1921-1933* (New York, 1960), largely superseding the older *The Incredible Era* (Boston, 1939), by S. H. Adams, and *This Was Normalcy* (Boston, 1948), by Karl Schriftgiesser. For a briefer treatment see Leuchtenburg, *Perils of Prosperity*, and Shannon, *Between the Wars*. A recent volume in the "Making of America" series that covers the years 1920-1960 is *The Urban Nation* (New York, 1965), by George E. Mowry.

Politics is surveyed in Eugene H. Roseboom's *A History of Presidential Elections* (New York, 1957). A recent biography of President Harding, by Andrew Sinclair, *The Available Man* (New York, 1965), rescues that much maligned chief executive from some of the charges hurled by his many critics. Robert K. Murray, *The Harding Era* (Minneapolis, 1969), goes even further, presenting Harding as far more informed and active than usually conceded. Francis Russell, *The Shadow of Blooming Grove* (New York, 1968), is more critical of Harding's leadership and moral lapses. Randolph C. Downes, *The Rise of Warren Gamaliel Harding, 1865-1920* (Columbus, 1970), reveals that Harding's nomination in 1920 did not result from political accident. Two older biographies of Coolidge, William Allen White's *A Puritan in Babylon* (New York, 1938), and C. M. Fuess' *Calvin Coolidge* (Boston, 1940), must give way to a thoroughly researched study by Donald R. McCoy, *Calvin Coolidge, the Quiet President* (New York, 1967). Further light on that perhaps not so reticent politician is provided by Howard H. Quint and Robert H. Ferrell, eds., *The Talkative President: the Off-the-Record Press Conferences of Calvin Coolidge* (Amherst, 1964); and Robert James Maddox, "Keeping Cool with Coolidge," *Journal of American History*, LIII (1967), 772-780. H. G. Warren, *Herbert Hoover and the Great Depression* (New York, 1959), has written the best analysis of the last of the Republican triumvirate. Burl Noggle examines the political effects of the principal Harding scandal in *Teapot Dome* (New York, 1962). The rise to political consciousness of the urban masses and the reorientation of the Democratic Party are depicted by Oscar Handlin, *All Smith and His America* (Boston, 1958); and by David Burner, *The Politics of Provincialism: The Democratic Party in Transition, 1918-1932* (New York, 1968). Arthur S. Link in chapters in his *American Epoch* (New York, 1955), and "What Happened to the Progressive Movement in the 1920's?," *American Historical Review*, LXIV (1959), 833-851, scrutinizes the era and its political cross-currents. Also see Russel B. Nye, *Midwestern Progressive Politics* (East Lansing, 1951); Paul W. Glad, "Progressives and the Business Culture of the 1920's," *Journal of American History*, LII (1966), 75-89; and Peter G. Filene, "An Obituary for 'The Progressive Movement'," *American Quarterly*, XXII (1970), 20-34.

Reevaluations of Republican foreign policy are found in two books by Selig Adler: the previously cited *Isolationist Impulse*, and *The Uncertain Giant* (New York, 1965), a survey of diplomatic history from 1921 to 1941. Economic foreign policy is handled by Joseph Brandes, *Herbert Hoover and Economic Diplomacy* (Pittsburgh, 1962), examining the overseas role of the Commerce Department; Herbert Feis, *The Diplomacy of the Dollar* (Baltimore, 1950); H. G. Moulton and Leo Pasvolsky, *War Debts and World Prosperity* (New York, 1932); and William A. Williams, "The Legend of Isolationism in the 1920's," *Science and Society*, XVIII (1956), 1-20. Burton I. Kaufman, "United States Trade and Latin America: The Wilson Years," *Journal of American History*, LVIII (1971), 342-363, describes America's wartime displacement of the British in Latin America. Carl P. Parrini, *Heir to Empire: United States Economic Diplomacy, 1916-1923* (Pittsburgh, 1969), follows a New Left point of view in connecting Wilsonian to Republican foreign policy as a quest for markets and the open door by different means. D. F. Fleming, *The United States and World Organization* (New York, 1938), traces relations with the League of Nations. Ventures in arms limitations are related by Merze Tate, *The United States and Armaments* (Cambridge, 1948); and B. H. Williams, *The United States and*

Disarmament (New York, 1931). Thomas H. Buckley, *The United States and the Washington Conference* (Knoxville, 1970); Harold and Margaret Sprout, *Toward A New Order of Sea Power* (Princeton, 1940); and R. G. O'Connor, *Perilous Equilibrium* (Lawrence, Kansas, 1962), examine the Washington treaties and the London Naval Conference of 1930. J. Chalmers Vinson, *The Parchment Peace* (Athens, Ga., 1956), deals with the role of the Senate and the Washington Conference; and his *William E. Borah and the Outlawry of War* (Athens, Ga., 1957), traces the influence of one influential Senator on the Pact of Paris. Robert James Maddox, *William E. Borah and American Foreign Policy* (Baton Rouge, La., 1969), finds Borah more practical than usually recognized. Also see R. H. Ferrell, *Peace in Their Time* (New Haven, 1952). In addition to the previously listed biography of Secretary of State Hughes by Pusey, see Betty Glad's *Charles Evans Hughes and the Illusions of Innocence* (Urbana, 1967). L. E. Ellis, *Frank B. Kellogg and American Foreign Relations, 1925-1929* (New Brunswick, 1961), views Kellogg as a mediocre head of the State Department. More favorable is R. H. Ferrell's biography in Vol. XI of *The American Secretaries of State and Their Diplomacy* (New York, 1963). He also presents a reappraisal of Secretary Stimson in the same volume. A. W. Griswold, *The Far Eastern Policy of the United States* (New York, 1938), is still the standard survey of that subject; also consult Okira Iriye, *After Imperialism: The Search for a New Order in the Far East, 1921-1931* (Cambridge, 1965). For a recent interpretative study of American diplomacy that concentrates on the present century, see Richard W. Leopold's *The Growth of American Foreign Policy* (New York, 1962).

For accounts of postwar labor unrest, nativism, and the anti-Communist hysteria, consult David Brody, *Labor in Crisis* (Phila. and New York, 1965); R. K. Murray, *Red Scare* (Minneapolis, 1955); A. S. Coben's biography of *A. Mitchell Palmer* (New York, 1963), the red-hunting Attorney-General; William M. Tuttle, Jr., *Race Riot: Chicago in the Red Summer of 1919* (New York, 1970); Robert H. Zieger, *Republicans and Labor, 1919-1929* (Lexington, Ky., 1969); *Strangers in the Land* (New Brunswick, N.J., 1955), by John Higham; Kenneth T. Jackson's *The Ku Klux Klan in the City, 1915-1930* (New York, 1967); and David M. Chalmers, *Hooded Americanism: The History of the Ku Klux Klan* (New York, 1965). Louis Joughin and Edmund M. Morgan, *The Legacy of Sacco and Vanzetti* (Chicago, 1948), is an exhaustive legal and literary study that concludes that the two aliens did not receive a fair trial. Foster Rhea Dulles, *Labor in America* (New York, 1949), is a good survey; briefer is *American Labor* (Chicago, 1960), by Henry Pelling. Irving Bernstein, *The Lean Years* (Boston, 1966), writes movingly not only of union activity but of the condition of workers from 1920 to 1933. George Soule, *Prosperity Decade* (New York, 1947), gives the most detailed examination of the startling economic changes in the 1920's. Valuable chapters are also found in Thomas C. Cochran and William Miller, *The Age of Enterprise* (New York, 1942). Also see James W. Prothro, *The Dollar Decade: Business Ideas in the 1920's* (Baton Rouge, 1954). Otis Pease, *The Responsibilities of American Advertising* (New Haven, 1958), casts a searching light on that socio-economic industry. On the use of press agency, consult Alan K. Raucher, *Public Relations and Business, 1900-1929* (Baltimore, 1968). John B. Rae, *The American Automobile* (Chicago, 1965), is a readable account of that industry. Social and intellectual aspects are covered in Harvey Wish's *Society and Thought in Modern America* (New York, 1952); Henry Steele Commanger, *The American Mind* (New Haven, 1950); Merle Curti,

The Growth of American Thought (New York, 1943); and Stow Persons, *American Minds* (New York, 1958). Clarke A. Chambers, *Seedtime of Reform* (Minneapolis, 1963), shows that progressive social work and thought continued to develop during the 1920's. Brief but excellent surveys of urban growth are by Constance McLaughlin Green, *The Rise of Urban America* (New York, 1965); and Mowry, *The Urban Nation.* Colorful descriptions and analyses are in *Only Yesterday* (New York, 1931), and *The Big Change* (New York, 1952), by Frederick Lewis Allen. R. S. and H. M. Lynd, *Middletown* (New York, 1929), and *Middletown in Transition* (New York, 1937), study the evolution of a typical midwestern town. Frederick Hoffman, *The Twenties: American Writing in the Postwar Decade* (New York, 1955); and Frank L. Mott, *American Journalism* (New York, 1962, 3rd ed.), are useful surveys of their subjects. *Literary History of the United States* (New York, 1948, 3 vols.), by Robert Spiller, et al., is the standard reference for literary development throughout the periods covered in this volume, as is Oliver W. Larkin's *Art and Life in America* (New York, 1949), for art and architecture. For accounts of the expatriates and Greenwich Villagers, see Malcolm Cowley, *Exile's Return* (New York, 1951, rev. ed.); and Matthew Josephson, *Life Among the Surrealists* (New York, 1962). George E. Mowry, ed., *The Twenties: Fords, Flappers & Fanatics* (Englewood Cliffs, N.J., 1963), contains good introductions to a variety of fascinating contemporary selections illustrating the range of the decade. James R. Mc-Govern, "The American Woman's Pre-World War I Freedom in Manners and Morals," *Journal of American History*, LV (1968), 315-333, points out that a revolutionary shift in manners and morals began, not in the 1920's, but during the Progressive Era and especially after 1910. See too *The Woman Movement: Feminism in the United States and England* (London, 1969), by William L. O'Neill. Norman Furniss, *The Fundamentalist Controversy, 1918-1931* (New Haven, 1954); and Paul A. Carter, *The Decline and Revival of the Social Gospel, 1920-1940* (Ithaca, N.Y., 1956), are invaluable on the religious scene. Also see Lawrence W. Levine, *Defender of the Faith: William Jennings Bryan, the Last Decade, 1915-1925* (New York, 1965). On recreation, consult Foster Rhea Dulles, *America Learns to Play* (New York, 1940). Prohibition is examined by Charles Merz, *The Dry Decade* (New York, 1931); Herbert Asbury, *The Great Illusion* (Garden City, 1950); Gilbert M. Ostrander, *The Prohibition Movement in California* (Berkeley, 1957); and Andrew Sinclair, *Prohibition: The Era of Excess* (Boston, 1962). *Prohibition and the Progressive Movement, 1900-1920* (1963), by James H. Timberlake, traces the origins of that reform. Chapters in John Hope Franklin's general history of the Negro in America, *From Slavery to Freedom* (New York, 1960, 2nd rev. ed.) deal with the Negro during World War I, the 1920's, and the Great Depression. Also see S. P. Fullinwider, *The Mind and Mood of Black America* (Homewood, Ill., 1969).

III.   The Great Depression:

Three books listed in the previous section provide useful brief sketches of the Great Depression: Hicks, *Republican Ascendency*; Leuchtenburg, *Perils of Prosperity*; and Shannon, *Between the Wars.* John Kenneth Galbraith, *The Great Crash, 1929* (Boston, 1955), has written the most lively account of the stock market debacle, which he views as a major contributor to the depression. Robert Sobel, *The Great Bull Market: Wall Street in the 1920's* (New York, 1968), concludes that stock prices were not unreasonably high nor a crash inevitable. Broadus Mitchell, *Depression Decade: From the New Era Through the New Deal, 1929-1941* (New York, 1947), is a detailed treatment of economic developments. For the social aspects, see Dixon Wecter, *The Age of the Great Depression, 1929-1941* (New York, 1948). David A. Shannon, *The Great Depression* (Englewood Cliffs, N.J., 1960), has edited a graphic collection of contemporary materials. A journalistic account is by Edward Robb Ellis, *A Nation in Torment: The Great American Depression, 1929-1939* (New York, 1970). For the intellectual currents, see Leo Gurko, *The Angry Decade* (New York, 1947); Daniel Aaron, *Writers on the Left* (New York, 1961); and Harvey Swados, ed., *The American Writer and the Great Depression* (Indianapolis, 1966). Charles and Mary Beard, *America in Midpassage* (New York, 1939, 2 vols.), is an older study in the inimitable Beard style. Good coverage of the political currents of the era can be found in Samuel Lubell, *The Future of American Politics* (New York, 1951); and Walter Johnson, *1600 Pennsylvania Avenue: Presidents and the People, 1929-1959* (Boston, 1960). For farmer unrest and third party movements, see Theodore Saloutos and John D. Hicks, *Agricultural Discontent in the Middle West, 1900-1939* (Madison, 1951); and Donald R. McCoy, *Angry Voices: Left-of-Center Politics in the New Deal Era* (Lawrence, Kansas, 1958). T. Harry Williams, *Huey Long* (New York, 1969), presents a close description and analysis of Long's state and national roles. See also *Demagogues in the Depression* (New Brunswick, 1969), by David H. Bennett. George Wolfskill, *The Revolt of the Conservatives: A History of the American Liberty League* (Boston, 1962), examines that anti-New Deal movement. Carl Degler, *Out of Our Past* (New York, 1959); and Richard S. Kirkendall, "The Great Depression: Another Watershed in American History?," in John Braeman *et al., Change and Continuity in Twentiety-Century America* (New York, 1966), 145-189, offer stimulating but differing interpretations of the Hoover and Roosevelt administrations.

The most detailed re-evaluations of the Hoover administration are by H. G. Warren, *Herbert Hoover and the Great Depression*; and by Albert U. Romasco, *The Poverty of Abundance* (New York, 1965). Also see Jordan A. Schwarz, *The Interregnum of Despair: Hoover, Congress and the Depression* (Urbana, 1970), and the older works by Ray Lyman Wilbur and A. M. Hyde, *The Hoover Policies* (New York, 1937); William Starr Myers, *The True Republican Record* (New York, 1939); and *The Memoirs of Herbert Hoover* (New York, 1951-1952, 3 vols.). The previously cited books by Hofstadter, *The American Political Tradition*, and *The Age of Reform*, and Goldman's *Rendezvous with Destiny*, are also useful here. Basil Rauch, *The History of the New Deal, 1933-1938* (New York, 1944), is a valuable pioneer study. Rexford Tugwell's *The Democratic Roosevelt* (Garden City, N.Y., 1957), is by a member of F.D.R.'s brains trust. Robert E. Sherwood, *Roosevelt and Hopkins* (New York, 1948), largely relates to the war years but has a section on the domestic New Deal. Arthur M. Schlesinger, Jr.'s *The Age of Roosevelt*, of which three volumes have now been published, is brilliantly written and indispensable for the student of the period: *The Crisis of the Old Order* (Boston, 1957); *The Coming of the New Deal* (Boston, 1959); and *The Politics of Upheaval* (Boston, 1960), carry his account through 1936. Frank Freidel's *Franklin D. Roosevelt* (Boston, 1952-1956, 3 vols.), is an uncompleted study now through the election of 1932. The best single-volume study is by William E. Leuchtenburg, *Franklin D. Roosevelt and the New Deal, 1932-1940* (New York, 1963). Also see his "The New Deal and the Analogue of War," in John Braeman, ed., *Change and*

Continuity, 81-143, which indicates the influence on the New Deal of the ideas and governmental agencies of World War I. James MacGregor Burns' *Roosevelt: The Lion and the Fox* (New York, 1956), is a first rate political biography. For other studies, consult Mario Einaudi, *The Roosevelt Revolution* (New York, 1959); and Dexter Perkins, *The New Age of Franklin D. Roosevelt, 1932-1945* (Chicago, 1957). A. J. Wann, *The President as Chief Executive: A Study of Franklin D. Roosevelt* (Washington, 1968), concludes that FDR was a creative and able administrator, often underrated by his critics, and he praises his plans for executive reorganization. James T. Patterson, "A Conservative Coalition Forms in Congress, 1933-1939," *Journal of American History*, LII (1966), 757-772, deals with the end of New Deal reform after the Court fight; and see his broader study, *Congressional Conservatism and the New Deal* (Lexington, Ky., 1967). *Back to Back: The Duel Between F.D.R. and the Supreme Court* (New York, 1967), by Leonard Baker, is an account by a journalist. A. T. Mason has written two sound studies of Supreme Court justices: *Brandeis: A Free Man's Life* (New York, 1946); and *Harlan Fiske Stone* (New York, 1956). Also consult the previously listed biographies of Charles Evans Hughes by Pusey and Leopold. Roosevelt's Republican opponent in the 1936 election is examined by Donald R. McCoy, *Landon of Kansas* (Lincoln, 1966). George Wolfskill and John A. Hudson, *All but the People: Franklin D. Roosevelt and His Critics, 1933-1939* (New York, 1969), provide a full study of New Deal critics and criticism.

Economic and political thought and policy are covered by E. W. Hawley, *The New Deal and the Problem of Monopoly* (Princeton, 1966); and Howard Zinn, ed., *New Deal Thought* (Indianapolis, 1966). Zinn's introduction is particularly worthy of careful reading, and Hawley points out the confusion and ambivalence in New Deal economic thought. Edgar E. Robinson, *The Roosevelt Leadership, 1933-1945* (Philadelphia, 1955), provides a reasoned critique from the conservative point of view. Also see Bernard Sternsher, *Rexford Tugwell and the New Deal* (New Brunswick, N.J., 1964); and his edited selection of writings about the nature of Roosevelt's policies, *The New Deal: Doctrines and Democracy* (Boston, 1966). Otis L. Graham, Jr., *An Encore for Reform: The Old Progressives and the New Deal* (New York, 1967), concludes that of 105 progressive leaders in the New Deal era, 60 opposed it and 40 supported it. Those who in the Progressive Era had been identified with social reform were most likely to endorse F.D.R.'s relief and reform measures, while those who had been progressive businessmen and lawyers concerned largely with more efficient city government opposed the New Deal as statist and encouraging class divisions. W. H. Droze, George Wolfskill, and William E. Leuchtenburg, *Essays on the New Deal* (Austin, 1969), write on the Shelterbelt project, New Deal critics and the Supreme Court fight. For a guide to recent literature, see Jerold S. Auerback, "New Deal, Old Deal, or Raw Deal: Some Thoughts on New Left Historiography," *Journal of Southern History*, XXXV (1969), 18-30. Roy Lubove, *The Struggle for Social Security, 1900-1935* (Cambridge, Mass., 1968), is a study of the origins of that movement. The following are detailed studies of New Deal agencies and reforms: *The Civilian Conservation Corps, 1933-1942* (Durham, N.C., 1967), by John A. Salmund; *Minister of Relief: Harry Hopkins and the Depression* (Syracuse, 1963), by Searle F. Charles; *Food and Drug Legislation in the New Deal* (Princeton, 1970), by Charles O. Jackson; *Crisis in Agriculture: The Agricultural Adjustment Administration and the New Deal, 1933* (Berkeley, 1969), by Van L. Perkins; *Securities Regulation and the New Deal* (New Haven,

1970), by Michael E. Parrish, a good study that emphasizes the role of the New Deal in preserving capitalism; and *Federal Relief Administration and the Arts* (Columbus, 1969), by William F. McDonald. James V. Patterson, *The New Deal and the States: Federalism in Transition* (Princeton, 1969), reveals the lack of state social services. Edward L. and Frederick H. Schapsmeier, *Henry A. Wallace of Iowa: The Agrarian Years, 1910-1940* (Ames, Iowa, 1968), emphasize Wallace's practicality as well as idealism. J. Joseph Huthmacher, *Senator Robert F. Wagner and the Rise of Urban Liberalism* (New York, 1968), is useful in the transformation of the Democratic Party. See also George Q. Flynn, *American Catholics and the Roosevelt Presidency* (Lexington, Ky., 1968); and Raymond Wolters, *Negroes and the Great Depression* (Westport, Conn. 1970), that emphasizes the impact of the New Deal upon blacks. Barton J. Bernstein, "The New Deal: The Conservative Achievements of Liberal Reform," in his edited *Towards a New Past*, 263-288, writing from the New Left viewpoint, depicts the New Deal as primarily conservative and faults it for failure to do much for groups outside of the middle class, which he attributes to the non-adoption of "a meaningful egalitarianism." Richard S. Kirkendall, "The New Deal as Watershed: the Recent Literature," *Journal of American History*, LIV (1968), 839-852, is a thoughtful analysis of trends in interpretation of the Roosevelt era.

There are a number of memoirs of the Roosevelt period. Among the best are the following: James Morton Blum, ed., *From the Morgenthau Diaries* (Boston, 1959); Harold Ickes, *The Secret Diary of Harold Ickes: The First Thousand Days, 1933-1936* (New York, 1953); Raymond Moley, *After Seven Years* (New York, 1939); Frances Perkins, *The Roosevelt I Knew* (New York, 1946); and Eleanor Roosevelt, *This I Remember* (New York, 1949).

IV. Depression Diplomacy and the Coming of World War II:

Serious study of the diplomacy of the Hoover-Roosevelt era should begin with Robert Ferrell, *American Diplomacy in the Great Depression* (New Haven, 1957). The general studies of F.D.R. and the New Deal, cited in the last chapter, are also useful: Burns, *Roosevelt: The Lion and the Fox*; Leuchtenburg, *Franklin D. Roosevelt and the New Deal*; and Perkins, *The New Age of Franklin D. Roosevelt*. Also see Sherwood's *Roosevelt and Hopkins*. Robert A. Divine, *Roosevelt and World War II* (Baltimore, 1969), depicts FDR as caught between internationalist and isolationist inclinations during the early New Deal years. Interpretative essays on Secretaries of State Hughes, Kellogg, Stimson, and Hull are found in Graebner, ed., *An Uncertain Tradition: American Secretaries of State in the Twentieth Century*. The Bemis series is brought closer to date in the previously cited lengthy essays by Ferrell, "Frank B. Kellogg" and "Henry L. Stimson" in Vol. XI of *The American Secretaries of State and Their Diplomacy*; and Julius W. Pratt's two volume study of "Cordell Hull" in the same series, Vol. XII and XIII (New York, 1964), edited by R. H. Ferrell and S. F. Bemis. Also see L. Ethan Ellis, *Frank B. Kellogg and American Foreign Relations* (New Brunswick, 1961); the critical biography of *Secretary Stimson* (New Brunswick, 1954) by Richard Current; and Elting Morison's *Turmoil and Tradition, A Study of the Life and Times of Henry L. Stimson* (Boston, 1960), a moving and well written study. The *Memoirs of Cordell Hull* (2 vols., New York, 1948), provide a good insight into his moralistic and salty role in shaping New Deal foreign policy.

An older but still the best study of American diplomacy in the Pacific, as noted earlier, is by Griswold, *Far Eastern Policy of the United States*. A recent reinterpretation is by Warren I. Cohen, "From Contempt to Containment: Cycles in American Attitudes toward China," in John Braeman, ed., *Twentieth-Century American Foreign Policy* (Columbus, 1971), pp. 502-559. Armin Rappaport's *Henry L. Stimson and Japan, 1931-1933* (Chicago, 1963), subjects the Manchurian crisis to close scrutiny and provides valuable correctives to previous accounts. Dorothy Borg continues the account of Japanese-American controversies in *The United States and the Far Eastern Crisis, 1933-1938* (Cambridge, 1964). Also see her *American Policy and the Chinese Revolution, 1925-1928* (New York, 1947). Herbert Feis' *The Road to Pearl Harbor* (Princeton, 1950) is a judicious study that briefly sketches earlier Japanese-American difficulties before concentrating on 1937 and after; Frederick C. Adams, "The Road to Pearl Harbor: A Reexamination of American Far Eastern Policy, July 1937-December 1938," *Journal of American History*, LVIII (1971), 73-92, stresses 1938 as a turning point in FDR's policy toward Japan. Naval aspects are treated in Gerald E. Wheeler's *Prelude to Pearl Harbor: The United States Navy and the Far East, 1921-1931* (Columbia, Mo., 1963). No serious student of Japanese-American relations should miss the provocative and interpretative work by William L. Neumann, *America Encounters Japan* (Baltimore, 1963). S. F. Bemis, *Latin American Policy of the United States*; Graham H. Stuart, *Latin America and the United States* (New York, 1938); Arthur P. Whitaker's perceptive *The Western Hemisphere Idea* (Ithaca, 1954); and Dexter Perkins, *A History of the Monroe Doctrine* (Boston, 1955), are useful for America's relations with its hemispheric neighbors during the 1920's and 1930's. Also see J. Fred Rippy, *The Caribbean Danger Zone* (New York, 1940). Alexander DeConde, *Herbert Hoover's Latin American Policy* (Stanford, 1951), gives much credit to Hoover as the originator of the Good Neighbor policy, versus the traditional account by Edward Guerrant, *Roosevelt's Good Neighbor Policy* (Albuquerque, 1950). The interpretative study by Bryce Wood, *The Making of the Good Neighbor Policy* (New York, 1961), examines closely the Latin American relations of the New Deal and builds a convincing argument that Roosevelt's Good Neighbor policy was an original contribution. For Mexican problems, see E. David Cronon, *Josephus Daniels in Mexico* (Madison, 1960). David Green, *The Containment of Latin America: A History of the Myths and Realities of the Good Neighbor Policy* (Chicago, 1971), presents a New Left critique that emphasizes economic factors. Lloyd Gardner, *Economic Aspects of New Deal Diplomacy* (Madison, Wisc., 1964), offers a New Left analysis of Rooseveltian economic foreign policy. Relations with Soviet Russia are briefly surveyed in George Kennan's *Russia and the West under Lenin and Stalin* (Boston, 1960); Thomas A. Bailey's sprightly written *America Faces Russia* (Ithaca, 1950); and the previously cited critical interpretation of American policy, *America-Russian Relations*, by William A. Williams. The authoritative study of the 1933 recognition is by Robert P. Browder, *The Origins of Soviet-American Relations* (Princeton, 1953). Also consult Donald G. Bishop, *The Roosevelt-Litvinov Agreements* (Syracuse, 1965); and a recent article by Robert E. Bowers, "Hull, Russian Subversion in Cuba, and Recognition of the U.S.S.R.," *Journal of American History*, LIII (1966), 542-554. For an account of the connections between foreign policy and domestic Communist activities, see Irving Howe and Lewis Coser, *The American Communist Party* (New York, 1957); and Theodore Draper, *The Roots of American Communism* (New York, 1957).

Isolationist sentiment and diplomacy are carefully analyzed in two works by Selig Adler, previously listed: *The Isolationist Impulse*, and *The Uncertain Giant*. Manfred Jonas, *Isolationism in America, 1935-1941* (Ithaca, N.Y., 1966), closely analyzes the thought and beliefs of the several types of isolationists. The best treatment of the London Economic Conference is in Schlesinger's *Age of Roosevelt: The Coming of the New Deal*. Crucial stages on the road to World War II are examined by Brice Harris, Jr., *The United States and the Italo-Ethiopian Crisis* (Stanford, 1964); F. Jay Taylor, *The United States and the Spanish Civil War* (New York, 1956); Allen Guttman, *The Wound in the Heart: America and the Spanish Civil War* (New York, 1962); and by Richard P. Traina, *American Diplomacy and the Spanish Civil War* (Bloomington, 1968). Hitler's attitudes and policy toward the United States are covered by H. L. Trefousse, *Germany and American Neutrality, 1939-1941* (New York, 1951); and in a stimulating article by Gerald L. Weinberg, "Hitler's Image of the United States," *American Historical Review*, LXIX (1964), 1006-1021. A recent article throws new light on domestic political considerations and the Spanish Civil War: J. David Valaik, "Catholics, Neutrality, and the Spanish Embargo, 1937-1939," *Journal of American History*, LIV (1967), 73-85. Also see Robert H. Rosenstone, *Crusade of the Left: The Abraham Lincoln Battalion in the Spanish Civil War* (New York, 1969). Arthur D. Morse's *While Six Million Died* (New York, 1967) is a graphic portrayal of American governmental inaction in regard to the plight of Jewish refugees and victims of Naziism. Henry L. Feingold, *The Politics of Rescue* (New Brunswick, 1970), presents a more carefully researched and balanced account of the same subject. Robert Divine, *The Illusion of Neutrality* (Chicago, 1962), and *The Reluctant Belligerent: American Entry into World War II* (New York, 1965); and Donald Drummond, *The Passing of American Neutrality, 1937-1941* (Ann Arbor, 1955), examine the enactment of the neutrality laws and their subsequent repeal. John E. Wiltz, *In Search of Peace: The Senate Munitions Inquiry, 1934* (Baton Rouge, 1963), concludes that the Nye hearings had no direct influence on the 1935 neutrality legislation. Valuable insights into agrarian isolationism and the movement for neutrality legislation are presented in two studies by Wayne S. Cole, "Senator Key Pittman and American Neutrality Policies, 1933-1940," *Mississippi Valley Historical Review*, XLVI (1960), 644-662, and *Senator Gerald P. Nye and American Foreign Relations* (Minneapolis, 1962).

For the non-interventionist or "revisionist" critique of Rooseveltian foreign policy, see Harry Elmer Barnes, ed., *Perpetual War for Perpetual Peace* (Caldwell, Idaho, 1953); Charles A. Beard, *American Foreign Policy in the Making, 1932-1940* (New Haven, 1946), and *President Roosevelt and the Coming of the War: 1941* (New Haven, 1948); and Charles C. Tansill, *Backdoor to War* (Chicago, 1952), a well documented but biased study. Bruce M. Russett, *No Clear and Present Danger* (New York, 1972), casts a sceptical view on the arguments that the United States had to oppose Japanese and Nazi expansionism. Basil Rauch, *Roosevelt from Munich to Pearl Harbor* (New York, 1950), depicts F.D.R. as always an internationalist and counters the revisionist interpretations of Beard. William L. Langer and S. Everett Gleason, *The Challenge to Isolation, 1937-1940* (New York, 1952), have written a detailed and balanced account of the breakdown of neutrality. Robert Freeman Smith's essay, "American Foreign Policy, 1920-1942," pp. 232-262, in the previously cited *Towards A New Past*, edited by B. J. Bernstein, is a neo-Beardian reappraisal of the major tendencies of foreign policy from the perspectives of New

Left historians. Smith rejects older interpretations of isolationism and a revival of internationalism under F.D.R. Instead, he sees one of the basic American policy interests throughout this period, and indeed since the late 19th century, as the "establishment and maintenance of a world order" favorable to America's economic and political interests.

Appendix

Population of Continental United States

Year	Population
1910 –	91,972,266
1920 –	105,710,620
1930 –	122,775,046
1940 –	131,669,275

Presidential Elections (all minor parties are not included)

Year			Popular Vote	Electoral Vote
1912	Woodrow Wilson	Democrat	6,293,454	435
	Theodore Roosevelt	Progressive	4,119,538	88
	William H. Taft	Republican	3,484,980	8
	Eugene V. Debs	Socialist	900,672	–
	Eugene W. Chafin	Prohibition	206,275	–
1916	Woodrow Wilson	Democrat	9,129,606	277
	Charles E. Hughes	Republican	8,538,221	254
	A. L. Benson	Socialist	585,113	–
	J. F. Hanly	Prohibition	220,506	–
1920	Warren G. Harding	Republican	16,125,200	404
	James M. Cox	Democrat	9,147,353	127
	Eugene V. Debs	Socialist	919,799	–
	P. P. Christensen	Farmer-Labor	265,411	–
	Aaron S. Watkins	Prohibition	189,408	–
1924	Calvin Coolidge	Republican	15,725,016	382
	John W. Davis	Democrat	8,386,503	136
	Robert M. LaFollette	Progressive	4,822,856	13
	Herman P. Faris	Prohibition	57,520	–
	William Z. Foster	Workers	36,386	–
1928	Herbert Hoover	Republican	21,391,381	444
	Alfred E. Smith	Democrat	15,016,443	87
	Norman Thomas	Socialist	267,835	–
	William F. Varney	Prohibition	20,106	–
	William Z. Foster	Workers	21,181	–
1932	Franklin D. Roosevelt	Democrat	22,821,857	472
	Herbert Hoover	Republican	15,761,841	59
	Norman Thomas	Socialist	881,951	–
	William Z. Foster	Communist	102,785	–
	William D. Upshaw	Prohibition	81,869	–
1936	Franklin D. Roosevelt	Democrat	27,751,597	523
	Alfred M. Landon	Republican	16,679,583	8
	William Lemke	Union	882,479	–
	Norman Thomas	Socialist	187,720	–
	Earl Browder	Communist	80,159	–

Party Affiliations in Congress

Year	Congress	House	Senate
1913-1915	63d	D-291, R-127, Other-17	D-51, R-44, Other-1
1915-1917	64th	D-230, R-196, Other-9	D-56, R-40
1917-1919	65th	D-216, R-210, Other-6	D-53, R-42
1919-1921	66th	R-240, D-190, Other-3	R-49, D-47
1921-1923	67th	R-301, D-131, Other-1	R-59, D-37
1923-1925	68th	R-225, D-205, Other-5	R-51, D-43, Other-2
1925-1927	69th	R-247, D-183, Other-4	R-56, D-39, Other-1
1927-1929	70th	R-237, D-195, Other-3	R-49, D-46, Other-1
1929-1931	71st	R-267, D-167, Other-1	R-56, D-39, Other-1
1931-1933	72d	D-220, R-214, Other-1	R-48, D-47, Other-1
1933-1935	73d	D-310, R-117, Other-5	D-60, R-35, Other-1
1935-1937	74th	D-319, R-103, Other-10	D-69, R-25, Other-2
1937-1939	75th	D-331, R-89, Other-13	D-76, R-16, Other-4

Index